DSL

A Wiley Tech Brief

Jennie Bourne

Dave Burstein

Wiley Computer Publishing

John Wiley & Sons, Inc.

NEW YORK · CHICHESTER · WEINHEIM · BRISBANE · SINGAPORE · TORONTO

Publisher: Robert Ipsen
Editor: Carol Long
Developmental Editor: Adaobi Obi
Managing Editor: Micheline Frederick
Text Design & Composition: Benchmark Productions, Inc.

Designations used by companies to distinguish their products are often claimed as trademarks. In all instances where John Wiley & Sons, Inc., is aware of a claim, the product names appear in initial capital or ALL CAPITAL LETTERS. Readers, however, should contact the appropriate companies for more complete information regarding trademarks and registration.

This book is printed on acid-free paper. ♾

This publication is designed to provide accurate and authoritative information in regard to the subject matter covered. It is sold with the understanding that the publisher is not engaged in professional services. If professional advice or other expert assistance is required, the services of a competent professional person should be sought.

Library of Congress Cataloging-in-Publication Data:

Bourne, Jennie, 1951–
    DSL : a Wiley tech brief / Jennie Bourne, Dave Burstein.
        p. cm — (Wiley tech brief series)
    ISBN 0-471-08390-9 (pbk. : alk. paper)
    1. Digital subscriber lines. I. Burstein, Dave, 1951– II. Title. III. Series.

TK5103.78 B68 2001
004.6'4—dc21   2001046621

Printed in the United States of America.

10 9 8 7 6 5 4 3 2 1

Wiley Tech Brief Series

Other books in the series:

Tom Austin, *PKI*. 0471-35380-9

Steve Mann and Scott Sbihli, *The Wireless Application Protocol (WAP)*. 0471-39992-2

Ray Rischpater, *Palm Enterprise Applications*. 0471-39379-7

Chetan Sharma, *Wireless Internet Enterprise*. 0471-39382-7

Traver Gruen-Kennedy, *Application Service Providers*. 0471-39491-2

Jon Graff, *Cryptography and E-Commerce*. 0471-40574-4

William Ruh, Francis Maginnis, and William Brown, *Enterprise Application Integration*. 0471-37641-8

For my mother, I miss her most when I do my best, my father who had DSL before I did, and steadfastly held on to a vision of me writing a book until I actually did it, and Dave whose brilliance and generosity inform every word of this book.

Jennie

For Jennie, who keeps me strong while we chase our dreams, and for our friends who are delivering the fast Internet around the world.

Dave

Contents

Acknowledgments

· ·

Just over two years ago, we entered a new industry, DSL, just as the worldwide rollout began. The welcome to a stranger was extraordinary, whether from ordinary engineers or the chair of the DSL Forum, Hans-Erhard Reiter. North-Point CEO Mike Malaga and Bell Atlantic leaders Jeff Waldhuter and Pete Castleton were among the first to encourage us, and virtually every company leader in the industry has graciously answered our (almost incessant) questions. Reporters Lee Goldberg, Loring Wirbel, and Annie Lindstrom were the first to show us the ropes, and Peter Meade one of the first to introduce us.

Matt Davis of the Yankee Group, videoconference guru Jim Harper, top industry consultant Danny Briere of Telechoice, Java expert Eric Lazarus, MBlast's Jamie Samilio and science fiction writer Michael Burstein wrote special items for this book. Vic Jayasimha and Patrick Kusior of Analog Devices contributed the remarkable illustrations of the inside of a DSLAM and a modem, with detailed explanations. Trish Boccuti and Scott Eudy of Paradyne, Richard Washbourne of Copper Mountain, Sandra Yocura of Netopia, Brooke Houston and Cheryl Ertel of Lucent, Kelly Karr of Virata, Steve Gleave of Jetstream and several others created illustrations for the book. The troubleshooting chapter was reviewed by folks from Verizon, BellSouth, Covad, Panix, Netopia, Alcatel, Efficient, and especially Telocity and Earthlink, where folks spent hours helping us get things right. Emmanuel Goldstein and half a dozen cohorts in the 2600 crowd confirmed the security chapter had it right, and who would know better than the top hackers? Bruce Schneier gave us a hand there as well, and his book, *Secrets and Lies* (a Wiley book), was an inspiration.

John Cioffi, Tom Starr, and Jim Southworth are our technical gurus. Another inspiration was Jeff Raskin, who demonstrated what a dedicated author could do even in the computer book genre with The Humane Interface. We wrote most of the book on the computer he designed, the Macintosh. Richard Wurman's Information Anxiety 2, Jan White's *Graphic Design for the Electronic Age*, and Karen Schriver, *Dynamics in Document Design* (a Wiley book) were our key design sources.

We are remarkably lucky with our friends in the industry, more than 300 of whom read chapters or gave us comments for the book. We haven't slept in the last two months, finishing this book, and we apologize for the mistakes. Correct them with an email to book@DSLPrime.com.

Introduction

● ●

Welcome to the Fast Lane

Digital Subscriber Line (DSL) exploded onto the scene in 1999, and three years later it has reached 10,000,000 customers. Soon, over 100,000,000 people will connect to the Internet through DSL, because the world wants fast, cheap access to the Internet. We report from the eye of a hurricane. The DSL landscape is constantly changing. For this book, however, we stopped and asked ourselves, what is most important for the user to know about DSL? We hope you find the result useful.

Three years ago, Dave created *DSL Prime*, which quickly became the industry newsletter for DSL. It was wonderful to be part of one of the hottest businesses on Earth. There were great hopes and plans, and many people got very rich very quickly. Companies went from IPO to $10 billion in months. Two years later, the same companies were near failure and we reported some of the agonies of 100,000 customers cut off in NorthPoint's bankruptcy. This is a brand new, wide-open field. We reported what we learned from field technicians, customers, and CEOs. It was heady stuff when then FCC Chair Bill Kennard explained to us that he had personally made SBC's commitment to universal service a requirement of the Ameritech merger approval. Joe Nacchio, CEO of Qwest, told us that video quality VDSL made economic sense, when every analyst was saying it was unaffordable. Now 50,000 homes in Phoenix are signed on to VDSL, and Qwest is considering how to expand.

If you're reading this book, we probably don't have to convince you that DSL is a good thing. We *can* help you choose a provider and get the most out of the service you pay for. We'll tell you how to watch security and what you can really expect, from the initial installation to the performance of the network. We'll give you particulars of how to decide on a provider, make sure you get the best deal, and advise you on troubleshooting down the line. While we'd like to impress you with our knowledge of the field, it's more important to us to provide the practical advice you need in language that's easy to understand whether you're corporate or an individual user. We'll do our best not to bore you as so many technical books do. We know you need information, but we also know you'll understand it better if we talk about what's happening in the real world instead of regurgitating the theory you can find in any good textbook. These are exciting times, and we are privileged to know the people making it happen; we'll take you on a journey into their worlds.

Because DSL is fast, you can do things you couldn't do before and other things, like sharing music files over a peer-to-peer network, with much greater ease. Because it's cheap, the average middle-class American and even the smallest of offices can afford it. The Internet does not change everything, but don't underestimate the impact.

Who should read this book? Everyone who uses DSL in their work: Network managers dealing daily with the ins and outs of DSL, tending a system that may extend around the world. Providers, and their sales staffs who have to sell it. Hard-working tech support people who have to explain DSL and make it work all day every day. Small business owners looking for a fast connection to the Internet. Anyone who has DSL and anyone planning to get it, for your office, school, church, or to make bringing work home easier.

We start by giving you the basics of how DSL works; for many of you this will be old hat, but you may find our brief explanation helpful when introducing others to the joys of the fast Internet. Next, we take a tour of the business landscape and introduce you to the companies that you'll be buying DSL from. This practical guide includes tips on how to distinguish a good provider from the bad ones, and gives you an idea of the options and services available. Our equipment chapter follows. If you have service now or even if you're just getting it, you'll want to know how the equipment works and what your choices are.

Chapter 6, "Troubleshooting," provides both a quick and dirty guide to getting up and running, and a more detailed description of the problems you may encounter and tips on how to fix them. Chapter 4, "Technology," is for you geeks out there. Hey, we admit it, we love this stuff.

OK. You have it, it's working, and you understand how it works with perfect clarity. The next half of our book focuses on all the incredible things you can do with DSL and how to configure it for your needs. Voice over DSL, videoconferencing, application service providers (ASPs), and video. We have a special chapter for enterprise users, and one for small office, home office, and telecommuters. We end with a look toward the future. Where will the technology go? How will the business fare? Will the rest of the world embrace DSL? We asked the experts and looked into our bones and shells; the results are optimistic and fascinating.

If you're a pro in this business, jump right to the chapter on the future. You'll find thoughts you agree with (we presume), some disagreements (we're sure), and some perspectives that we hope will intrigue you enough to read the rest of the book.

If you're new to DSL, start at the first chapter, which highlights what's most important. Then follow your interests.

We're true believers. DSL was integral to the research and writing of this book. We're here to tell you that the dream of working at home on your own terms with a fast Internet connection is real. Most of this book was written in an apartment overlooking Central Park where we didn't have to wear any clothes that we didn't want to.

We know everyone who is reading this will have heard the horror stories. *DSL Hell* has been a headline in half of the newspapers in the United States. The real experience is rarely that bad. We'll show you how to avoid the pitfalls *and* explain why they happen.

We wrote this book so you can understand it if you're not a geek. We firmly believe it is possible to write about technical subjects clearly. Our job is not done if we fall into jargon and obscurity. We use the term *telcos* to describe Pac Bell (Pacific Bell) and Verizon, not ILECs. We explain every technical term in context, so you don't have to flip to the glossary—but it's there if you need it.

This book does not stand alone, www.DSLPrime.com is where you'll find the news of what's happening in the industry today, what's changed since we wrote this book, and answers to the questions we know many of you will be writing us. We know some mistakes will slip through, and welcome corrections. Email us at book@dslprime.com. In our day-to-day work on *DSL Prime*, we rely on our readers—many are professionals in the field—to keep us honest. They've proved an incredible resource for our reporting and for this book. Please send us your comments and corrections.

Jennie Bourne

Dave Burstein

CHAPTER 1

DSL

D SL is spreading like wildfire and we write this as a warning to the world. An Internet connection at speed, once tasted, is something you'll never want to give up. Making the fast Internet cheaper and near ubiquitous is creating a fundamental shift in the way millions do business, allowing every branch office to have the fast connection that few could afford before.

Public access to information shifts the balance of power, and DSL makes it affordable. It's changing the way we do business and the way we learn. Fortune 500 companies log on for meetings and news, libraries are moving online, and students halfway around the world are taking courses at MIT.

High speed Internet, always on, is a glorious thing. However, not everything is so rosy. We report on how to avoid *DSL Hell,* a part of every U.S. computer user's working vocabulary. Networks are being built around the globe at an accelerated pace, but in the U.S., competition is dying and the telcos are moving very slowly. Many U.S. cities had at least five DSL providers active in 2000; by August 2001, NorthPoint and Rhythms had shut down, and competitors around the globe were suffering. Regulators had a wonderful dream, that they could allow competition and Adam Smith's *invisible hand* would ensure progress. In fact, strong government involvement in Korea, Canada, and Japan is producing the best systems and fastest growth.

From These Beginnings

The technology at the heart of Digital Subscriber Lines (DSL) was invented in the 1940s. However, it wasn't until the 1990s that engineers at Bell Labs/Bellcore and scientists around the world came together to create the technology that makes the industry what it is today: practical to produce and cheap enough to deliver high bandwidth connections to the Internet to millions over copper telephone wires.

By 1993, the American telcos led by Bell Atlantic were looking for ways to bring the cost down, primarily to deliver movies on demand to all their customers. Every telco in the world went into advanced trials and intense planning to kick start the industry and encourage suppliers to bring down prices. The American telco giants came together for a joint procurement of DSL equipment in one single massive order.

Alcatel, a French manufacturer with little presence in the U. S., seized the opportunity. They bid below their costs expecting that with volume they would be profitable. This ensured that their chosen technology, dynamic multi-tone coding (DMT) prevailed. DMT breaks the frequencies that travel over copper wire into 256 separate bands. The divisions or *channels* provide robustness by insuring that interference on some frequencies does not prevent the data on others from being transmitted accurately. As a result, asymmetric DSL (ADSL) dominates the market. The vast majority of the lines installed today are standard full-rate ADSL lines at up to 7 Mbps.

A second version of DSL, symmetric, was championed by a new group of companies, competitors empowered by the 1996 Telecommunications Act. The premise of the act was that allowing competition among phone companies would better serve the public interest than regulation. The act made provisions for competitors to share existing telco's infrastructure because it would be impractical and an enormous waste of resources to require competitors to tear up the streets for new wires and replicate the services of thousands of phone company local central office switching stations and other facilities.

Requiring the telcos to unbundle their services and sell access to their facilities, the act made competition attractive and feasible to the new DSL companies and spurred an industry. The new companies could rent the local loop wire and a small space in the telco office (CO) to which it connects. Government policy and early successes in the long distance market, including Sprint and MCI, inspired investors to pour tens of billions of dollars into the new companies.

Early in 1999, three DSL companies—Rhythms, NorthPoint, and Covad—raised hundreds of millions each to begin their network buildout. In 18 months, each reached all the major cities in the United States, covering 40–50 percent of the populations at a cost of about $1 billion each. They were among the hottest stocks of the Internet boom with a combined value of $15 billion by early 2000 despite few customers and little revenue.

These specialty DSL companies, over a dozen regional or small city focused peers, and several dozen Internet service providers (ISPs), were the darlings of Wall Street. Using business plans that had interesting ideas and minimal revenue, they raised billions more. Focused more on business service and looking for the customers who would pay more, these companies provided customers with one great advantage over the telcos. The telcos did not, and often still do not want to sell DSL to their business customers because they see DSL as cannibalizing the business from T-1 lines, which they sell at four to ten times the price.

Closely examined, these T-1 lines differ only slightly in technology from DSL and are no longer significantly more expensive to deliver, which makes them among the most profitable products each telco has to offer. They are sold with better service guarantees and better service, but most of the cost difference is billions of dollars in pure profit that the telcos are unwilling to give up.

Inspired by the multi-billion dollar market, dozens of mostly small companies raced feverishly to create the equipment needed. In a few cases, brilliant individuals created this technology. They include Joe Lechlider, who in the 1980s at Bellcore first provided the concept. Overwhelmingly, however, most DSL technology was created by corporations usually inspired by a driven businessman with a strong technical background. Throughout this book, we will describe for you the key companies with which you'll be dealing. We know that the details of their products will change as will some of the key people, but we believe that the culture and emphasis of the companies will change much less. Moreover, based on our work covering the industry for *DSL Prime* we're uniquely qualified to provide an inside-the-industry perspective.

Connecting the world seemed imminent early in 2000. U.S. telcos were wiring feverishly, while billions of dollars flowed to DSL providers in many countries. The American Covad, Rhythms, NorthPoint, NAS, and DSL.net reached a stock market value of $11 billion, with another dozen funded in the hundreds of millions and looking to go public. In Japan, Tokyo Metallic and eAccess attracted several hundred million dollars; QSC, KPNQwest, VersaPoint, First Telecom, Colt, and a dozen others were working on the

European continent. British Prime Minister Tony Blair proclaimed *Broadband Britain*. England had a dozen viable players, fighting amongst themselves for space in telco offices. The Internet was the future, and DSL would be the key enabling technology. Huge fortunes had been made, and more were on the way.

Then the bubble burst. The Internet boom had been the greatest Ponzi scheme in history, drawing in over three trillion dollars from investors unconcerned with actual profits. Stock values were at unprecedented highs by 1998 ("The Internet changes everything"), but belief in a new economy was sustained by the emergence of a new class of billionaires. Prices kept rising, new companies were formed more interested in going public than making profits, and thousand dollar bottles of wine were opened to celebrate the deals. We, like everyone close to the action, dreamed of riches. It was great fun for everyone in the boom days, and we had many fine lunches as the companies visited New York to promote their businesses.

The boom couldn't last, and the money suddenly disappeared. DSL, like all telecom services, requires enormous capital. With money hard to raise, even monopoly telcos are struggling and slowing down; competitors are generally going out of business.

Companies and networks disappeared soon after. NorthPoint had wired half the U.S. at a cost of over $1 billion; 100,000 users were shut down when no one wanted to buy the company in bankruptcy, at any price. (AT&T bought the physical system at about a tenth of its construction cost, and may restore it in 2002.) Rhythms shut down, Covad went into bankruptcy. Tokyo Metallic ran out of money, VersaPoint shut down, and none of the dozen planned British networks have been lit for full service.

By late 2001, as we write, some patterns are clear. Some countries are moving rapidly, driven by competition or government policy. Korea's President believes the fast Internet will help his country grow, and "guided" the industry through effective competition. In Canada and Germany, the telcos expect strong cable competition, and are moving rapidly. In Japan, Softbank, an Internet conglomerate that controls Yahoo, decided to gamble, and priced service at $22, hoping to attract millions of customers. The telco had to drop the price by half to stay in the game. Where there is less competition, prices are higher and growth slower. In the U.S , after the competitors were beaten down, the telcos raised prices; in the U.K. and France, the telcos effectively blocked others, and have kept the price high. Our publication, *DSL Prime*, does not want the U.S. to fall behind. We (with a smile) urged Son to move to America, and drive down prices. As an alternative, perhaps everyone in

Chicago should move to Toronto, where Bell Canada charges half what SBC/Ameritech bills—and gives better service.

A network that provides DSL service includes three key components: a DSLAM or remote which aggregates your DSL line with your neighbors, a local megapop, serving a metro area, and a network operations/control system. DSLAMs originally cost $20,000 or more, so they were first placed where they can serve the most customers, the large telco offices. Businesses and homes in densely populated cities are always the first to get DSL. Equipment costs have come down dramatically, with small DSLAMs now costing $5,000 and remotes for the field even less. Telcos can now profitably serve less dense areas; by year-end 2001, Germany's Deutsche Telekom will reach 90 percent of the country, while Bell Canada and BellSouth will be at 70 percent. 75–90 percent of customers can be profitably served without government aid, making telco requests for subsidies a taxpayer rip-off unless they extend beyond that core. The pending proposals in the U.S. and England do not promise universal service, and legislators armed with facts should turn away the lobbyists.

DSL Essentials

First, let us introduce the system reduced to its essentials. For those new to DSL and for the pros that need a simple way to explain it to others, the illustrations on pages 6 to 8 offer an explanation of how DSL works. We discuss the equipment and technology at the core of DSL at greater length in Chapters 3 and 4, but for now, let's get you up to speed on the basics.

DSL provides high-speed access to the Internet. A DSL modem or router connects over an ordinary phone line to a DSLAM in the phone company office.

The DSLAM functions like a bank of modems, connecting to up to hundreds of lines in the neighborhood, and aggregating the traffic to send over fiber to a network center or megapop. (A typical megapop has a control system (often, Redback Subscriber Management) and a fast switch that sends your packets directly to the Internet or to your ISP.)

DSL works because your phone line can carry 20 times (or more) as much data when carried as a digital stream rather than as an analog signal. The digital data can use a much wider range of frequencies. Analog connections use only the lowest 4K of bandwidth, which is all an ordinary modem can utilize. DSL modems use the higher frequencies as well.

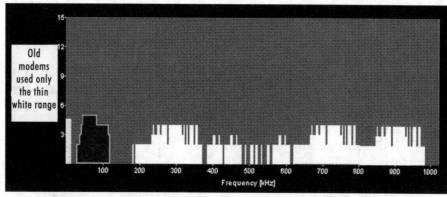

Phone Upstream   Downstream ADSL bandwidth (grey areas are blocked by interference)
on   in black
analog   **DSL modems use the entire band to the far edge**
modem
first   This chart shows the test mode of the Virtual Access router.
4K   The far left in white is the phone and analog modem band.
only   The dark area next to it is the upstream ADSL.
                The light area that fills to the right is downstream ADSL.
                Some areas, as use can see, are blank due to interference.

ADSL, for example, uses 256 channels of 4K each. With coding, that transmits as much as 12 megabits over a short, clean line. In practice, DSL is usually 10 times as fast as a 56K modem, and sometimes 50 times as fast. Asymmetric DSL (ADSL) offers fast downloads, 7–10 Mbps at 6–8,000 feet, 1.5MB twice as far. Uploads to the provider are slower, 384K to 1 Mbps. It's great for surfing the Internet.

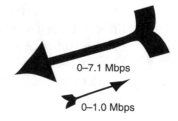

Symmetric DSL (SDSL and the newer G.shdsl) can go as fast as 2.3 Mbps upstream, no faster downstream. Businesses needing to send large files prefer symmetric bandwidth, but many do fine on the less expensive ADSL connection.

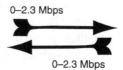

Unfortunately, signal strength drops with distance, and is affected by the line conditions and the other wires in the bundle. If you're more than about a mile from your DSLAM, your maximum speed will fall. At three or four miles, DSL won't work without a repeater.

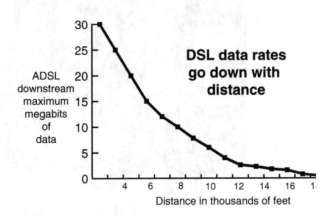

DSL is so much cheaper ($40–400) than traditional data lines (T-1s) ($400–2000) that you can install it in every small or home office. A midrange DSL line (500K to 1.2 Mbps) costs $150–250, and can provide enough Internet bandwidth for a 20–50 person office.

DSL, Cable, Wireless, Fiber—Which?

DSL is the most popular, but not the only, way to connect a business to the fast Internet. It's less expensive than any other business-oriented service, which doesn't always mean it's right for you.

Cable has outsold DSL two to one for consumers partly because of its two-year head start. The actual cable connection doesn't reach most office buildings or business districts. and the cable companies have overwhelmingly concentrated on consumers. Two bugaboos about cable connections—security and speed when the network is busy—have rarely been problems in practice.

Downstream speeds in most networks have been at least as fast as DSL for most of the day, and the occasional peak demand has not proven more of an issue than with DSL networks which themselves share bandwidth for all but the last mile. Traffic is encrypted and there has been no objective evidence showing that break-ins have been more common over cable than over DSL.

This means that cable is a reasonable choice if you have a good local provider and don't need much speed upstream to the Internet, which is where cable is severely limited. Most cable networks have business-unfriendly policies such as prohibiting connection to your corporate VPN. Few have the type of customer support for business that better DSL providers offer. It is also not possible to get a static IP address, so even running an e-mail server for a small business is problematic.

Higher security standards and more reliable quality of service are built into the newer cable modems and networks, and they look to be an even stronger competitor in the future.

Fixed wireless is making its way from the labs to the field, and as companies gain more practical experience, promises to become a major contender. Direct connections like line-of-sight microwave have long been ideal for campuses and favorable geography. One major advantage of wireless is that you don't have to tear up the streets to install it.

What's new are services like the one XO/Concentric is offering in Silicon Valley, and Sprint is offering in a dozen cities as part of ION. A large antenna shares 2 to 10 megabits per second of bandwidth with multiple users delivering a few hundred kilobits of bandwidth to each. Users from miles around need merely a good path, not perfect line of sight. Improved techniques like Cisco's Orthogonal Frequency Division Multiplexing (OFDM) mean that trees, clouds, and rain are less an obstacle than before. Early results from the field are encouraging, and everybody in the business expects rapid growth when the bugs are resolved.

Satellite is the only broadband Internet service available in many places and is dropping dramatically in price and improving in speed and reliability. Where you have alternatives, it is rarely the best choice for interconnection, typically being higher in price and slower than the alternatives.

T-1 and traditional frame relay services have years of proven reliability, generally better support, wider availability, and markedly higher costs, typically three to ten times as much as DSL. For the last ten years, nearly all new T-1 lines have actually been delivered on the early DSL standard HDSL. When you're buying a T-1 line today, you're essentially buying a DSL line with a promise of better service. A DSL loop, for example, may carry a three-day guarantee of repair, while a T-1 promises a four-hour guarantee.

Because it's the high-priced business service and users have always been more demanding, T-1 lines get more intense management and testing as well as priority for repairs. They almost always get the promised speed of 1.5 Mbps rather than the variable speed, not guaranteed, so common with other DSLs. Most T-1 lines work over two pairs of wires. Since the early 1990s, the service has usually been delivered using two lines of HDSL, an early version of DSL with 784 Kbps on each wire. The newer standard can work on a single pair.

T-1's have a distinct advantage over DSL. They can deliver megabit speeds over five or six miles using repeaters to extend their reach. T-1s also work with most equipment in existing telco networks, including the remote terminals that serve a quarter of America but block most DSL. Until your DLC is upgraded, which will take much of this decade in some places, a T-1 may be your only choice.

The alternative traditional connection, frame relay, also receives priority service, but a 56K frame relay line costs as much as a megabit of DSL. (Frame relay originally connected the *main distribution frames* in the telcos offices, and the name remains.)

ISDN is an older, slower, generally more expensive digital data system that is being supplanted by DSL throughout the world. DSL offers several times the performance and lower prices. In most places you pay by the minute for ISDN, which adds up to prohibitive bills if you spend much time on the Internet. If you are too far from the telco office to get regular DSL, you may be able to get IDSL, a special flavor of ISDN that is always on and usually less expensive unless your Internet use is very light.

Fiber, without a doubt, is the best and highest speed connection, but not available in most locations at low cost. If inexpensive fiber is a choice where you need service, consider it. Look at Yipes, Cogent, and Telseon in many major metro areas, expanding rapidly.

Need to Know—Some Jargon and Ideas

We wrote this book with as little jargon as possible, but are stopping here to introduce the central ideas and equipment. Therefore, when this book uses an industry-specific term not explained here, we'll explain it in context.

DSL enhances an ordinary phone line with equipment on each end to process digital data. This results in data transmission up to 10 times faster than analog modems. Under the best circumstances, DSL can be hundreds of times faster. DSL technology takes advantage of the fact that voice phone calls use only a fraction of the bandwidth copper phone lines can carry. DSL modems translate digital data from your computer or network into an analog signal that can be transmitted over the unused bandwidth in existing copper wires. DSLAMs change the data back into a digital form and send it via fiber optic network on to an ISP or directly to the Internet. ADSL, for example, uses a megabit of frequency to deliver up to 11 megabits per second of bandwidth, compared to 56 kilobits delivered by an ordinary modem. This means that more digital data can be delivered and it can be sent faster. Lines between phone offices were already digital; the innovation was to deliver digital data to home and office customers—hence, DSL, Digital Subscriber Line.

The equipment in your office is a DSL modem, gateway, or router.

DSL modems take the data from your computer or network and transform it into a specialized analog signal that can be transmitted over a phone line to your provider. Modems can be connected to a single computer or through a router or a hub to a network. The actual modem circuitry is credit card sized, which means it can be a stand-alone unit, on a card, or built in to your computer or other equipment.

A *DSL router* makes DSL available to several computers on your network. Unlike a hub, which simply shares a single IP address across the network, a router creates individual addresses for each computer on your network internally. As chips become more powerful and cheaper, many modems are adding the functions of a router. These hybrid machines are sometimes called DSL gateways (see *DSL gateway*).

DSL gateway is a new term, often used in different, confusing ways. In this context, a gateway is a combined modem and mini-router, designed for smaller networks. However, the same word is used to describe a router with voice functions added, and deeper in the network a gateway connects from a DSL/data network to deliver phone calls to a voice switch. Gateway is a general term for a connection between systems, so we'll try to be careful to make clear what we mean.

These devices are connected over your phone wire using several different protocols.

ADSL (asymmetric DSL) is dominant, over ninety percent of DSL lines. You can deliver approximately twice as much data carrying more in one direction (downstream from the Internet) than in the other direction (upstream to the provider and hence the Internet). By separating the signals coming and going, interference is reduced and lines can carry more than twice as much data. The same line that can carry 8 megabits asymmetrically (7M downstream and 1M up) can only deliver 3 megabits symmetrically (1.5 megabits in each direction). Asymmetric service works for users who download more large files from the Internet than they upload to it.

G.SHDSL is the latest variant of SDSL, and will become a common business offering in 2002-3.

HDSL is the older flavor of DSL used to deliver T-1 lines over two pairs of wires. HDSL2 does the same over one pair of wires. The technology is similar, but the marketing and support very different. For most practical purposes, T-1 service is a different market, and not the subject of this book.

IDSL lines deliver DSL technology over ISDN lines. It is most often used to provide DSL to customers more than about three miles from the nearest CO. The speed is limited to 144K. Today, several companies manufacture repeaters that allow ADSL and SDSL to go 30,000 feet and more, although few providers are deploying them in the field. In other contexts, ISDSL stands for International Society of Divine Love, International Sea Drilling Limited, or the International Symposium on Digital Libraries.

SDSL (Symmetric DSL) is appropriate if you need to send as much data as you receive. Examples of companies that need SDSL include a graphic design firm, or a company doing extensive videoconferencing. Creative marketing by providers has spread the myth that most businesses need the more expensive symmetric service, but many offices are well served by less expensive ADSL lines instead. In practice, most SDSL providers have focused on business connections and delivered better service to their higher paying customers. The older type of SDSL will very rapidly be supplanted by the new G.SHDSL standard, promising speeds up to 2.3 megabits.

VDSL (Very High Speed DSL) can carry as much as 53 megabits per second, but only over shorter distances of well less than a mile. VDSL is used to deliver video over phone lines to subscribers. Because a project that's wired 50,000 homes in Phoenix is the only large installation in the world, most of our discussion of VDSL is in Chapter 11, "The Future."

The other side of the connection is the phone network, either in the central office or closer to you in a remote.

CO (Central offices) of the telephone companies serve entire towns and neighborhoods, and until the 1980s were the standard way to bring you service. In these offices, hundreds, sometimes thousands, of local phone lines are converged and connected to the phone company's fiber optic network. They also act as switching stations. In a densely populated city like New York there can be as many as 20 COs, while a small town may have just one.

Today's technology has dramatically reduced the size of phone equipment, leaving plenty of room for the telcos to install DSLAMs and make space available to competitors. Typically, competitors locate their equipment in a 10' by 10' enclosed collocation cage, or *colo*. The distance from the CO to a subscriber's location determines whether they can get DSL. A customer must be within about three miles or 15,000 feet of the CO.

DLC remotes (DLCs, digital loop carriers) serve hundreds or thousands of lines from a small box in the field, and became the standard way to serve new or growing communities in the 1980s. Electronics by the 1980s made it possible to compress most of the functions of the phone office into a large closet deployable quickly and inexpensively, and connect back to the CO on a few fibers. This is much cheaper than building new COs. While they save the enormous cost of running hundreds or thousands of wires to the CO or building new ones, they sometimes create an obstacle to DSL. Unfortunately, older DLCs were not designed to handle DSL, and require upgrading. Probably half the lines currently not served by DSL are blocked by a DLC not yet upgraded. DLCs handle voice, T-1, ISDN and other services, with the latest including DSL built-in.

DSLAM (Digital Subscriber Line Access Multiplexer) is a mechanism at a phone company's central location that links many customer DSL connections to a single high-speed ATM line. Hundreds of subscriber lines can converge at a DSLAM. The signals are received by the equivalent of a bank of modems, and the data from as many as 64 lines can be decoded by the circuitry on a single card. All the data is joined (aggregated) and then sent over a single connection (multiplexed) to the provider and the Internet. By law, independent companies can rent space in the phone company's offices to install their DSLAMs. The newer DSLAMs include more functions, including equipment that facilitates line testing, video multicasting, and voice transmission.

Basement DSLAMs are what we call what the manufacturers like to call MDU/MTUs, multiple dwelling units/multiple tenant units. The pizza-box sized units are typically installed in a basement telephone room, serving clients in the building with a wired DSL connection. A single high speed connection goes back to the provider. In many cases, this is more efficient than running individual wires for each client.

The underlying data can be handled in two fashions, ATM and IP.

ATM (Asynchronous transfer mode) is the highly digital protocol that currently controls most of the phone network, and is the most common way to serve DSL. ATM breaks up data into 53-byte packets. The uniform size of the packets allows faster and more reliable control, which makes a significant difference in quality of service. "The future may be IP, but ATM works today" is the heart of the argument for its use. No ATM cash machine jokes, please.

IP The Internet runs on the Internet Protocol (IP), which assembles the data into packets, addresses them, and attaches other information. IP packets vary in size, making them appropriate for the diverse systems on the Internet but much harder to control or prioritize. When your computer sends data to the Internet, it is structured as IP packets. There's definitely a waste translating the IP packets to ATM, and some DSL networks are designed for pure IP.

Reliability Counts

DSLAMs, except for those produced by Alcatel, were developed by small entrepreneurial companies like George Hawley's Diamond Lane and Rick Gilbert's Copper Mountain. Even Paradyne, one part of mighty AT&T, was independent in this era. Most are now part of giants. Nokia bought Diamond Lane, Cisco purchased NetSpeed, Lucent Ascend, and Nortel Promatory. Recently, the largest modem manufacturer, Efficient, was sold to Siemens for $1.5 billion.

DSLAMs for independent DSL providers are located in what are called co-location cages, spaces rented to them at the telco's central offices (COs). From the CO your DSL provider typically sends all the traffic in one metropolitan area to a megapop, a large point of presence that controls the network throughout the city. At the megapop is a subscriber management unit that handles all the traffic including your login and IP addressing. Behind that is typically a big switch that connects directly to the Internet. Soon, video servers, distributed Internet services, and voice over DSL (VoDSL) equipment will be added at the COs and at the megapop to bring the Internet to you locally and therefore faster.

We've described the system partly so you can understand why setting up your service can be problematic. Each of these units must be provisioned accurately with all your circuit and wire information; literally hundreds of millions of dollars are being spent developing computer systems to make each component of the DSL system automatic. Progress is being made, but the complexity of operations support systems has been a major hurdle. Meanwhile, everything from an illegible fax to a 23-year-old inaccurate record of the wiring in the phone office can cause delays and problems.

The only downside to DSL is reliability. Providers have grown too fast, cut too many corners, and delivered service known as DSL Hell. We'll tell you how to protect yourself.

DSL Hell does not come from technical problems. The similar HDSL system for T-1 lines has worked reliably for most of a decade. Rather, it stems from provisioning problems and the difficulty of training rapidly the tens of thousands of field installers, CO technicians, and customer support people as the demand for DSL explodes.

 Like any connection to the Internet, you have to plan for security, backup, and occasional troubleshooting.

Everybody understands that there will be some problems with a new technology. It's now time for these problems to be solved. We say this meaning no disrespect to our many smart and hardworking friends in the industry. There is a common perception that the staff at the telcos is less capable than at the independent Internet companies. We've met too many on all sides to believe that.

Once you have a faster connection, you'll never want to go back. The crucial equipment is the DSL modem/router, which controls your end of the line. It takes the digital data from your computer, processes it intensely, and encodes it as an analog signal that is transmitted across the phone line. At the other end in the DSLAM is the equivalent of a bank of modems reversing the process and translating your data back into a digital form. The DSLAM also takes hundreds of local phone connections and aggregates the traffic onto a single digital line that carries it to your ISP and then to the Internet.

Around the World

THE UNITED STATES

... leads the world in DSL deployment with more than half the world's lines through the summer of 2000. By the end of 2001, U.S. lines will represent less than a third of DSL worldwide, and in a few years will be only a small fraction of the market. The telcos apparently fear no competition, and have been raising their rates despite a dramatic drop in the cost of equipment. Field operations have been an enormous burden, with *DSL Hell* costing hundreds of millions of dollars, as well as company reputations and customer trust. SBC, the largest of the U.S. telcos, dropped its 2001 plans 40 percent, and shows little evidence of returning to planned growth schedules. To reach the 30M projection in 2005, DSL would have to catch up with cable, and a majority of American homes would have to sign on to broadband. If the telcos feared competition, they could meet planned projections—but their actions suggest otherwise.

CANADA

... has two telcos, Bell Canada and Telus, strongly being challenged by cable. While the U.S. telcos have jumped from $40 to $50 per month, Bell Canada is still at $27 US. They've invested in video, have advanced trials of voice over DSL, and we think will continue to grow rapidly.

KOREA

... is a remarkable success story, with Korea Telecom leading the world and Hanaro performing dramatically. Korea's president Kim Dae Jung, has led his country to the fastest deployment of broadband in the world. Korea installed more lines, with fewer problems, than all the giant telcos in the United States. President Jung, believes strongly that spreading the fast Internet to all Koreans will pay off economically and socially, with distance learning and better access to government. His goals include building community and education through distance learning. He made building broadband a national policy promoting fierce competition between two telcos (Korea Telecom and richly financed Hanaro) and Korea Thrunet cable. By 2001, a third of all Koreans had broadband putting Korea far ahead of any other country, and KT, Hanaro, and cabler Thrunet are racing ahead. There's a limit approaching in a few years, of course, when nearly everyone is wired.

JAPAN

... did nothing until 2001 after the government, prodded by Sony's president, forced NTT to begin deploying DSL, and to accept competition from eAccess, Tokyo Metallic, and KDD. NTT had long-range plans for fiber, and was therefore reluctant to invest in DSL. However, financial issues in a troubled economy meant that NTT's fiber deployment would be limited until late in the decade. Officially, the government's motivation was that fast Internet connections would help the economy; unofficially, it was intolerable for former colony Korea to grab the world lead in this sector. Plans are ambitious, although their 2M goal for 2001 got off to a slow start. Microsoft made a major investment in Japanese cable; suggesting competition will heat up.

CHINA

... is everyone's fantasy market, with unlimited potential depending on the economic growth of the country. Internet use is booming, and China Telecom has a large contract with Alcatel for DSLAMs. There's been more talk than action to date, and it's very hard to find a firm basis for prediction.

TAIWAN'S

... telco, Chungwa, signed a contract with Alcatel for 1.7M lines in 2001, demanding a price—$175 including DSLAM and modem—that astonished the world. With the government encouraging competitors in a very price-centric market, competition is fierce, and prices are dropping. That's a good recipe for demand.

INDIA

... as few outside recognize, is one of the ten largest industrial economies in the world, with engineers and entrepreneurs whose skills reign in Silicon Valley as well. The telephone monopoly has been able to resist government pressure, so progress has been and is likely to continue to be slow.

GERMANY

... saw a rapid deployment by CLECs across the country in 2000, and Deutsche Telekom finally jumped in with plans for 2 million lines in 2001. This was partly inspired by a government requirement that DT spin off their cable operation, creating another possible competitor. Initial rollout is running behind plans slightly, but huge volumes are the goal.

FRANCE

... has kept competitors out, but France Telecom now offers wide service. With government backing, they wired the country for data with Minitel, and there's every reason to believe DSL will replace it.

THE UNITED KINGDOM'S

... British Telecom (BT) did much of the basic work on DSL, and the engineers were ready to lead the world. The Prime Minister, Tony Blair, made rousing speeches about Broadband Britain predicting that Britain would lead Europe in five years. Hundreds of millions of pounds were spent by Kingston, First Telecom, UUNet, and a half dozen others building networks for DSL. Hopes were very high, and motivation strong—cable has made dramatic inroads, taking 2 million voice lines.

BT management's primary response was to effectively block out others. The regulator, OFTEL, allowed BT to virtually make competition impossible, with engineering charges up to $1,000 to install lines and no access to BT offices in the major cities. The result: All competitors decided to take their losses and drop out of providing DSL to residential consumers, while a handful hope to build a business customer base. BT itself is late and slow, with prices designed to protect their other products, not to grow broadband.

Other countries have bright prospects, because DSL is a moneymaking service for any telco with standard facilities in place. If you already have the copper lines, central offices, and fiber connecting them, the cost of adding DSL is low and dropping. All of Scandinavia will have high penetration, with Telenor and Swedish competitor B2 planning some of the most advanced services in the world. Spain's Telfonica has ordered over a million lines of equipment, some of which are destined for subsidiaries in Brazil and Argentina. Telstra in Australia has promised to offer service to 90 percent of the country by 2002, under pressure from cable companies and competitive telcos. We know of plans in Pakistan, Vietnam, and the United Arab Emirates. Capital constraints are holding back telcos around the world, but the primary alternative, fiber, is even more expensive to deploy.

Environment of DSL

The environment around DSL is a complicated, regulated universe, where understanding change, and separating useful information from hype is important. We'd need another book to describe it all, but can't discuss DSL in a vacuum. Next, we present some highlights, to put the remainder of this book into a context and guide your understanding of DSL both as an industry and as a technology. Here we've mapped key factors that shape the DSL industry and its users. This unconventional approach is more like a road map than a treatise. Browse it as you would a Web page, selecting only the topics that interest you or most fit your needs.

If the technology stood alone, everyone could have DSL at megabit speeds and minuscule cost. However, a worldwide industry with investments (and eventual revenue) in the tens of billions doesn't develop just from technology; governments, bankers, analysts, and press play a major role in determining the likely future. Sony, Bill Gates, and the Motion Picture Association are actively involved, and so are the key Internet freedom organizations. You take all these factors into account to understand your future choices.

Your Information Sources

Understand that they lie to us, and we don't always catch them.

Much of what you read—sometimes including *DSL Prime*—is incorrect, despite a good, conscientious reporter. That's always true, of course, because reporters are human and make mistakes. In this field you have to be especially careful. Neither we nor most others have the time to track many stories in depth, especially the *instant reporters* rushing to get to press and the Net. The companies are often the primary source, and it shows.

Deliberate misinformation is far too common. The FCC Chair came to an investor's meeting in New York, seeking to hear things that were different from what they were telling him in Washington. He had a wonderful term, *regulatory arbitrage*, for the lies they tell. SBC and Verizon are on Wall Street saying they are going full speed ahead on DSL, for example, while in Washington they say they can't proceed without getting more favorable rules. Rarely does a reporter hear both of these presentations, and rarer still do you have the time and experience to sort out the contradictions. Reputable public companies can and do lie.

MAJOR NEWSPAPERS

All have dedicated telecom reporters, and many of them are excellent. The *Wall Street Journal* and the *San Jose Mercury* have strong teams, and the Chicago, L.A. and San Francisco papers have had strong coverage of SBC in particular. However, their beat is wide, their time is short, and their readers are more interested in earnings than service stories—so rarely is their coverage deep. When the *New York Times* or *Wall Street Journal* break a major story, the impact can be huge, with immediate moves in the stock price and numerous copycat stories in other media. What the *Times* or *Journal* reports in the morning often is on *Moneyline* that evening, typically with the same folks quoted. We speak from experience.

Telecom reporters are assigned to the business desk, and spend most of their time with the industry. They know their primary audience is investors, not the users of the service. The result is that telco earnings announcements get wide coverage, but issues like service reliability aren't reported unless the problems are extreme. In addition, the Internet press and the wire services report fast, and everyone's under pressure. The result, alas, is that far too many stories result from press releases with perhaps an analyst or two commenting; rarely can they take the time to do proper research.

LOCAL PAPERS

Local newspapers are great sources of information on hometown companies, and easy to access on the Web. We've gotten some of our best stories on Qwest from the *Denver Post* and the *Rocky Mountain News*, for example, and the *Chicago Tribune* has been the primary source for SBC's service problems in the Midwest.

CNET AND CBS MONEYWATCH

The Internet has some strong reporting; the rest, as well as financial news outlets like CNN and CNBC, rarely have reporters with telecom experience, and the work shows it. Generally, the "instant reports" on these sites, as well as from Dow Jones and Reuters, followed avidly by investors and treated as primary news, are rushed out so fast that they contain little that's not in the press release or a single analyst's comments.

PHONY CITIZEN GROUPS

In the real fight for your interests it's very hard to separate genuine consumer concern from the self-interested lobby of giant companies that pose behind innocent names like *Consumers Voice* and pretend to speak for the public interest. When *Voices for Choices*, speaks of global monopolies, the industry knows that's really the opinion of their primary financial sponsor ATT.

When *iAdvance*, in the persona of former White House spokesperson Mike McCurry, claims there is healthy competition, we know his bills are being paid by the Bells. When *iAdvance*'s former Congress member Susan Molinari talks DSL, she's being financed by SBC and Bell Atlantic. That makes particularly important to the public debate those without corporate giant backing like Consumers Union, the Electronic Frontier Foundation, and we hope the authors of this book.

ANALYST PACK

About 150 professional analysts, most working for large brokerages, have an extraordinary effect on the market. One morning, Dan Reingold of Credit Suisse was dissatisfied by Verizon's financial report, and downgraded them. The stock promptly lost over $2B. Smaller companies are typically followed by only half a dozen analysts, and if any of them issues a new recommendation, the stock may move 5 or 10 percent within the hour.

Most are extremely smart and diligent, and their reports are invaluable research for us. Analysts lie in their ratings, reporting "hold" or "market perform." Generally, their companies make more money on investment banking (IPOs, corporate bonds, mergers, and acquisitions), so they are reluctant to criticize their prospective corporate clients.

Hint: The analyst's favorite tool, and usually the best source of corporate information, is the quarterly financial conference calls most companies hold, which now are often broadcast on the Internet. The CEO and CFO are usually on the call, reporting in depth to the folks who will have an enormous influence on their stock price. They often answer questions they would never accept from reports, afraid to raise doubts by ducking. If the company doesn't Webcast the call, try e-mailing their investor relations department for the time and toll-free number of the call.

Business Decisions

CABLE VERSUS TELCO WAR

The nightmare of the phone companies is that the cable guys will take away the voice customer when they install high-speed data; in fact, the cable companies in England have taken millions of customers. That fear is the only reason most telcos moved strongly to DSL, Telcos are generally slow and cautious beasts, likely to spend half a decade testing, training, and planning before undertaking such a large deployment. Cable telephony slowed down in 2001, as many of the operators, especially AT&T, faced financial problems and decided to slow down.

The result was dramatic: a month after AT&T, the largest cable operator, announced it would concentrate on profits, not growth in areas like voice over cable, SBC responded by raising the price of DSL. This was particularly outrageous, because the costs of delivering DSL were going down 40 percent in six months.

BANKRUPTCY FEAR

Everyone's afraid their provider will go bankrupt as NorthPoint did, stranding tens of thousands of customers despite federal law prohibiting such abrupt termination. That's a legitimate worry that will make it increasingly hard for competitors to do business. Fortunately, in the United States at least, the law is clear, and even in bankruptcy customers must be given notice. NorthPoint collapsed before the system was ready to protect users, but Rhythms shut down with 30 days notice, allowing you to switch. As we write, Covad is in a bankruptcy proceeding, from which they expect to emerge. Because their service has been so much better than the Bells, we'd take a chance and go with them. In the event of catastrophe, there should be time to find an alternative.

DOCSIS AS CABLE ADVANTAGE

DOCSIS is the cable modem standard; one reason cable is ahead is that they all united behind Denver's cable labs to make standard equipment sold by the millions. The newer versions 1.2 and 2.0 contain security provisions important to corporate customers, and quality of service tools to support voice and video. This will make cable an even more formidable competitor to DSL.

BUNDLING

Bundling was expected to be the way cable and phone companies compete. AT&T did a marketing trial, bundling video, long distance, a cable modem, and three or four lines of full-featured local telephony for about 30 percent off. That amounted to over $100/month per home, a profitable customer and one taken away completely from the telco. Add wireless and expected extra services, such as video on demand, and the average revenue per customer skyrockets. The initial investment and marketing costs were so high that AT&T backed away, deciding instead to split the company into three parts.

VDSL STANDARDS BATTLE

VDSL can go 50 meg or more, five times as fast as ADSL. 50,000 customers are in service in Phoenix, and the technology has been working for several years. The equipment is inherently cheaper than ADSL, with simpler chips that draw less power. Because it only works up to 4,000 feet, it's not right for everyone, but it should be in much wider use. It has been stalled in the marketplace partly by the industry's inability to choose between standards. CAP/QAM (a single-carrier standard design supported by the VDSL Coalition (www.VDSL.org), Broadcom, and Next Level) with two years of field experience in Phoenix, finally looks to be emerging the winner. Till now, VDSL was stalled in standards committees, as the VDSL Alliance, led by Alcatel and Texas Instruments, fought for an alternative, DMT. DMT chips should have advantages of compatibility with ADSL, but both Alcatel and TI are more than a year late delivering working chips. Nearly everyone supports the need for a standard, but could work with either. Battles like this are one reason why the industry is behind the cable guys.

WALLED GARDENS ARE REALLY PRISONS

Walled garden is a term used by cable folks to give preference to the programming they choose or choose not to carry. On the Internet, everyone has access to all programs. Access, however, is limited by the fact that required speeds for video are not universally available. Networks are closed at the edge and may not provide sufficient speed inside, creating a defacto walled garden limiting access and making the Internet more like cable television.

AOL and Time Warner can keep Disney and ABC off their cable Internet Roadrunner service by demanding a steep toll to connect at video speeds. We discuss this crucial freedom of speech issue in Chapter 11.

Finance

VENTURE CAPITALISTS

Venture Capitalists made and lost tens of billions of dollars between 1997 and 2001 investing in DSL providers and equipment manufacturers, and generally have effective control of most independent companies. They were the royalty of the New Economy. They took enough profits to do well, but generally were the largest shareholders after the crash as well. In good times, they allowed management to be the face of the companies, and make most decisions. However, when the crash came, they stepped in, often replacing the CEO in quiet board coups.

WALL STREET AND "THE MONEY"

As in so many businesses, Wall Street calls the shots. Enormous profits were made in DSL companies—billions by 1999—so everyone with money jumped in, in many cases funding far more companies than could ever be successful. This was the Internet and telecom boom, and everyone was making so much money that all common sense was lost.

FREEDSL

Winfire had a million people on their waiting list, although only about 10,000 were connected when the money ran out early in 2001. There's no question that the demand for DSL would be enormous at any reasonable price, and we believe that Bell Canada's rate of $27 (US) is about right for large consumer deployments. Canada's price is low, because the telco is responding to strong competition from cable. With less aggressive cable competition, the U.S. telcos instead raised the price in 2001 to about $50, resulting in a much slower ramp.

Laws and Regulations

THE 1996 TELECOM ACT

The 1996 Telecom Act changed all the rules for U.S. telcos, who are required to open certain facilities in return for diminished regulation and the right to expand, especially into the long distance market. FCC Chair Reed Hundt brokered the deal, believing that competition would spread in local telephony. Many agreed, and literally tens of billions of dollars poured into new companies, the CLECs (Competitive Local Exchange Carriers), which became one of the hottest areas of the Internet/dot.com boom. We watched some really wild glory days, as data-oriented CLECs NorthPoint, Rhythms, Covad, DSL.net, and NAS went public in 1999, and climbed to a combined value of over $17 billion. The telephony-oriented competitors, including Allegiance, Winstar, Teligent, and ICG, raised the nominal market value of the sector over $40 billion, and early investors claimed returns of 10 and 20 to 1 in a few years. Hundt, after leaving office, joined the board of North-Point, and made over $10,000,000.

By 2001, the bubble had burst, with NorthPoint's bankruptcy in early 2001 the conclusive proof that things weren't working. The 1996 Act itself was part of the problem, because it turned out not to require any real competition. The law had a 14-point checklist that was supposed to permit competition, but no requirement that the competition actually occur. For practical matters, for consumers and most businesses, reality is there is no competition. The result, a monopoly without regulation, is the worst of both worlds.

COMPETITION IN EUROPE

The Council of Europe required that all Common Market members open telecom to competition, including DSL, but left the details to the individual states. Competitors moved rapidly in Germany, Sweden (especially B2), and Holland, where the regulations were reasonable. The telcos have answered back, with Deutsche Telekom investing to acquire more subscribers the next few years than the entire rest of the continent. However, Britain's regulator OFTEL allowed British Telecom to set rules and pricing that chased away a slew of planned competitors, while moving slowly itself. The situation is similar in Italy, France, and Spain—little effective competition, slow telco deployment. Ireland is even further behind—nothing, at least until 2002.

Bill Gates of Microsoft believes the one thing holding back new technology and services is the cost of broadband access, and Microsoft has invested billions of dollars in DSL and cable modem providers around the world, including the now bankrupt NorthPoint, and struggling Rhythms and DSL.net. Like Intel, they know that faster Net connections will inspire many users to buy new, faster computers.

NAPSTER

Music sharing was the key application driving the demand for broadband. Traffic rose 30–100 percent the weekends before Napster's court hearings, as folks, we included, rushed to download MP3s before the court interfered. Broadband costs come down dramatically with volume, so every application that creates more demand for broadband will drive down the prices that everyone will pay.

JAPANESE REGULATORS

In Japan, regulators faced a bind trying to persuade politically powerful telco NTT to allow competition, lower prices, and provide advanced services. Powerful business leaders, headed by Sony President Nobuyuki Idei, believed that NTT was holding back the Japanese economy, causing cabinet-level intervention. The resulting antitrust investigation was surprising, because NTT was majority owned by the Japanese government, but political pressure forced open the market in early 2001, with plans for the fastest deployment in the world in the next few years. Cynics add that Japan had little choice but to expand DSL, embarrassed by the fast growth in former colony Korea.

ECONOMISTS

Richard Posner and other Chicago School economists have been enormously influential, providing the intellectual basis for eviscerating antitrust law. Posner's "The Regulation of Natural Monopolies" essentially challenged a century of antitrust law, arguing that "monopolistic" behavior was rarely significant or damaging. Anyone who watched the monopoly telcos wipe out most of the competition in the last few years knows better, just as everyone in the computer business knows that Microsoft has used monopoly power. However, it's almost impossible to bring a successful antitrust case, and competition is dying.

DSL Heaven—Creating Opportunity, Changing Lives

As a Black woman I look forward to a future when computers connected to the fast Internet will be as ubiquitous as television sets in the African American community. The fast Internet has taught me more about access than any equal opportunity program. Although I worked for many years as a journalist and filmmaker, the fast Internet is where I feel at home. It's the world's greatest classroom and for those who have access, it represents the power to change lives.

I'll never forget my first experience. After waiting in line at the Science and Business branch of New York's public library to spend an hour on the Internet I was swept away by the speed of the connection. In that hour I did more than I'd been able to do in six on my dial-up connection, in days as a researcher in *Newsweek's* vast *morgue*. I was hooked. Surfing the Net at speed was like a drug. It unleashed my imagination. I made connections quickly, bringing back the real excitement of investigative reporting. Today I can't imagine how I practiced journalism for 20 years without it.

Too many young minds are trapped in inferior inner city schools. They deserve the bright future the Internet can help to unlock for them. Every library, every school, every church should have DSL, a tool that can help students pursue their dreams. Every bright inquisitive student deserves access. Every woman who wants to return to school should have the option to take classes over the Internet. I took a break mid-career to go back to Journalism School at Columbia. It was expensive and hard to manage. If I'd been a mother with children to support, I probably couldn't have done it. Today, Harvard and MIT are delivering their curriculums via the fast Internet; others will follow and the world will open for those who have access.

As an online journalist and Web producer I hear many smug comments about technologically advanced families. While I'm proud to say I come from one (my father in his 70s was an early adopter of DSL), I'm concerned that this is just one more way of separating the *haves* from the *have-nots*. These days I have to restrain myself from accosting children in the street and sending them to the library, not just to read books, but to know what I know. The world can come to your doorstep over a high-speed Internet connection that provides access to an endless supply of information, and it isn't that expensive when you consider that information is power and knowing how to find it can change your life.

Jennie Bourne

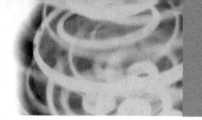

CHAPTER 2

Choosing a DSL Provider

C ompetition for your DSL account has been decimated in 2001. In 2000, most American cities had three to five choices, with the local bell, three national networks, and two dozen regionals all active. England, Germany, Japan, and Scandinavia had companies proclaiming similar plans. The Internet/telecom boom ended, financing dried up, two national networks (NorthPoint and Rhythms) shut down, a dozen smaller ones failed, and choices became much more limited. The pattern was worldwide; no British competitor widely offers consumer service, and few are available for business. *The Empire Strikes Back* was one explanation, as the incumbents universally made it difficult to enter the market, but financing issues are clearly crucial. DSL, like most tele-com services, requires 4-7 years of losses building networks and acquiring enough customers to break even. If the money isn't available, even the best run company fails.

You have fewer choices today, but in larger cities businesses are still served by more than just the local phone company. First thought suggests you choose the telco, sure to be around and not facing co-ordination problems because of the many parties involved. Facts, however, suggest otherwise. The dedicated DSL specialists, such as Covad, have consistently delivered far superior service. A good ISP with a company like Covad providing the actual lines is far more likely to provide a smooth install and support you down the line. Covad, as of this writing, is in Chapter 11 proceedings with a good chance to emerge as a healthy company. We hope they do—evidence is over-whelming that today's telcos work best with a competitive spur.

There are many things to consider when choosing a DSL provider, among them, provider reputation, price, speed, service guarantees, and support. In this chapter, we'll help you to understand all the components of DSL service. Then we'll take you on a guided tour of the DSL landscape and give you some insight into the major companies providing DSL.

Choosing a provider is only the beginning. We're not going to lie to you. So many people have gone through installation and startup problems that DSL Hell has become part of the vernacular. Choosing a good provider, one that won't make you feel like you're being punished for wanting high-speed Internet access without paying T-1 prices, also requires some street smarts, so we've included a section at the end of this chapter on avoiding DSL Hell.

A Good Provider Means You'll Never Walk Alone

A good DSL provider will make sure you have what you need for the installation, coordinate things so it's more likely to happen on time, and answer the phone when you have a question or a problem. A bad one will cancel the installation and refuse to serve you the minute they run into a problem.

Installations are getting better, but there are 20 individual steps that can and often do go wrong. Stuff happens, and it's good to know that your ISP will be behind the scenes negotiating on your behalf. A good ISP may also provide faster service, better connections to the Internet, and more reliable equipment.

Your ISP secures your DSL service and provides other services, including access to the Internet, security, and e-mail. Your connection to the Net might be provided by a business DSL specialist like MegaPath, a midrange local outfit like Panix in New York, or a huge national one like AT&T, Sprint, AOL, or Earthlink.

When you need service or support, you will call your ISP, but they may not actually provide your DSL. Unless your ISP is also a phone company, they will subcontract your DSL line from a wholesaler like Covad, Rhythms, or your local telco, and add to it the Internet connection, e-mail, and other services like Web hosting.

The telcos get over three-quarters of the business, most of which they direct to their own ISPs (80 percent in SBC territory). Covad, the strongest independent provider, serves independent ISPs, but now they too keep some customers for themselves.

This complicated arrangement means that your ISP will act as an intermediary between you and the actual service provider. Don't jump to the conclusion that you can avoid problems by buying DSL directly from a telco ISP. The evidence is overwhelming that buying directly from telcos will not ensure you better service. Apparently, their own divisions don't communicate any better with each other than they do with their competitors who subcontract lines from them.

By far the best independent source for quality ratings is *DSL Reports*. Seven thousand individual users contributed their experience to the following chart, including many who were happy with their service. Independents, Bell Canada, and BellSouth do much better than the telco giants, Verizon and SBC. Earthlink, which is largely a reseller of the telco DSL services, draws much higher ratings than the telcos that own ISPs. Instead of using these numbers, from June of 2001; get the current ratings at www.dslreports.com/gbu.

DSL Reports data is excellent, but not perfect. They have enough responses that a few exceptions won't skew the ratings, and they have proven exceptionally ethical. While they accept ads from providers (as *DSL Prime* does), *DSL Reports* does not hesitate to publish negative information about advertisers. We suspect the XO rating is skewed low, perhaps by unrealistic expectations by gamers, a very demanding audience. We know Telocity has some of the best policies for consumers, including static IPs and advanced troubleshooting, so we would give them more credit than those answering the poll did.

One conclusion is clear: Some providers are better than others, and the mega telcos SBC and Verizon are exceptionally disappointing. We meet and get enough e-mail from users to be absolutely sure that's accurate, although we're amazed that the problems continue. We know many of the key people, and they are dedicated, hard workers. We often get e-mail late at night and on the weekends.

Lots of smart, dedicated people are working to fix the problems, but the results so far are dismal. The telcos have been consistently unwilling to provide trade publications like *DSL Prime* and journalists covering the field, with basic data, on network speeds, reliability, uptime, latency, install times, churn, and the like. If things aren't as bad as they are reported to be, why are they hiding the real data from everyone?

We ask the telcos to start releasing basic data to prove to you that they are living up to their claims. Verizon, for example, boasts "Verizon Online Internet access as dependable as your telephone. Fast, reliable Internet access is just a click away." They will not provide any data to back up the words *dependable*, *fast*, or *reliable*.

Hundreds of ISPs may want your business, but they are all reselling the service of a handful of actual DSL providers. Mid-sized and regional providers, like DSL.net and Arrival, often sell direct as well. Prices are leveling off, and we suggest you go for quality, not a small price advantage.

The Good, the Bad, and the Ugly—June 2001

NAME	AVG /5	DAY WAIT	S	I	R	T	SV	V	REVIEWS FROM
Mpower Communications	4.02	29	B+	B-	A-	B	B	B+	TN GA CA FL (18 reviews)
SPEAKEASY.net	3.99	25	A-	B+	B+	B	B+	B	AZ MD IL TX PA MI OH NJ CA MO VA GA WA OR NY MA (842 reviews)
MegaPath Networks	3.94	37	B+	B	B+	B	B+	B	IL PA TX MI NJ CA VA GA CO NY WI (340 reviews)
Cincinnati Bell/ Broadwing	3.65	14	C+	C-	A	B	B-	A-	OH (22 reviews)
Bell Canada	3.65	9	B-	B-	A-	C-	B	B+	(124 reviews)
Network Access	3.63	43	B-	B+	B-	B-	B-	B	(18 reviews)
BellSouth	3.58	29	B-	B-	B+	C+	B-	B	MS AL NC GA KY TN FL SC LA (769 reviews)
Qwest	3.55	18	B-	C+	B	C+	B	B	AZ WA OR CO MN NM (user quotes and 104 reviews)
EarthLink	3.43	35	B-	C	B	C+	B	B	NY FL WI MA (1342 reviews)
DSL.net	3.35	32	B	C	B	C+	B-	B-	NY (user quotes and 46 reviews)
US West	3.33	25	C+	C+	B	C	B-	B-	WA (user quotes and 137 reviews)
Southwestern Bell	3.19	30	C+	C+	B-	C-	C+	B-	AR OK MO KS TX (663 reviews)
XO/Concentric	3.04	43	C+	C+	B-	C	C+	C	IL NY CA (145 reviews)
Verizon/GTE	2.99	36	C+	C	C+	C-	C+	C+	WA CA IN TX (233 reviews)
Pacific Bell/SBC	2.99	33	C+	C	B-	C-	C	C+	CA (846 reviews)
Ameritech/SBC	2.97	34	C+	C	C+	C-	C	C+	OH IL IN WI MI (373 reviews)
DIRECTV/ Telocity	2.90	38	B-	C	C	D+	C	C	NY TN WI FL LA MA (1461 reviews)
SNET/SBC	2.90	31	C+	C	C	D+	C+	C	CT (148 reviews)
Verizon Online	2.78	31	C+	C	C	D+	C	C	RI VA MD WA ME IN TX PA NJ NY CA FL DC MA (1469 reviews)

From *DSL Reports*

S = Sales Rating   T = Tech Support
I = Install Experience   SV = Services (Email,DNS,News etc)
R = Reliability   V = Value for Money

Getting the Best Information

We hope you find this book useful, but things are changing so fast that no book can be completely current. Therefore, here are some sources that will be updated in Internet time:

www.dslprime.com is our site, where the provider page will be regularly updated. We report weekly on the industry, supplemented by hundreds of e-mails from users. Although we accept advertising, we do our best to make sure our editorial serves our readers first.

www.dslreports.com produced by Justin Beech is invaluable. Justin filters the results of thousands of user responses. By and large, his data confirms what everyone inside the industry knows: Many telco customers feel like they are in DSL Hell, the imperfect service from their competitors, and the enormous variability between different ISPs. In particular, no one should buy DSL without checking this page

www.dslreports.com/gbu (GBU = Good, bad, ugly) breaks the larger providers into greens (consumer ratings of 3.5 or higher out of 5), yellows (3 to 3.5), and reds (under 3). It is disheartening to see companies with the skills of Bell Atlantic, Telocity, Rhythms, and Ameritech in the worst categories—but accurate.

The rating includes this disclaimer, "No automatic rating system is foolproof! Do Your Own Research! Smoking Kills! Do not put your pet in the microwave!" In particular, consumers are more likely to report than businesses, and some ratings, such as XO/Concentric's, we suspect come from unreasonable consumer expectations.

www.point-topic.com is the best site for international information, although it's much less detailed. Conscientious and well done.

Many sites that claim to offer recommendations are simply fronts for agents. www.everythingDSL.com, www.telcoexchange.com, and the other sites that provide DSL recommendations (especially DSL.com) have not convinced us they give equal coverage to providers they don't have resale or advertising relationships with, although the first two are generally conscientious.

Reading the vendors' Web sites is generally unenlightening. They all know what the main customer concerns are, and give answers that seem to address them. However, on the real issues—actual speed, reliability, repair time—you find weasel words like *up to*, obsfuscations, and no guarantees. Verizon is typical—their terms of service specifically deny what all their advertising and promotion claims.

Universal Broadband

Service areas are defined geographically, a legacy of the telcos whose regions were defined when AT&T was forced to divest itself of local phone companies. In major cities where 55 percent of all U.S. businesses are located, you have the option to choose between your local telco and several competitors. There are still areas where only the local telco provides DSL and others where DSL is not yet available.

The telcos have not yet extended DSL service to customers of many of their smaller central offices (COs), and the buildout to the 20 percent or more of users served by remote field terminals (DLCs) is lagging far behind projections. SBC promised 80-percent coverage in 2002 with Project Pronto, but is already more than a year behind schedule. Verizon and BellSouth expect to be able serve 80–85 percent in their territories before SBC meets its goals, although Verizon is slipping as well.

SBC, which serves one-third of the United States, has promised universal coverage throughout "soon after 2002," and Verizon claims that universal service is "a strategic goal" but provides no timeline. BellSouth has committed to universal broadband in North Carolina by 2003.

At least 80–90 percent of customers can be served profitably, so it is just a matter of the telcos delaying deployment. DSL equipment costs $200–500 per customer, easily recovered in a service that sells for $400 or more per year. Serving the remaining few by satellite adds only a small cost, as evidenced by the ability of Earthlink and AOL to sell satellite service at little more than the cost of DSL. Four separate companies offer repeaters, which can more than double the DSL reach, and neighborhood gateways keep dropping in price. If SBC, Bell Canada, and Telia in Switzerland can serve everybody, so can your telco.

Evaluating Your Provider

You will order your DSL service through an ISP, which in most cases will be a division of your regional telco or the direct sales arm of a provider like Covad. Deciding which company to work with can be tricky. Marketing and PR claims often bear little relationship to the truth. Like used car salespeople and purveyors of carnal pleasures, DSL companies tend to overstate what their product can reliably deliver.

If you're a corporation or even a medium-sized company, you're in luck. Every company has a special sales division for enterprise-level customers, and many DSL providers focus exclusively on the lucrative business market. You'll get better; more informed sales help and better deals. You'll also have a wider range of choices of services from ADSL, to VDSL and options for security.

If you are a small to medium-sized business, we suggest you seek service from the enterprise division of your provider. Because they support major customers, salespeople in enterprise divisions typically have more clout, but generally there are no firm rules about minimum size that prevent you from working with these more professional teams.

Even if you've tracked your company's current Internet usage, calculating your need for bandwidth involves making an educated guess about the future. Your needs *will* expand with broadband. The question is, how much? Once accessing the Internet is less of a waiting game, your employees are likely to use it more often for research, e-mail, and in other unexpected ways. Applications like teleconferencing, collaborating online with visual editing tools, and rich media will also increase the demand on your connections.

Most providers will upgrade your service to a higher bandwidth, for a price. A good rule of thumb is to buy double the bandwidth you think you'll need. There are other considerations. If you are planning on videoconferencing, or need to send or serve many large files, you'll need a more expensive symmetrical service. If performance isn't critical, the inexpensive ADSL will probably be fine.

DSL connections fail. They also sometimes slow down so much that it interferes with their basic functions. Few networks are designed for the kind of reliability we take for granted in our everyday phones. You should choose a provider based on a proven record of reliability. Even with the best provider, you must have a contingency plan so that your business isn't badly hurt if your line goes down even for several days.

Quality of Service

DSL technology has come a long way since its inception. Chipmakers are adding more functionality every day. However, it is difficult for such a new industry to keep up with selling and supporting the wide range of features they can now offer. A good provider won't offer more than they can effectively deliver and support. Two measures of quality will help you to evaluate potential providers: technical prowess and service.

The Quick-and-Dirty Buying Guide

Avoid these common mistakes:

Buying from an inferior provider, with many documented complaints. Investigate your provider. Online resources like www.DSLPrime.com and www.DSLReports.com are frequently updated, and can help you decide which providers to avoid. Other sources, like this book and colleagues you respect, can also help.

Assuming you'll be up and running in no time. Don't expect your installation to go smoothly. Use our guide to avoiding *DSL Hell* to prepare for a smooth install. You can be happy and surprised if it does go according to schedule. In particular, don't make plans based on your provider's promised delivery date for working service. Wait until you see it actually working.

Installing DSL without backup. If DSL is important to your business, you should have some kind of backup system in place and a plan for switching over when the service has problems. This can be as simple as an ISDN or dial-up modem built into the router, if your staff is trained how to cut over temporarily. Restoring service after it goes down often takes longer than it should—you must be ready.

Making your choice:

Don't take the easy way out, make service a priority. DSL specialists (like MegaPath or Covad direct) and good regional ISPs (like Panix in New York and Boston) generally provide better service. While there's a dramatic difference in the service and the support you get, the prices are not very different. If you choose to go with the big telcos, seek out their major business teams, and build a relationship with a salesperson that has the clout to get you help when you need it. Verizon and SBC have been particularly disappointing on service quality.

Don't buy more bandwidth than you need. You can always upgrade business DSL, because your modem or router is designed for maximum speeds. If you need more speed than you thought (most businesses will), your provider can upgrade you from their control panel, and you won't need to wait for an installer.

Choose your DSL to match the way you work. If you regularly upload large files, as a graphics designer might, you need faster upstream speed, and will want symmetric service. However, the standard recommendation that businesses buy the more expensive symmetric service (SDSL or the newer G.SHDSL) is not well thought out. Asymmetric (ADSL) upstream speeds can go to 768K and higher, and typically cost half as much. Better providers like Covad limit the over-subscription on business lines, typically sold as SDSL—but that's not because of the technology.

Avoid web hosting. Don't plan to use DSL to host servers that will get a lot of public traffic. DSL just isn't reliable enough, and it turns out that professional Web hosting is much cheaper than doing it yourself. *DSL Prime*, for example, supports 30,000 visitors per month on a $40-per-month account at XO (Concentric) that includes 5 gigabytes of traffic, redundant Net connections, a server that can handle peak loads, and a professional staff to take care of it 24/7.

Don't be bamboozled into buying a VPN if you don't need it. Virtual private networks (VPNs) ride over a private network that's twice as fast as the public Internet, and are backed by professional security. Beware, many ISPs use the same term to describe business-level service that includes security and sometimes virus protection for service running over the public Internet. Most ISPs promise more security than they deliver; often they just turn on security features built into your router and Windows software. Typically, the charge for a VPN is double that of basic business DSL. If you can handle security and virus protection yourself, you can save money.

If security is a serious concern, get managed service. If you want security strong enough to keep out a serious cracker, bring in a security professional, or a managed service provider. However, understand that securing your DSL line does not secure your business. Serious hacking problems are rare, and what many providers call a VPN is just an excuse to charge you more. Insiders are far more likely to create security problems, and the forms of attack blocked by firewalls are only a small part of the problem.

Wear a raincoat. Install virus protection and keep it updated. Never leave your network unprotected from viruses. Virus problems are more common than security breaches.

Don't sign your life away for a "free" modem. Don't sign a contract for more than a year. Most providers will give you a good deal without a longer commitment. If you do decide on a long-term contract, make sure you are getting the best deal possible. Equipment and deals change fast, and you don't want to get stuck with outdated equipment and a long-term contract with a provider you hate.

Technical Prowess

> ➤ *Actual delivered speed—the big lie of the DSL business.* As publisher and contributing editor of *DSL Prime,* we want to keep our friends in the business, but speed claims are often untrue and sometimes border on the preposterous. To put it nicely, speed or more accurately, bandwidth, can vary widely depending on how much your provider oversubscribes the shared lines of its network and backbone connection. Few providers will guarantee a specific bandwidth, and nearly none consistently deliver the speeds they advertise. Our 512K line from Earthlink and Covad consistently runs faster than our *640K* line from the local telco.

> ➤ *Reliability.* If your provider's network is badly engineered, your speed will vary dramatically with high packet loss and distorted peaks. This makes little difference when downloading e-mail, but as we move to the third Internet—broadband fast enough to support video and other rich media—this inconsistency can be crippling.

> ➤ *Latency.* Latency measures how long it takes your data to get from point a to point b. When there is congestion on the network, the equivalent of an Internet traffic jam, data transmission can slow down. The same problem develops if your provider has poor connections to the high-speed fiber-optic network that makes up the Internet backbone. The contractual deals made between owners of segments of the Internet backbone are called *peering.* Poor peering relationships are like low-cost airline travel. Your data might have to travel to Des Moines and Dallas to get from New York to Denver instead of taking a more direct route.

> ➤ *Packet loss.* Internet transmission of hypertext data depends on a sophisticated system of feedback between your browser software and the computer serving the requested Web site. Files are sent and resent until the server receives acknowledgement from the browser that they were received. This works fine for text and static images, but streamed audio and video files must be received in sequence without more than a fraction of a second delay to maintain continuity. The term *packet loss* describes the percentage of data packets delayed and re-sent. The percentage of *packet loss* can be as high as 30 percent on a bad network. On the other hand, Concentric's quality of service guarantee promises less than 1 percent. Packet loss can happen because of congestion inside the network, or at Internet exchange points that are too limited for today's volume. Better providers avoid congestion with direct connections to the other major networks.

> ➤ *Quality of connection to the Internet backbone.* The design of the network and the quality of your ISP's connections or *peering* relationships determine your performance with other Internet service providers.

➤ You can't just measure speed inside the network; a good connection highly peered to good backbones yields better service. *Edge caching* or storing content files inside a network or on servers in several major cities for more efficient access, can improve on all of the quality standards listed above. Akamai, Digital Island, and others provide this service. Alternatively, you can cache on your network using an Inktomi server or similar technology to speed performance.

Support, Testing, Monitoring

The telco DSL providers give no guarantees that they will deliver the bandwidth they promise. They also hedge when it comes to specifying length of time before repair. The nominal standard is typically three days, unacceptable, and they have refused to release any data showing they are in fact living up to that standard.

Earthlink may soon provide a bandwidth meter for customers, and influential chip designer Aware offers Dr. DSL, a software package, which allows users to see data about their lines including packet loss, latency and speed at any time. You can also check your bandwidth at http://DSLReports.com.

Your service provider has all these tools and more. They monitor the network closely, know when there are outages and slowdowns, and measure latency, packet loss, jitter, and congestion. However, they don't share that data with you, the customer. Instead, they claim *high speed*—but refuse to inform you, regulators, or the press what that high speed is.

A good provider, like Panix, a New York City ISP, will share their findings with you. Panix puts out a regular message of the day and updates its customers when there is a problem. If, for example, the news server is having problems, they'll put a message on their Web site, where you log on to the server, and in some cases send you an e-mail alert.

UUNET/MCI posts a weather map of its entire network on its site so any user can see where there is congestion, bottlenecks, or trouble. In addition, they promise to extend sophisticated line testing now applied to T-1 lines to DSL. MCI's DSL service includes several features that help to insure reliability, including technology that checks your line every five minutes to find any problems and sometimes fix them. They also constantly send test signals to your modem, so if someone accidentally kicks your modem plug out of the wall, they can call you right away. DSL chips are very sophisticated, and many modems have these advanced capabilities, but providers are not supporting all of them at present.

Software now on the market allows you and your provider to test and measure your line. You'll see the speeds and any problems on your line. Teradyne's Net-Flare helps you to quickly determine the source of any problem on your DSL. It automatically measures throughput, checks it against the bandwidth and packet loss standards promised by your ISP, and lets you know about the problem. However, tools like this require support from your provider, and most ISPs haven't made them available to customers.

Conversely, some telcos, like Verizon, are notorious for withholding information. It can be difficult, for example, to find out why the e-mail server hasn't been responding for days at a time or when the problem will be corrected. Even we as press were unable to get accurate answers on Verizon's e-mail problems, which got so bad that the *New York Daily News* ripped into them: "Frustration, thy name is Verizon.com. Tens of thousands of Verizon e-mail customers in New York City who were promised warp-speed DSL Internet connections are saddled with a service that's often so slow, users would do better to walk the message across town."

Speed Bumps

Are you really getting what you're paying for? With apologies, we offer Verizon as an example. The network's promised 7.1 Mbps bandwidth sounds good on the surface, but is their network configured to deliver it consistently? They're not making any promises. Start by reading the small print. You'll find statements like "Due to the sophisticated nature of DSL, Verizon Online cannot guarantee uninterrupted or error free service" and "Your actual speed will be lower due to various network factors."

On another page of the same Web site, Verizon confesses that speeds quoted describe the speed between your premises and their CO, and even those numbers are defined as a comparison to 56K modem speeds, a totally meaningless equation. Five times faster, or 25 times faster than what, you might ask? What you need to know is your speed to the Internet. What they can deliver remains unclear.

In general, independent companies that specialize in working with business customers offer better service and support than the traditional phone company providers. Independent companies developed to sell broadband, like Covad and Rhythms, provide a higher quality of service. We'll be delighted if we have to change this paragraph in the second edition of this book, but first the telcos have to solve their service problems.

Technical support is a key area in which your ISP can make a big difference. Getting support from telcos may require waiting on hold for long periods of time to speak with a support center trained for consumer questions. Business-oriented ISPs like XO/Concentric are designed to be more responsive.

The CEO of Panix, a New York based ISP, says, "If I serviced customers like the telcos do, I'd be out of business fast. Verizon, for example, consistently has been having trouble with e-mail, going down for days, sometimes. But I designed my system with enough redundancy so that if we have a problem, the customer is protected. In 11 years, there hasn't been a single 24-hour period the mail server was down." We would like to confirm that record. We haven't noticed even a two-hour outage or delay in the three years we've used Panix for e-mail.

Asking colleagues for advice and recommendations is great, but the odds are that you don't know any experts in this fast changing field. That's why we strongly recommend you check reliable independent sources like those we've listed at the beginning of this chapter for informed objective advice. However, unlike the telephone industry, DSL is not regulated by the government. One result is that accurate statistical information is hard to come by.

We'd like to call special attention to *DSL Reports*, www.dslreports.com. This online publication does a superb job of gathering user experience, and providing data, including a number of surveys, to provide you with information so you can judge the providers for yourself. However, be aware that the site has some built-in limitations. Happy customers sometimes don't take the time to write in about their service, so some of the best providers are not rated, and consumers reporting to the Web site are a self-selecting group. That said, none of the other sites (EverythingDSL, Telcoexchange) has *DSL Reports'* proven record of independence. Some of its strongest recommendations go to providers who neither buy ads nor pay commissions to the publication.

Our experience is that the best service has come from independent ISPs, primarily business-focused Covad resellers. A set of regional providers receive dramatically better ratings than any national service, and the biggest telcos, SBC and Verizon, consistently do poorly.

Even if you are using an outside consultant or an inhouse IT specialist, consider carefully which provider you choose. After all, you have to live with your choice and make it continue to work for you.

Sometimes an ISP will tell you exactly what to expect. Bell Canada's Web site prepares customers for the installation process. It clearly states what their technicians will do during an installation: "The technician will bring, install and configure the DSL high-speed modem, the Ethernet card, the phone filters and the Bell Sympatico High Speed Edition service software. Once the installation has been completed, the technician will perform tests to ensure connectivity to the Internet."

The site also helps customers prepare for the installation. "You must have your Windows 95/Windows 98 or Macintosh system CD-ROMs, as these may be required to complete the installation." Whoever your provider is, make sure you see the DSL connection working in your browser and verify your speed with an online bandwidth meter before the installer leaves your premises.

If your adoption of DSL requires substantial changes in your LAN or connecting an extensive VPN, you'll need a specialist, to make sure your DSL is efficiently shared and you have adequate security to protect your system. We recommend following the advice of the experts, especially someone you will work with in the future. If they've signed on to the choice, they are far more likely to deal appropriately with any problems that come up. However, you still need to be informed to manage the process and make decisions. *Keep reading*.

DSL Providers

As we write, the DSL scene is changing rapidly. For all practical purposes, the telcos have beat out competitors and are taking the lead in DSL, but a few hardy competitors survive, and we hope will continue to play an important role diversifying and driving the market.

These giants have 80 percent of the market. However, the service quality has been consistently weak. News articles about the telcos continue to report that customers are having hellish experiences getting connected. They serve millions of customers, some not very well.

The DSL specialists discussed in the following sections have generally done a better job than the mega-telcos, Verizon and SBC. Within each region, telcos have the widest networks, and often the lowest prices. If you choose to work with a telco, information is your best defense. To get the best service, you need to understand how DSL works, and the steps you'll go through to qualify for service and get it installed. Knowing what to expect once your service is up and running helps too, but that's why you're reading this book.

All the telcos have divisions dedicated to corporate data sales, which specialize in higher margin frame relay, T-1, and T-3 data lines. The sales staff is usually higher paid, and has better access to corporate resources. They can also sell you DSL, usually at the same price, often with more courtesy and knowledge than the *business DSL* division. Expect them to try to sell you the higher-priced products, but DSL is a part of the product line.

Bell Canada. Facing strong cable competition, Bell Canada has the broadest DSL network of any large telco in North America, already able to serve 70% of their customers. The CEO promises to offer service to the vast majority of his customer base. With over half a million customers in 2001, twice as many Canadians have DSL as do people on this side of the border. Their low prices ($27 (US) for consumers and $55 for business) were inspired by strong cable competition. They were one of the earliest providers to offer Very High Speed DSL (VDSL) and Voice Over DSL (VoDSL) trials, and their Aliant group serving eastern provinces creating advanced video technology. Service has consistently been above average.

BellSouth. The style is well-starched and buttoned, but their DSL deployment, reaching 70% of their users by late 2001, is more aggressive than the others in the U.S. Moving to data service, they brought in some young folks with a different style, and promoted them for results. They originally planned to go straight to fiber, so they were very late in DSL. We agree that fiber is the right long-term move, but it would have taken a decade to build and more investment than U.S. telcos are willing to make. Our first draft of this chapter contrasted the telcos with the independents, noting the general inferiority of the telcos. We were wrong. Two mega-telcos, Verizon and SBC, have severe problems. BellSouth and Qwest have proven, to the contrary, that a telco can do a decent job. BellSouth faces a technical obstacle offering DSL, 35,000 remote terminals that serve almost half their territory.

Qwest. A hard-driving company, with an ever-involved CEO who invites everyone to e-mail him directly at joe@qwest.com. While he doesn't read most of the e-mails himself, someone *is* delegated to answer mail and help you out, and the invitation sends a powerful signal that this CEO is a hands-on kind of guy. Qwest gobbled up baby bell US West in 2000, laid off 6000 people, and pushed out most of top management. The purge, at least so far, hasn't stopped them from improving the service of the telco dubbed "US Worst," by consumers, while they continue to build networks worldwide.

Qwest has by far the most aggressive national plans of any telco, offering business DSL and telephony in cities around the country, with a $3 billion target for 2003 sales. In their region, US West was the early leader in DSL, whose 30,000 customers at one time may have been more than the entire rest of the industry. In Phoenix, they have 40,000 VDSL subscribers, the most advanced deployment in the world. They were the first telco to add Video on Demand (from Intertainer), have experimented with Internet gizmos, and are experimenting with high-speed gaming.

However, if you're in a smaller town in US West territory you could be out of luck. They've chosen not to deploy DSL to smaller sites (except state capitals, an obvious political ploy.) Qwest's CEO says, "Qwest is going to put our investment in the most profitable location, whether it's Boise, Boston, or Berlin." We support the folks in Idaho who believe the phone company has an obligation to offer service, even if the return on investment is only 15 percent, rather than the 35-percent plus that Qwest demands.

SBC. In 1999, SBC's CEO boasted that they were going to build the best, not just the biggest, network in the world, inspiring our industry publication, *DSL Prime* to choose SBC as *Company of the Year*. They launched Project Pronto, with a $6 billion budget, that would bring DSL to 80 percent of their users by the end of 2002, and promised 100 percent would get broadband in the next few years (DSL, wireless, satellite, or whatever it takes). $1.5 billion of that was slated for an ATM backbone that "would reliably deliver the speeds we promise" (Chang), which included a 6MB data rate to 60 percent of their customers. That commitment to universal service is unique in America, and was negotiated by the former FCC Chairman Kennard along with the Ameritech merger.

Unfortunately, the next 18 months were extraordinarily humbling for SBC, which services one-third of the United States. (They also own a major share of Bell Canada and Telmex, and have worldwide investments.) In March of 2000, the CEO told Wall Street that they were "ahead of schedule" in their million-subscriber goal. But as he spoke, a backlog of 170,000 orders was building up, and installation problems were frequently nightmares. A corporate reorganization that summer was a disaster, with 30,000 orders lost in the computer and needing to be re-entered. By year end, they only reached 770,000, and were cutting back plans around the country.

For three successive quarters, SBC told Wall Street that earnings would not reach their excessively optimistic expectations, and the stock dropped $20 billion in one day. Those financial problems probably explain why SBC cut back all expansion out of district, and raised the price of DSL more than 25 percent in order to reduce demand. This amazing step came in January 2001, as the price of equipment needed to deliver the service dropped 30 percent in four months. DSL subscribers are a burden the first year because customer acquisition and startup expense is high, reducing profits temporarily. Slowing DSL deployment will actually raise reported earnings four to seven cents a share, but reduce opportunities for their customers and hurt the company over time.

SBC still calls DSL the "etone of the future," and remains the largest U.S. provider. The Koreans are deploying twice as many lines, and the company has a long way to go to recapture momentum. Just before we went to press, SBC announced they were canceling their plans to deliver broadband to all their customers, and that Pronto was dead. As late as September 2001, they had denied that, but our subsequent reporting had demonstrated that SBC had stopped building in early 2001, and was simply disingenuous. CEO Whitacre is under pressure from his board, and a new COO, politician Bill Daley, has stepped in. We hope he will at least be honest.

Verizon. The telco for a third of the U.S. offers DSL to about half their customers, after slowing the rollout in the GTE areas and to the 20 percent of customers served through DLC remote terminals. They had 720,000 subscribers early in 2001, with plans for 500K more over the year. You can get service directly from Verizon's own ISP, or through Earthlink, Telocity, and other resellers. Service quality has been an enormous burden for Verizon, with many DSL Hell stories. Service has been down far too often, and e-mail has been a problem a half-dozen times. Business service is aggressively priced, but still facing operational challenges.

In 1999, Verizon crowed "We're going to beat cable" in the *New York Times* and claimed, "We're now a data company, not a phone company," while predicting that a third of all homes would sign up for DSL. However, 2000 was a disappointment; they ended the year 30 percent below target amidst many reports of DSL Hell.We hope by the time you are reading this book that the problems are behind them..

Little Telcos. About one-sixth of the United States depends on smaller companies, including Broadwing/Cincinnati Bell, whose 40,000 ZOOMTOWN DSL subscribers were the first in the United States to receive video on demand. They aim to make Cincinnati *Zoom City*, using advanced telecom services to help the city grow, and with Intertainer are the first to offer Video on Demand over DSL.

Century, Alltel, Citizens, and many of the smaller companies, like Roseville Telephone Cooperative, offer their territory more comprehensive DSL services than the Bells.

Ahead of the telcos, three inspired companies, Covad, NorthPoint, and Rhythms, raised a billion dollars to build networks covering almost half of the United States in less than two years. They have generally delivered better service than the telcos. However, the Internet boom collapsed, taking with it the second billion dollars needed to build the customer base and carry the operation to profitability. NorthPoint failed after Verizon welched on a merger deal, and now is a shell hoping for success in a billion-dollar lawsuit. Rhythms followed, shutting down in September 2001. Covad, in bankruptcy as we write, has a good chance of surviving, and we hope they do; they have generally delivered better service than the telcos, and remain the best choice for most.

Covad. The largest national wholesaler is in Chapter 11 proceedings as we write, but we hope will emerge successfully. They've had shaky financial going, but generally have delivered much better service than the Bells. Pricing varies depending on which ISP you sign up with, and they offer consumer-level service as well, at $50–60. SBC has committed to $600 million in wholesale volume. Nearly all the mid-sized and smaller ISPs base their service on Covad's.

They grew fast, signing up resellers without strong finances. However, when the Internet boom ended, funding wasn't there, and the ISPs couldn't pay their bills. They serve hundreds of thousands of customers who are getting generally superior service, but the future is uncertain.

New Edge Networks. Built on the premise of service to smaller cities, New Edge Networks raised $77 million in 2001, which could be enough to carry the network to profitability. If you need facilities in any of the 500 cities they serve, they are the obvious choice.

Regional providers are dedicated to small and medium-sized businesses. Often, they build a reputation for superior service, and usually have dedicated sales forces that are encouraged to build relationships with customers.

The highest ratings on *DSL Reports* go to regional ISPs that understand customer service, and a few national ISPs who are mostly Covad resellers. MegaPath has held the highest scores on the national ratings (around 4 out of 5), and the regionals listed next all score above 4.5. That's why we recommend that most folks choose one of the better ISPs, like the one listed next. Whatever the theory, these are the folks who have delivered, as of midyear 2001. However—check the Web for current info.

MegaPath. *MegaPath's* CEO proclaimed he would offer quality service, and MegaPath's consistent position near the top of the national *DSL Reports* chart suggests he has delivered. California based, their rates are usually only slightly above companies whose service is deplorable. *Speakeasy* grew from an Internet Café in Seattle into a 50-city provider that gets generally good ratings. *XO/Concentric* is a national Internet provider that had a strong reputation for quality, and superior service monitoring and service level agreements. Their customer support declined drastically during 2001. *Panix* is a regional favorite in New York and Boston. They were one of the first ISPs in the world. A recent *DSL Reports* rating was 4.74 out of 5.

AOL. 30M+ members are one-third of the Internet, and AOL knows they will lose them to others unless they ramp up broadband. They've committed to resell over a million lines from Verizon and SBC, but by early 2001 hadn't signed more than 10,000 or so, as they seek a strategy and alliances. They bought Time Warner, the second largest cable company, and are constantly negotiating for ways to serve AT&T as well. A Billion Dollar investment in satellite gives them another option, but the result, as we write, has been virtual paralysis.

The quality of AOL's DSL service will depend on the backbone quality they provide, and their record is dismal. We are closely watching AOL for major developments. Until they decide their strategy, they are offering DSL only in very limited territories, and early experience has not been good.

Earthlink. The second largest ISP in the United States has always had a reputation for friendly service. They are now the largest independent reseller, (over 300,000 lines) and generally have delivered better service than the telcos do directly. We have an Earthlink line, backed up by Covad, and they've done a good job. Most new customers, however, will get lines resold from the Bells. They also have services appropriate for many small businesses. In March 2001, they became the first major provider to offer home gateways as a regular product, working with 2Wire.

Microsoft Network (MSN). The third largest U.S. ISP had ambitious plans, but their $30 million investment in both NorthPoint and Rhythms proved disastrous, with thousands of customers shut down in the NorthPoint bankruptcy. Since then, they've cut a deal with Qwest to become the ISP for Qwest's 500,000 subscribers, and recently announced they will also use other Bells for resale.

Telocity/DIRECTV DSL. They've some of the most customer-friendly policies, offering static IP's, an advanced gateway of their own design, and no contract requirements. They were purchased by Hughes/DIRECTV, which itself is owned by General Motors. Caught heavily in the downfall of Rhythms, their actual service hasn't lived up to their plans. We hope their problems are behind them by the time you read this book.

AT&T. Ma Bell, now more of a cable company than a telco, purchased facilities in 1700 telco offices in the NorthPoint bankruptcy early in 2001, reaching almost half the United States. They immediately shut down the network, and expect to rebuild it with an emphasis on voice alongside data. Until they have the new network up and running (target is early 2002 but they'll probably miss it), they are a minor provider, primarily reselling Covad.

AT&T spent $100 billion, and four years, building America's largest cable network, planning to offer bundled data, video, local and long distance. Now, they're spending billions more splitting the company in three parts, all of which will offer high-speed data. AT&T Broadband will focus on cable, but may fill in gaps and business districts with DSL. AT&T Wireless will soon have high-speed data and continues to work on Project Angel, which would put a small, fixed wireless box on every home. AT&T Business and Consumer will use DSL as a primary product, presumably in a voice + data bundle rolling out heavily in 2002. They will offer a mix of their own facilities and resale (of Covad and the Bells.)

AT&T's own fiber backbone, along with the facilities obtained with the IBM Global Network, gives them enormous capacity, and a base of 60 million customers gives them enormous potential. The long-distance business is shrinking rapidly, and AT&T as a company has no choice but to expand into local telephony and data. Their current efforts (largely Covad resale) are so small that we can make no judgments about their quality. DSL-Prime.com will publish updates as the rollout gains steam.

Sprint. They built possibly the largest DSL network in the world, 2000 offices, but may never turn it on, as Wall Street pressures them to cut back and just sell the company. If the company remains independent and on track, however, ION – primarily a DSL voice and data network – is crucial to company survival. With millions of consumers in their long-distance and wireless division, as well as their own Internet backbone, potential is extraordinary. Until then, they are moving slowly, city by city, to actually offer services, under the ION product name. They're also the furthest along in field deployment of fixed wireless, and will use whichever technology works best for the location. They are the local telco in Las Vegas and cities in 18 other states, and offer DSL in most of their territory.

Wall Street analysts are doing their best to sabotage the service, because the uncertainty of a four-year ramp discourages investors or a merger and its related fees. ION continues to have technical problems, and might be cancelled. We hope instead that they become a strong competitor.

DSL Hell

Verizon executives were taken aback when they opened their *New York Times* one day last year to find the caption, "Night of the Living DSL" atop a full-page horror movie spread. The problem is real, type "DSL Hell" into Google, and it returns 18 pages of references. Our job is to suggest how to avoid it.

DSL is still a very young industry. The 9-million plus users are essentially early adopters who faced the typical problems of a technology working out the kinks. Collectively, these and other problems prominent in the industry are known as DSL Hell:

➤ Delays getting qualifying for and scheduling installations

➤ Installation problems

➤ Problems getting lines

➤ Problems with micro-filters

➤ Coordination between the telco and ISPs

➤ Not getting advertised speeds even off peak

➤ Bandwidth bottlenecks during prime time

➤ Poor support during outages

➤ No support for network problems

The First Circle: They Say You Just Can't Get DSL

Thousands of customers are just out of reach for DSL service. Many of these are in locations served by DLCs. Each telco has its own schedule for adding technology to extend service to these customers.

Problem

DSL standards were designed for 18,000 feet of wire and more, but some companies will refuse you service beyond 12,000 or 15,000 feet because a minority of the longer lines have trouble, and they just don't want to bother taking care of customers.

Solution

Check your distance from your telephone company Central Office (CO) on your provider's Web site. If the distance is 10,000 to 16,000 feet, there's a good chance you can be served if you persist. Here's the catch: Telcos use a mapping program to check the *wire distance*, much less accurate than actually testing the line itself. If a check of your map distance at *DSL Reports* shows you are between 12,000 and 17,000 feet, insist they perform an actual test of your line. Interference from load coils or bridge taps can also prevent you from getting DSL. In most states, the Phone Company is required to remove these impediments. Good luck. The first level of support probably won't even understand the issue (they'll just tell you you're not qualified). DSL is wonderful if you can get it; fight to speak with a senior, better-informed representative.

Problem

You're behind a remote terminal. Twenty to 30 percent of Americans receive their phone service through a neighborhood connection, rather than directly from the phone office. Telcos have been slow to upgrade DLCs to support DSL.

Possible Solution

Bell South has upgraded 5000 remote terminals, and SBC is installing tens of thousands of new ones, ready for data, as part of Project Pronto. If your neighborhood is not scheduled for an upgrade, complain directly to your local newspaper, politicians, and state utilities commission.

The Second Circle: Installation Delays and Bad Scheduling

One of the most common complaints is an installation rescheduled without notice. Another is poor coordination. The ISP shows up to hook up your DSL, but the required phone line is not installed or isn't working.

Installations are getting better, but there are at least 20 steps to the installation process, and things can and often do go wrong at any one of them. For starters, your ISP may not provide your DSL. Many ISPs buy DSL from a wholesaler like Covad, Rhythms, or a local telco who you probably won't ever talk to even if things get really fouled up, which isn't all that uncommon.

Several ISPs may be vying to sell you the same repackaged service in your market. A good ISP will track your installation. This includes making sure you have all the equipment you need, coordinating with the phone company and DSL provider so it's more likely to happen on time, and keeping you informed of any problems. Keeping track of scheduling is crucial.

In addition to coordinating things so they are more likely to happen on time, a good ISP will answer the phone when you have a question or a problem.

Possible Solutions

Make sure the telco installing your line has no problem getting access to the telephone room in your building.

If the telco doesn't show up to install your line on schedule, call at 2 P.M. when they can still rectify the situation, rather than at 5:00 P.M. when it is too late.

Let your ISP know about any missed appointments right away so they can reschedule the installation and adjust their schedule for getting you up and running.

The Third Circle: Can't Get Answers

All service representatives are helping other customers. Your estimated waiting time is two hours. After that, we may cut off your call, refer you to another division of the company, or be unable to help you.

Hours on hold only to get a technician who can't help you is a complaint we've heard frequently as companies sell DSL faster than they can train support people.

Possible Solutions

Make sure your ISP provides 24-hour support, seven days a week. Call off peak, or at the start of the business day, for faster service.

Take down the name and direct number of the technician as soon as you are connected so you can call back if you are disconnected.

Try suggested fixes while you are on the phone to avoid having to call back.

If the person you're talking to can't solve your problem, ask for a supervisor or someone who can.

We have included, with each provider, our advice on what to do when the support people can't solve your problem. Verizon, for example, has a special presidential support team. The Qwest CEO invites you to e-mail directly, where a team is standing by to solve problems.

If necessary, appeal to someone at the top of the corporate ladder by sending an e-mail, a certified letter, or a FedEx to the CEO or head of DSL.

Businesses can and should ask to be assigned a salesperson. Ask your sales rep to run interference for you and get help from inside.

Always have the facts of your problem outlined clearly, and try to sound reasonable. You're not likely to get a good response if you let your anger loose.

The Fourth Circle: It's Not Working, and Nobody Can Get Any Work Done

You want a provider that's designed a system likely to have fewer problems. Superior service costs more to deliver, but price doesn't always correlate with quality of an ISP. We have two DSL providers: one has been reliable and supportive, and the other has had persistent problems and been unhelpful when we needed assistance. Although the price is similar, and the offerings comparable, the experience has been very different.

Possible Solutions

Make sure your service is working correctly before the installer leaves your premises. Run a speed test using the bandwidth meter. If you use more than one browser, test them both. Don't take the installer's word that it works until you see it work on your computer.

Your downtime may be the result of poor planning. Installing redundant systems is part of the territory with DSL. Your backup system, whether it is a dial-up modem, an ISDN line, or an alternate DSL line, should be ready to go. Establishing procedures for switching over prepares you for a smooth switchover when your DSL goes down.

Try to diagnose where the problem is when you go down. First, make sure the problem isn't in your own network. Then, contact your provider to see if there is any trouble on their network, or in any of their servers.

The Fifth Circle: Lies about Bandwidth

DSL is advertised as a fast, always-on connection to the Internet, and that's what your provider should be delivering. Many lie. If you are having intermittent problems with the connection going down, or not delivering close to the promised speeds, document it clearly. Tech support will likely disregard your complaint, saying, "sometimes the Internet is slow." Often, the problem is inside the provider's network, and they should be able to fix it. Downloading files from the provider's own Web site emphasizes the problem.

Document your speeds using a bandwidth meter and other tools we'll introduce in Chapter 6, "Troubleshooting." If you can show that the problem with your connection is persistent, you can make a case for remedies, but you'll have to insist strongly. Often, a router is overloaded, or an ATM switch inadequate, but the telco does nothing about it.

The Sixth Circle: Finger Pointing

Hey, we know what we're talking about from experience. Covad came to install our service and found a line was bad. They said "we'll have to work it out with the Phone Company and get back to you." We're still waiting. They cancelled the order. Miscommunication is a big problem industry wide. Some companies keep their on-time delivery records pristine by canceling any jobs where they encounter problems.

It might seem like cutting out the middleman and going with the telco's ISP would solve the problem, but it doesn't. Communication between divisions of the telcos is just as bad as it is with outside ISPs. Sources as respected as the *New York Times* made this mistake, recommending you deal directly with the telco throughout. Sounds logical, but it doesn't work that way in reality. The largest telcos, Verizon and SBC/Pac Bell, have given the worst service consistently.

Possible Solutions

When registering a complaint or asking for resolution, ask for the name of the person who will be calling the supervisor at the other company and press him or her to make the call. Generally, professionals at that level will work together to solve problems.

Every company has a team dedicated to relations with other companies. Make sure they're working on your problem, rather than allowing low-level people to give you a runaround.

The Seventh Circle: Billing Problems

Operations are the Achilles Heel of many companies jumping into DSL. Everything is so new and so complicated that they make lots of mistakes. For example, Verizon double billed thousands of customers.

Possible Solutions

Check your bill. Keep an eye out for additional charges. Basically, you should see sales tax added and little else. There have been abuses reported on universal service charges that should only be applied to voice phone lines.

Document, document, document. Keep a log of your attempts to solve billing problems, including the names of employees with whom you speak, their titles, the date and time, and any promises made. Tracking your efforts to provide the high-level executive who finally solves the problem offers clues to what happened and who is responsible.

We know that many users have not received proper support from their telco, despite making a good faith effort to go through channels. We asked all the major ones what a user with unsolved problems should do. Qwest had a responsive answer, to e-mail the CEO joe@qwest.com, and his office has a team to help you. Every other telco has a special support group for VIPs as well as customers they choose to help, but they refused to give us information on how to get that treatment. That means you, as a forsaken client, have no recourse except drastic measures. Don't abuse the process, and make sure you've checked everything you can. Sometimes, however, you'll have to go to the top.

If the errors are not resolved in a reasonable amount of time, speak first with your sales representative, and then with the company CEO or DSL head. Sometimes, registering your complaint in the form of a registered letter or FedEx gets more attention.

If the company doesn't respond, be thankful the telcos haven't completely eliminated the regulators. All state regulatory commissions have staff that would like to help, although they are not always successful. Also helpful, unless too many readers of this book use it, is a complaint to the FCC. You can do that in 15 minutes, and for now, the companies generally respond. Go to www.fcc.gov/cib/ccformpage.html.

Let the world know. Contact local press, trade press, and DSL Web sites like DSLPrime.com and DSLReports.com. Share your experience with others so the magnitude of the problem becomes visible and embarrassing to the company. When just a few companies dominate a market, you have no realistic alternative to using their services. Every company has an obligation of honesty and fair dealing; when you share a dominant market position, we believe they also have an obligation to treat customers properly.

CHAPTER 3

The Equipment that Makes DSL Work

A n ordinary phone line and a DSL modem or router is all it takes to connect to the wonderful high-speed world of DSL. You'll get 10 or sometimes hundreds of times the speed of a 56K modem. Like a dial-up connection to the Internet, DSL connects you through a phone line, but a DSL modem and the equipment it connects to at the phone company's central office (CO) are very different. DSL computer chips transform plain copper phone wire into a high-speed data pipe. One chipset is located in the modem or router that connects your computer or your network to the Internet; your provider needs complementary equipment on the other end to complete the connection. These fast chips housed in a DSLAM or DLC (see Chapter 4, "Technology") are the magic that makes DSL work.

Home users and many offices will receive DSL over the same phone line that they will continue to use for voice calls. Others will require a separate dedicated line. In addition to the line that carries your service, you'll need a modem, or a router/gateway with a modem built in to connect your line to a computer or an existing network.

Our focus in this chapter is on what DSL providers call *Customer Premises Equipment* (CPE), the equipment you will purchase and maintain inhouse. It includes your modem, router or gateway, your DSL line, and (if you're installing ADSL) one or more microfilters.

Equipment

Rule #1: Use the equipment your provider supports, unless you have a darn good reason not to.

Go with the gear suggested by your provider unless you have specific network or security concerns that make your provider's recommendation inappropriate. Generally, your provider will give you the option to choose the type of modem or router you purchase, but not the brand. Providers expect to subsidize the equipment cost, typically with an attractively priced bundle designed to sign up customers. However, even without the price incentive, we recommend sticking with equipment your provider knows and can support.

In the 1980s we all believed that DSL speeds were impossible over ordinary phone lines. Joe Lechlider's early theorizing seemed "too good to be true," an old-timer remembers. But by 1991, dozens were working on the technology, and soon they delivered working systems. Today, DSL equipment is assembled from off-the-shelf parts. The key difference is that today's inexpensive, highly integrated chips can do what took multiple circuit boards a decade ago.

DSL Lines

DSL lines are just plain old phone service (POTS) lines Copper phone wire is a twisted copper pair that transmits voice calls through the public switched phone network (PSTN). When it is used for DSL service, the wire itself (ordinary 24- or 26-gauge phone wire) can be either a special line *dedicated* to DSL, or it can share the existing line used for voice calls. Almost all consumer service is now line shared, as are the least expensive business choices.

Originally, for shared lines, a technician visited your office or home and installed a small box (a *POTS splitter*) to separate voice and data, but tests at US West proved that consumers could self-install. Now it is common to ask consumers to plug in their modems and install a small *microfilter* on each of their phones, which prevents interference between DSL and voice.

For business circuits, your ISP typically orders a dedicated line, which allows them to offer symmetric service with higher upstream speeds. They then pay the phone company $12–20 per month for the line, one reason your charge for SDSL is higher. However, many businesses will do just fine with less expensive ADSL service, which Covad and the telcos are offering. Upstream speeds of 384K and even 768K are practical with ADSL, and the savings can be large.

DSL Modems

DSL modems bridge your computer and your provider's wide area network, which in turn is connected to the Internet. The modem can be stand-alone hardware connected through an Ethernet or USB wire, a PCI card inserted into your computer or a component built into a router. In addition to decoding the data sent over the DSL line, the modem must compensate for the interference from the other lines it is bundled with in a binder group in the cable coming to you. This includes a whole lot of signal processing, echo cancellation, and adaptive equalization handled invisibly in the DSL modem and in the connection on the other side. When dozens or even thousands of lines are bundled together, the signal on each line can affect those on lines near it. This crosstalk problem is well known, and Tom Starr's T1E1.4 Standards committee has been establishing rules that should keep it manageable in future networks. Even though the problem will likely become more severe as more homes sign up for high-speed data. Wet cables, AM radio transmitters, and other interferers abound. Consequently, the DSL chips include both analog components to drive the signal and a digital signal processor that resurrects the original data and performs error correction.

We generally recommend Ethernet connections, because they are the most reliable and they are easy to link to an existing Ethernet network. Pete Castleton of Verizon convinced us that external modems are generally worth the extra cost. The advantage of an external Ethernet modem is that it can run independently of the host computer, which allows your DSL line to be tested even if your computer is the problem. This makes troubleshooting easier. Verizon provides external Ethernet modems for general use, despite the added cost of perhaps $50 per machine. Since he's responsible for over a million users, that adds up to quite a piece of change.

The disadvantage of an Ethernet modem is you may need to install an Ethernet card ($20–70). However, that's usually easy with typical Windows equipment. You just open the case, insert the card, and restart. Windows 98 or later *Plug-and-Play* is highly likely to recognize the Ethernet card and install all the needed drivers. Most Macs have Ethernet built in these days, saving that step.

Internal PCI cards are less expensive and can be preinstalled by the computer manufacturer. These allow BellSouth, Verizon, and SBC to send a fully configured package to the user, reducing technical problems at initial installation. Corporations with telecommuters may choose this approach to lower support costs.

USB modems are attractive because nearly all computers since 1999 have USB ports, with plug-and-play installation of USB add-on hardware. However, USB modems are dependent on the host computer, which makes troubleshooting harder. The technician sometimes can't determine whether the problem is the line or the computer. Individual telecommuters or those outfitting a small office or home office have the option of installing a PCI card into their PC, or using an external modem configured for USB. However, even for individual users, we recommend an Ethernet-based router. Even if you have to install an Ethernet card to make use of one of these more sophisticated modems, it's worth it.

In theory you could use any DSL modem to connect to any provider's DSLAM. Years of interoperability testing have gone into setting standards that help make the equipment interchangeable, but the reality is different. Modems and DSLAMs have subtle differences that can foul you up, and your provider may not support all the capabilities of another modem. Typically, your DSL provider will sell you a specific modem that they know works well with their equipment. While other modems may work, your provider may not know them intimately, leaving you in a lurch when you need support.

Figure 3.1 A DSL modem is a single connection to the Internet.
Courtesy: Aztech

Inside a DSL Modem

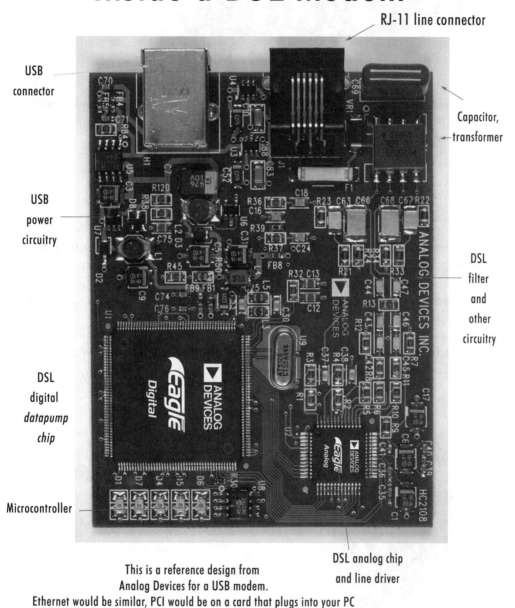

RJ-11 line connector

USB connector

Capacitor, transformer

USB power circuitry

DSL filter and other circuitry

DSL digital *datapump* chip

Microcontroller

DSL analog chip and line driver

This is a reference design from
Analog Devices for a USB modem.
Ethernet would be similar, PCI would be on a card that plugs into your PC

Figure 3.2   An Analog Devices board for the interior of a DSL modem showing the components of a typical modem.

Courtesy: Analog Devices

Figure 3.3   A router connects several computers to the modem. This Asante router can be connected behind a modem.

Courtesy: Asante

Routers

Routers with modems built in are the most common equipment used to connect a business DSL line, but other options sometimes make sense. Smaller offices (up to a dozen connections) can often be served by the gateways described later in this chapter, which are designed for ease of use. Larger enterprises often already have a routed network to which you can just add an industrial-strength modem called a CSU/DSU. However, calculate the cost carefully; most CSU/DSU *modems* cost almost as much as a new router with the modem built in.

Figure 3.4   Don't be fooled by the name; gateways like this one from D-Link aren't just for home use.

Courtesy: D-Link

What's Your Backup Plan?

Prepare for DSL downtime with a backup plan. Unless you have other equipment in place, a router with backup built in is the best choice. Nothing is more important for business reliability than accepting that occasionally your line will go down, and being ready to deal with it. The right router can make dealing with downtime much easier. A new breed of routers is emerging that can switch traffic between two DSL lines, from different providers. Another common solution is a router with a built-in ISDN or dial-up backup system. Netopia produces one of the best. The simplest backup solution for you telecommuters is to hold on to your phone modem and maintain a dial-up connection. For critical operations you'll also want to keep a backup modem or router on hand in case yours becomes defective.

ISDN lines provide an effective backup system that is inexpensive in most parts of the world. They deliver 128K in both directions without undue overhead for an effective throughput of more than double analog modems. When your DSL is down, you'll be charged for traffic over the ISDN line by the hour ($1–3), brutal for heavy use, but ideal for a backup used only occasionally.

Built-in test is now featured with chips from Aware, Virata, Infineon, and Conexant, and will be a standard feature of all units in a few years. You evaluate most of the basic parameters of the connection, including speed, packet loss, and latency of the network. Manufacturers are rapidly developing software to make that information accessible to users through browser windows. Virtual Access's router provides a preview of next generation technology. It uses sophisticated software that can often diagnose where the problem on the network is, even if the difficulty is the DSLAM, the subscription management server, or the provider's backbone router. The best providers know that this smart technology will reduce their support costs, and BT, BellSouth, and Next Level are using the unit.

What Security Do You Need?

Security choices may affect your equipment decision. Many large corporations are implementing IPSec, a high security system that integrates sophisticated management features. Check Point is the worldwide leader, Cisco another common choice. If that's your corporate standard, make sure to get equipment certified by the vendor of the corporate security system. If you use Check Point, for example, think first of Nokia's Ramp, tested and supported by

Check Point. Interoperability of IPSec systems is often claimed, but there have been significant problems in the field.

Encryption and other security features require significant processing, which can slow your data rate. For an office with heavy traffic, you should look for a unit that can process at *wire speed* or *line speed*, and the newer, more expensive models do. In some cases, external units or internal add-on processors are required for that speed.

Most routers have firewalls built in, but the extent of their features varies. Network address translation protects against many simple attacks, but Evan Solley, CTO of Netopia, recommends that if intrusion protection is important to you, you should "seek a broader range of security features, including intrusion detection and logging, denial of service prevention, blocking of access to/from specific sites, protocols, and other features."

Mac Users

We both prefer Macintoshes, and much of this book was written on a network that includes a PC and a Mac. Any equipment could serve a mixed network, but Netopia and Cayman stand out because they come from the Mac world. Their tech support people are far more knowledgeable about Macintoshes. Cayman's routers were the early Mac standard, and Netopia sells Timbuktu, a classic Mac communications package.

Home Gateways Are Right for Many Offices, Too

Although they call them *residential gateways*, the units in this section are really small routers designed for ease of use. Most can comfortably support a dozen or so moderate users, and may reduce support costs. Wireless models save the cost of running cable, often the most expensive part of installing a small network. The same engineering is involved, whether the units support three users or twelve, and a simple unit for a dozen users may be ideal for smaller offices.

Home gateways come with software to make the hook up easier and firewalls to give you some protection. 2Wire and Cayman were the first to market but all the home electronics manufacturers, Sony, Thompson RCA, Motorola, and the telecom outfits (Alcatel, Nokia) are jumping into this field as well. One by one, DSL service providers are choosing which gateways they'll support. Like other DSL equipment, choose the unit preferred by your provider to lower the support burden.

Small Offices May Be Well Served by a *Gateway* Designed for Home Use

While one person, one computer seemed like an impossible dream in 1985, now it's common in middle-class American homes. Some innovative products are aimed at this market. Cayman was probably the first to ship, modifying their business router for telecommuters, and recommended by Verizon's Enterprise division. 2Wire is working with Earthlink, SBC, and Verizon's consumer division, with both wired and wireless gateways. They have a physically attractive design, which looks good for a home or professional office, and designed both the manual and their Web site to provide help to an inexperienced installer.

The earliest units were designed to use either the phone wire you may already have in your house (HomePNA—Phone Networking Alliance) or standard Ethernet, which required running Category (CAT) 5 cable. Cayman shipped a wireless model (mid-speed, running HomeRF protocols) in 2000, and early in 2001 started delivering wireless units running up to 10 megabit utilizing the 802.11b wireless Ethernet standard, which looks like it will dominate the market.

Wireless units typically cost a few hundred dollars more, and require a $100 wireless adapter for each station on the network. One word of caution, beware of security problems with wireless. An employee of the *Wall Street Journal* found that he could easily tap Cisco's headquarters' wireless network from their parking lot, and someone we know replicated the test from the public street next to Columbia University.

DIRECTV DSL/Telocity delivers a customer unit that serves as a modem but was designed as a gateway. As they expand their offerings, they are turning on the home networking features.

Sony, Panasonic, Toshiba, Samsung, and RCA/Thompson, the large consumer electronics vendors, all have products they are quietly demonstrating to providers but have not yet announced. When they enter the market, around the end of 2001, look for plummeting prices, with full-featured units dropping to the $200–300 range, and simple ones much less expensive.

Software-based Routing and Why Not to Do It?

With prices on gateways coming down to about $100 more than modems, and inexpensive home routers at under $150, it's usually easier, faster, and more reliable to use hardware to network. However, if you already have a home or office network with a hub, you can do your routing through the PC connected to the modem. It's called *soft routing*, and its been built in to Windows since the second release of Windows 98. Consider carefully before you pursue this option. While soft routing saves money because it is built in to your operating system, it can be complicated to set up, run, and troubleshoot. It ties up some of the processing power of the host computer, and if that host crashes, all the other users are cut off from the Internet. Even inexpensive hardware routers have generally proven reliable, while we all have learned that PCs crash often.

 A modem can support the whole network through Microsoft's Internet Connection Sharing, but why bother when routers cost as little as $100?

The Chips They are 'A Changing'?

Chips are the core technology that determines the direction and new advances in DSL. Manufacturers are now promising new chips that will extend DSL's reach beyond the current limits. The labs are also promising 20–25 percent increases in throughput by about 2003. These changes in technology will allow U.S. telcos to serve 10 million more sites, to bring DSL to 10 or 15 percent more of the market, and to deliver faster, more reliable service to many millions more. The latest chip designs also include components that help providers to test lines more effectively, technology imperative to making service more reliable. Conexant has announced that they will produce a chip that includes a time-based reflectometer, a sophisticated tool that measures microsecond variation in signal response to identify problems on the line. Aware is already shipping chip designs that allow the modem/router to diagnose problems and display performance results on the user's or the support center screen.

Routers will become more capable and cheaper; and modems will include most of the features of today's routers. Prices will go down, and software modems will be built in to many of the computers for sale in five years. Those predictions are easy to make, because chips, the primary component, will continue to double in capacity every 18 months or so, following Moore's Law. The Semiconductor Industry Association produces a detailed *road map* of technology trends, and hence, the likely properties of the chips they can produce, measured by the size of the smallest design feature and the number of transistors on a chip. Most of the equipment described in this book is based on chips with a .25 micron design rule. That's about one four-hundredths of the width of a typical human hair. In 2002 and 2003, production will shift to .13 micron designs, supporting three to five times as many transistors.

Smaller chips run faster, allowing the on-chip logic to do more processing. As a result, the current modem chips will add the firewalls, encryption, and network address translation of the router. The functions of the other chips in the design can be integrated into the primary chipset, driving down the cost.

Professional routers are likely to plummet in price. Routers without voice capability mostly list for $500 to $800 in early 2001, but already manufacturers like Eicon and Zyzel are driving prices down toward $300.

Hardware modems will keep coming down in price, with Texas Instruments predicting that their 2002 chipsets will be so inexpensive that modem manufacturers will drop the price under $75 retail. Adding multi-user support, a firewall, and even SNMP management features will add little to the cost, bringing even to inexpensive units most of the gateway/router features, at continually lower prices.

Software-based DSL modems will be built into many computers, essentially replacing the hardware modem over three to six years, just as they have replaced dial-up modems. Motorola and PC Tel have demonstrated *soft modems* at trade shows, which use about 200 megahertz of the Pentium's processing power to replace much of the modem hardware. As CPU speed approaches and passes 2 gigahertz, that's a good tradeoff.

Manufacturers

Just a few manufacturers produced most of the DSL equipment used in the U.S. today. Often large contracts, including those from telcos and large ISPs, determine equipment features and set the trend for technology. Manufacturers leading the field provide a combination of reliability and innovation, but as components have become standard, look for many new players, especially Asian component vendors with efficient manufacturing.

Efficient, America's leading modem manufacturer, is an aggressive, sometimes brash Texas company with a reputation for reliability. Efficient became everybody's favorite by working with providers and DSLAM vendors early, and making special models to their specifications. Efficient bought FlowPoint to get the more commercial routers and a whole line of routers tailored for voice over DSL (VoDSL), and then was itself bought out by Siemens for 1.5 billion dollars in 2001. They make reliable modems and provide good support.

Westell from the beginning put extra smarts into their modems. The early models can be turned into mini-routers and do network address translation with a software upgrade sold on their Web site. However, Westell's long-term ties to the bells may be their undoing. They gambled and won the first, early Bell Atlantic contracts by pricing below costs, expecting that as chip prices went down and volume increased, they would make a profit. In the meantime, Westell had to reveal it in a 10K, "a single large contract, (Bell Atlantic) was being fulfilled with equipment that it cost us more to manufacture than we were charging the customer."

They had to take layoffs the next year, as orders came in slowly, but soon Bell Atlantic and SBC ordered large volumes, and Westell was the toast of Wall Street. However, disappointments at mega customer SBC may well be the death of the company. Cancelled SBC orders were so large that Westell had to write down $25 million in inventory. CEO Mark Zionts lost his job for what initially looked like a smart move—gearing up to match the forecasts of the company's biggest customer. The telcos have succeeded in shifting much of the technology risk to vendors.

Asian competition is gaining ground as modems become commodities and they are the low cost producer. Some of them are part of big companies like Creative Labs. Other specialists like Zyzel and Arescom have been consistently able to undercut the brand names and keep their prices driving down. Ambit, an independent division of Taiwanese electronic giant Acer, has won massive contracts from Chunghwa in Taiwan and Yahoo/Softbank in Japan that will make them one of the world's largest manufacturers. They have close ties with Alcatel, from whom they purchased a factory.

Router and gateway manufacturers continue to shape the DSL environment. A few have distinguished themselves by anticipating future market needs and creating products that can be upgrades with software or minor hardware adjustments. It's almost always easier and better to go with the customer premises equipment (CPE) that your ISP's tech support people know. Most routers come in two models, one with the DSL modem built in, the other without a modem that you just plug in to whatever modem your vendor provides. A separate box won't cause any technical problems and, if you're not getting any support from your ISP, is an excellent way to go.

Netopia is a charming, spirited company that comes out of the Mac environment. Their router has worked flawlessly for us, and the support they've given has been excellent. Still independent, with cash in the bank, we hope they prove to be one of the survivors.

Ramp also went up with the CLECs and was swallowed by Nokia. They distinguished their product line by making an early deal with Check Point and putting IPSec security corporate standard on their routers first.

Linksys, *D-Link*, and *Netgear* (a division of *Nortel*) specialize in no-frills inexpensive products that work just fine. In particular, their small routers are an easy way to take a modem or existing hookup and build a small network. The unit without the modem has most of the features you need, including a basic firewall, and the price is dropping, likely to under $100. They don't have the flash of the gateways described later in this chapter, but offer knowledgeable users most of the same functions at a very attractive price.

Adtran earned Dave's appreciation when they gave excellent support for the ISDN modems that he was using, and their new products, emphasizing the new symmetric standard, G.SHDSL, are well-built industrial-grade equipment. Adtran actively participated in developing G.SHDSL, which will replace much of their T1 product line.

Asante, like Netopia, has always been a favorite for Mac users, with reliable product and good support.

Eicon, based in Montreal but owned by I-data of Copenhagen, is pricing aggressively as it moves its products from ISDN to DSL.

Virtual Access sells to British Telecom, Bell South, and Qwest. They have the most advanced customer diagnostics of any unit on the market.

Efficient, *Westell*, and many Asian manufacturers are listed under modems, but also make routers. Efficient, in particular, has a large market share.

Polycom, *Avail*, and others emphasize Voice over DSL, so they are covered in Chapter 7.

Cayman, a quiet, engineering-oriented company in New England was the first to market. They modified their router, originally designed for the Mac, and priced it for the home and small office market. They built a reputation for strong products, but didn't have the flavor or the hype of a consumer company.

2Wire's founder, Brian Hinman, was a boy wonder when he built Polycom, a leading voice/video conferencing company. He dreamed of bringing video to the Net, but first he's delivering the gateway that's been chosen by Earthlink, Verizon, and soon others. The 2Wire gateway features a broadband portal, e-commerce option, and either wired or wireless networking. One model has four voice ports as well.

For the Pros

The chip vendors, who drive the research in this field, have spent years in testing to develop interoperability, and generally their gear works fine with other vendors compatible equipment. There remain subtle differences, however, especially between different chipsets. There are clear 10–15 percent performance differences that have been proven, and anecdotal evidence of minor reliability problems. That's another reason to stick to your provider's preferred equipment; they've probably tested all the equipment in their labs, and you'll do better following their recommendations.

Noise and interference within the modem/router make the actual design quite tricky. A small change, like moving a capacitor can make a significant difference. Therefore, most manufacturers rely heavily on the chip maker's reference design. Chip makers work hard to create an optimum design using their components, then give it away to the modem manufacturer in order to sell their chips. It is very detailed, and includes the actual CAD files for the circuit board. The manufacturer adds a case, packaging, software, sales support, and marketing, but the internal design may be nearly identical among a dozen modems. Numerous Asian manufacturers have jumped in, driving down prices of standard modems (to a quantity price of $50-75 in mid-2001). If their manufacturing is reliable, the products work very well, and many of the largest providers are now buying virtually generic products from Asia. In this market you must know your supplier, however.

CHAPTER 4

Technology

T he technology that makes DSL work can be traced directly back to Claude
Shannon, who in 1948 developed the theory of digital signal processing at
Bell Labs. At the time, the fastest computers in the world probably couldn't
handle the translation of a voice signal into digital bits, but his colleagues at
Bell Labs were developing the transistor, which brought practical form to his
theory. Fifty years later, this technology has come home as the foundation for
DSL, which can carry as much data as 50 phone calls over the same wire.

The first applications were in long distance, where the digital signals could
be regenerated across the continent without amplifying the noise. Within
three decades, most of the long-distance network was digital, and so were
many of the central office switches. A decade later, starting in 1986, it was
time to digitize the signal for the last mile, and Bell Labs developed ISDN.
The basic rate was only 144K; 10 times the modem speed of the day. The
higher-speed service, called T-1/E-1 or PRI ISDN, was considered far too
expensive for anything but high-end commercial service.

A Mathematical Theory of Communication (1948)

This pioneering paper on information theory begins by observing that "the fundamental problem of communication is that of reproducing at one point either exactly or approximately a message selected at another point." Shannon's images now seem intuitively obvious, just as Shakespeare's plays now seem filled with clichés. We include an excerpt for the pleasure of the historical document, and because it describes well the essence of your DSL network.

1. An information source which produces a message or sequence of messages to be communicated to the receiving terminal. The message may be of various types:

    (a) A sequence of letters as in a telegraph or Teletype system;

    (b) A single function of time f (t)) as in radio or telephony;

    (c) A function of time and other variables as in black and white television—here the message may be thought of as a function f (x; y; t)) of two space coordinates and time, the light intensity at a point x; y) and time t on a pickup tube plate;

    (d) Two or more functions of time, say f (t, g (t), h (t)—this is the case in "three-dimensional" sound transmission or if the system is intended to service several individual channels in multiplex;

    (e) Several functions of several variables—in color television the message consists of three functions f (x; y; t), g(x; y; t), h(x; y; t)) defined in a three-dimensional continuum—we may also think of these three functions as components of a vector field defined in the region—similarly, several black and white television sources would produce "messages" consisting of a number of functions of three variables;

    (f) Various combinations also occur, for example in television with an associated audio channel.

The *Information source* you're connected to might be a video server at your ISP or a bank of server computers across the Internet. That's a large view of the network. A more direct view would consider the DSLAM you're connected to the as the *source*.

2. A transmitter which operates on the message in some way to produce a signal suitable for transmission over the channel. In telephony this operation consists merely of changing sound pressure into a proportional electrical current. In telegraphy we have an encoding operation which produces a sequence of dots, dashes and spaces on the channel corresponding to the message. In a multiplex PCM system the different speech functions must be sampled, compressed, quantized and encoded, and finally interleaved properly to construct the signal. Vocoder systems, television and frequency modulation are other examples of complex operations applied to the message to obtain the signal. *See below for an illustration of a DSLAM line card that acts as a transmitter*

3. The channel is merely the medium used to transmit the signal from transmitter to receiver. It may be a pair of wires, a coaxial cable, a band of radio frequencies, a beam of light, etc.

4. The receiver ordinarily performs the inverse operation of that done by the transmitter, reconstructing the message from the signal.

Your modem is the receiver, and the computer or television is the final destination.

5. The destination is the person (or thing) for whom the message is intended.

The full paper is fascinating, and most is clear to a non-engineer. It's at http://cm.bell-labs.com/cm/ms/what/shannonday/paper.html

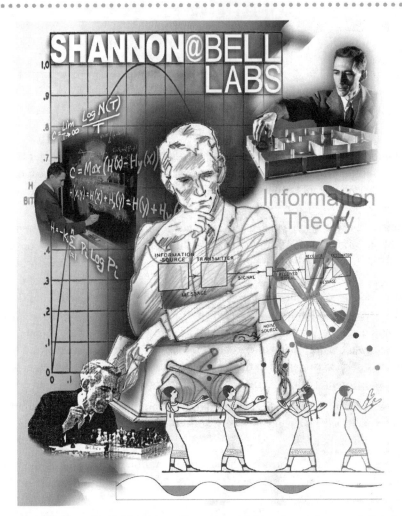

Figure 4.1 Claude Shannon, whose theories introduced the era of digital communications. Shannon was famous for juggling and riding a unicycle through the halls of Bell Labs.
Courtesy: Lucent/Bell Labs

"Accomplishing the Impossible Is an Engineer's Greatest Reward,"
John Cioffi and Tom Starr

Joe Lechlider at Bellcore, the Bell Labs spinoff, was the first to believe that DSL was practical, as chips became so powerful that soon they could do all the processing that required thousands of dollars of equipment at the time. In

1987, he inspired Stanford Professor John Cioffi to join the work despite general skepticism they could achieve real world results. Cioffi now remembers, "Experts said 144K ISDN was very near the capacity limit of telephone lines. We were the only two guys who believed in DSL." Lechlider was also the first to realize that asymmetry (running faster in one direction than the other) would lead to greater total bandwidth. Restricting the upstream and downstream channels to different frequency ranges reduces their mutual interference. The result is that a line that can carry 1.5MB in each direction, for a total of 3MB, can carry 7MB in one direction and 700K in the reverse, more than twice the total bandwidth.

Lechlider and Cioffi weren't alone for long. An enormous international effort was developing by 1991, when a journal edited by Cioffi featured Gavin Young of British Telecom, Wu-Jhy Chiu and team from Taiwan, and two dozen more from around the world. The names themselves resonate with regional flavor: Vedat Eyuboglu, Ahmad Aman, Nikolaos Zervos, Kamran Sistanizadeh, Kenneth Kerpez, and Pedro Crespo. This wonderful diversity continues in the industry today, where the names on our e-mail are often Faraj, Nabil, Mariam, Sundi, Krista, or Eitan.

By 1991, the main issues in DSL technology were already clear, and most were on the way to being solved. Lechleider's speculations had been confirmed; now the practical problems were to fall rapidly. Chiu and others actually tested the copper in the field, necessary to know what was practical. Samueli and Nicholas wrote from Pairgain, where they were soon to produce the early HDSL equipment, the *T-1 replacement* that was the first to market. Chen was working on echo cancellation, required to efficiently send data in both directions. Young proposed adaptive equalization, whereby the line would be automatically tested for its actual condition and interference, and the transmission adjusted for best results. Every DSL chip today has test functions built in; the latest generation announced by Conexant has built into each $20 chip the key functions of a $15,000 instrument, a *time domain reflectomer*, which can analyze the line based on nanosecond delays. Starr led the key standards group, T1E1.4 for the next decade, solving many of the toughest problems of interference, and was a key advocate of Ameritech and SBC.

The most contentious dispute was over the line code, how the bits were to be translated into an analog signal and carried over the copper wire. Werner and Samueli believed the simpler CAP/QAM coding would get to market faster, and prove more robust. US West and some smaller telcos still use that system, but standard ADSL evolved from John Cioffi's DMT code. *Discrete multitone modulation* divides the frequency range into 256 separate bins, so most of the signal gets through even if interference blocks a few frequencies. A decade later, the same folks are battling over standards for VDSL, but from changed positions in life. Cioffi is now an award-winning full professor at Stanford, whose ADSL patents have made him wealthy. Samueli and Nicholas founded Broadcom, now a major communications chipmaker, and have become billionaires. In researching DSL history, we've interviewed them all—and they are still arguing over who was right, and which is the better standard for the next generation, VDSL.

To honor the history, and to show how much research has been required, we've recreated the table of contents of that historic issue on page 73.

Today's DSL Systems

A decade after the theory was developed, ten million DSL lines are in service, with one hundred million likely over the next few years. Thousands of engineers worked to make the technology real, from the chips to the networking gear. In the previous chapter, we described the modems and routers for your DSL connection. In this chapter, we'll look at the chips inside those modems and your provider's network equipment.

In your office, the chips in a DSL modem do an extraordinary job, very precisely encoding, synchronizing, checking, error correcting, and decoding all the data. Your data crosses the wire to a DSLAM or a DLC, and from there by fiber to a metropolitan control center (megapop), which typically houses the network intelligence to handle customer logons, traffic management, and integration of each user into the Internet.

Inside the cloud of the Net is a wonderfully complicated, vibrant network that constantly adjusts to changes in traffic flow and the limitations of the equipment. The defining character of the Internet is that it continues to work despite failure of multiple components, automatically rerouting traffic, and requesting re-sent data when necessary. When the World Trade Center was destroyed, Dave was in D.C., not far from the Pentagon, while Jennie was in New York. The telephone lines were blocked, but we were able to exchange very reassuring e-mails without any problems. Congestion is part of the normal operation, and slow performance where capacity is short is an accepted fact of life.

The Internet connection itself should be broad, and the better providers purchase backbone connections that are close to the core of the networks and supported by excellent peering relationships.

IEEE Journal of Selected Areas in Communications, Volume 9, Number 6, August 1991

Figure 4.2a These *wire bundles* were installed in trenches to reconnect Wall Street to the world after the 7 World Trade Center collapsed, literally on top of Verizon's central office at 140 West Street. With five stories of rubble blocking access to the wires for repair, it was faster to crack the pavement and put in new lines temporarily. Each bundle of wires contains 25-100 twisted pair phone lines, which are connected on your end to the phone and in the central office to a DSLAM or DLC. (Your wires are much more carefully buried and protected, of course.) The wires are the crucial determinant of the top speed of your DSL connection. Signals diminish due to resistance in longer wires, which limits DSL to about 3 miles without repeaters. They vary in thickness and condition, with rusted splices a typical problem. The other wires in the bundle cause interference, especially T-1 data lines. That means it is impossible to determine your DSL connection speed unless and until your actual line is tested or equipment installed. The interference in the binder group can change over time, as additional services are turned on for your neighbors, which can reduce your connection speed, and need to be accommodated.

Figure 4.2b   Your telco CO is probably a much smaller building than this one, 140 West Street in Manhattan, which serves 200,000 lines near Wall Street and was built in the 1920s. By the 1950s equivalent capacity could be installed in a building a quarter the size; by the 1980s, remote terminals with fiber connections made new COs almost unnecessary. The debris from the collapsed building is also not a standard feature. These pictures are from six days after September 11, by which time 3,000 Verizon workers had most of Wall Street up and running, including 14,000 of the 15,000 circuits to the stock exchange itself.

. . . .

Chips Rule: All Else is Commentary

That's an exaggeration, but if you are looking to understand the technology, and guess the future, start with the chips. The core of a DSL chip/chipset is usually a digital signal processor (DSP), a specialized chip more efficient for the necessary calculations than a conventional microprocessor such as a Pentium. Typically, a second chip handles the analog functions, although every design is different. Intelligence may come from a controller chip, a microprocessor core (such as ARM), the computer's processor, or some combination thereof. The cost of the DSL equipment is also dependent on the smaller chips required—the better chipsets incorporate more of the other functions, reducing total cost and power. The leaders in DSPs are Texas Instruments (TI) and Analog Devices, who have applied that expertise to DSL. Dedicated design houses like Broadcom, Metalink, Globespan, Tioga, ITeX, Aware, and Centillium play important roles, while Motorola, Legerity, Conexant/Mindspeed, and Intel are also players. Inhouse operations at Alcatel, Siemens/Infineon, Samsung, NEC, and other large firms also have designs.

There are many different ways to design the chips for a DSL board, with significantly different requirements at the customer premise and the DSLAM. Customer premise equipment for PCs and most routers are not constrained by power or space, so compatibility, cost, and flexibility are key features. However, portable computers and USB modems are more restrictive; small size and low power draw are major advantages. At the telco office end, space and power are at a premium, so the smallest, highest-density chips, needing the least power, have a major advantage. With 20–30 percent of customers served by DLC remote terminals, the extreme space and power limits in boxes in the field become even more restrictive.

The different flavors of DSL are emphasized by different manufacturers. Conexant is the leader in the first-generation SDSL, the symmetric service initially favored by data CLECS. The newer generation, G.SHDSL, is standards based, and at least six companies are targeting the market. The larger ADSL market is dominated by Alcatel, whose DSLAMs are in telcos including Verizon, BellSouth, SBC, British Telecom, and Taiwan's Chungwa. Other makers of ADSL chips have demonstrated interoperability with Alcatel, including rigorous testing at the University of New Hampshire, so equipment vendors can choose freely.

In Chapter 11, "The Future," we predict that the reach and capacity of DSL will be extended 15–25 percent further. DSL can be extended to six miles or more if the telcos install repeaters. Improvements beyond that will require a technical breakthrough, perhaps from a multiwire method of measuring and compensating for noise.

Manufacturers

Alcatel Microelectronics leads the chip market, with large sales to independent modem vendors as well as their own DSLAM division. They and TI are the prime supporters of the VDSL Alliance, which uses DMT coding for ADSL compatibility.

Analog Devices is a major chip manufacturer whose SHARC DSP holds a major share of the market against TI and Lucent/Agere. They work closely with Aware, and deliver large volumes of modem chips around the world.

Aware designs chips, and then sells the designs as intellectual property to the actual manufacturers, including Analog Devices, NEC, Infineon, and STM. They were the first to announce on-chip testing, which they call Dr. DSL. The diagnostics made possible by the chip include speed and error correction.

Broadcom, one of the world's most innovative chip design firms, shipped the first Gigabit Ethernet chip. They supply most of the chips for cable modems. The founders, Henry Nicholas and Henry Samueli, were two of the pioneers of DSL. One of the reasons they founded Broadcom was that Pairgain, where they were working, refused to provide sufficient support for their vision of DSL. They released a VDSL chip in 1998, giving them a two-year lead in the field, and supplied all the chips for the world's largest deployment, in Phoenix.

Centillium made an initial splash with low-power, high-density chips, winning a series of design contracts in Asia. They worked for years with NTT to develop chips that could work with Japan's nonstandard ISDN network, and were rewarded with orders for millions of chips in 2001 when Japanese deployment picked up steam.

Conexant created and dominated the market for symmetric DSL, supplying the chips for most telco competitors. They also make ADSL chips, and their G.shdsl chip will have state-of-the-art testing capabilities.

Globespan is the largest *independent* DSL chipmaker, and may have passed Analog Devices to become the number-two DSL chipmaker overall, *including* those that are part of larger companies. An engineering-rich company, they are the primary supplier to Lucent and Cisco.

Intel has heavily targeted communications chips, but their early ventures, including the purchase of Level 1, have brought them few advanced designs or customer wins to date.

Ishoni's primary product is a *gateway on a chip* that will help drive down the cost of home gateways.

ITeX has designed chips that work with the Pentium for control of the DSL modem functions, using the computer's processing power rather than an on-chip processor core or DSP. This should lower system costs for motherboard manufacturers who seek to include a DSL modem. They are majority controlled by giant Taiwanese chipmaker TSMC, and have direct access to the TSMC production capabilities.

Legerity, spun off from AMD, has a high-voltage technology that is developing interesting chips that work for voice and data.

MetaLink, an Israeli company, did some of the pioneering work on HDSL2, and was one of the first to produce G.SHDSL chips as well. They developed the first chips designed for the VDSL 998 standard, and several DSLAM makers will be using the chip.

Motorola abandoned their CopperGold ADSL chipset, after design delays cost them most of their customer base, but continue to be a market leader in the controller chips that supply the intelligence for many modems. They are demonstrating a DSL soft modem, which will run software on the computer's Pentium to replace most of the chips now required for a DSL modem.

PCTel has built strong market share in 56K soft modems, and hopes to play a major role in DSL soft modems when that market develops.

Tioga was once part of DSLAM vendor Orckit, but now is independent and looking for other customers. They have a close relationship with Fujitsu, whose plant manufactures most of Tioga's chips.

Infineon is the former chip division of Siemens, one of the world's leading telephone switch vendors and a world-class semiconductor manufacturer. They have innovative chips to do data and voice on the same card, and are leading the way to VDSL, working with Savan of Israel.

STMicroelectronics, one of the largest European chipmakers, is the first to demonstrate the new generation of VDSL chips supporting the DMT coding used in ADSL as well. They have a close alliance with Alcatel.

Texas Instruments purchased Amati, the pioneer of DMT ADSL, whose John Cioffi defined DMT standard line coding, and Kim Maxwell founded the DSL Forum that brought the industry together. They are the world leader in DSP chips, and DSL chips are a natural addition whose volume they intend to grow.

Virata grew out of research at Cambridge University, and now specializes in highly integrated chips. Their initial strength was in the chips that control DSL modems, with which they included a complete suite of software. They now also make a version that integrates the digital functions of a DSL chipset.

DSLAMs are the Connection to the Net

A DSL *Access Multiplexer*, or DSLAM, connects hundreds of lines to your provider's network and hence to the Internet. It may be in your basement, or in the phone company's central office. Your wire terminates in *line cards*, which can handle up to 64 individual subscribers. All the traffic is combined, and then sent further up the network, typically through a fiber link to a central control point for your city. Your modem, the Internet backbone connection, and most other parts of the network can be readily upgraded, but replacing a DSLAM requires a *forklift upgrade* and would be so expensive that it's unlikely to happen. Therefore, the DSLAM is the long run limit on the services your provider can offer you. Older, less capable units mean video speeds or guaranteed speeds are harder to deliver.

Alcatel is the 800-pound gorilla in this business, with a 50 percent plus market share that's growing. They underbid everyone else for a Bell *joint procurement contract*, and won BellSouth, SBC, and Bell Atlantic/Verizon as DSLAM customers. That experience, and a willingness to bid as low as nec-

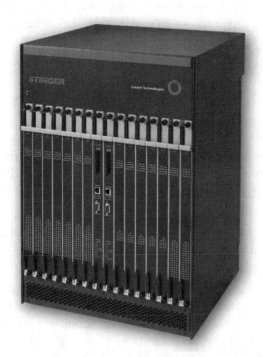

Figure 4.3   Lucent's Stinger DSLAM introduced in 1999 was the first of a new generation designed to be powerful enough to deliver video.

Courtesy: Cheryl Ertel/Lucent

essary to win contracts, added customers British Telecom, French Telecom, Telfonica of Spain, and in 2001, Deutsche Telekom, Chunghwa of Taiwan, and China Telecom. Their 7300 DSLAM, shipped in 2001, has video speed performance, built-in test, and an option for Voice over DSL, enabling future services. Ten million lines of the older units, with more severe limits, will restrict offerings in most of the United States for many years.

Cisco bought Netspeed, whose premier clients were Qwest and Cincinnati Bell, and added a major deal with SBC for parts of the U.S. midwest. They refused to drop prices sufficiently to hold the Taiwan contract, and have struggled to maintain their market share.

Copper Mountain is the premier independent, but has been struggling since their primary customer base, the telco competitors, failed.

Elastic Networks uses a somewhat different technology, based on Ethernet. They compete in the same market, however, and to the user are very similar to DSL. They scored a major contract win with Verizon Avenue to install their Etherloop equipment in buildings. They've had a hard battle, being nonstandard, but have had impressive results with increased bandwidth at medium distances.

Lucent's Stinger, introduced in 2000, was the first popular DSLAM of the second generation, with video capabilities and test. Sprint's troubled ION program is the largest customer, and they've made some progress in Qwest.

NEC has worldwide distribution, but has been unable to make many sales outside Japan.

Net to Net makes inexpensive DSLAMs, starting around $10,000 and less in quantity, that make it practical to deploy to smaller towns. When one telco claimed it was *too expensive* to serve all their offices, we asked the rhetorical question "How much does it cost to install a $10,000 DSLAM?" Rural districts can be profitably served, because nearly all of them are already connected with fiber to the larger networks, and an inexpensive DSLAM is paid off with 20 subscribers or fewer.

Nokia bought Diamond Lane, whose DSLAMs have proven reliable in the Covad network, and hoped to become one of the leading suppliers in the world. However, they have had a difficult time finding contracts.

Paradyne was part of AT&T when they developed the earliest DSL equipment, and now is an independent public company created by a Texas Pacific leveraged buyout. Their proprietary Reach/DSL has superior results in the field for customers two and three miles from the DSLAM. Paradyne was one of the first to deliver their 10,000th DSLAM, and has a diverse worldwide customer base.

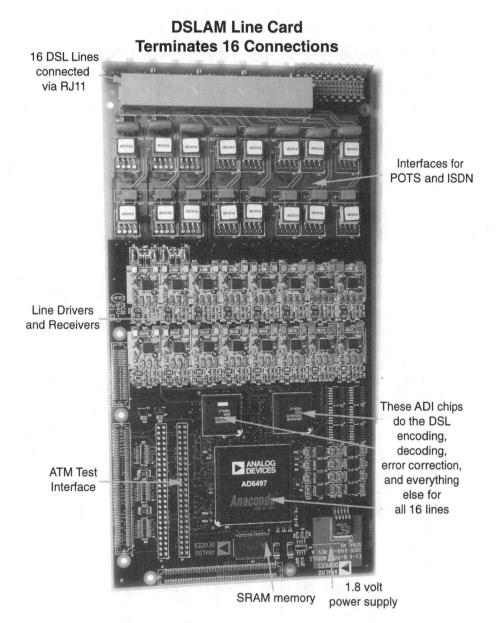

DSLAM Line Card
Terminates 16 Connections

16 DSL Lines
connected
via RJ11

Interfaces for
POTS and ISDN

Line Drivers
and Receivers

These ADI chips
do the DSL
encoding,
decoding,
error correction,
and everything
else for
all 16 lines

ATM Test
Interface

SRAM memory

1.8 volt
power supply

Figure 4.4   Your DSL line is connected to a line card like this. Take a look at the components.

Courtesy: Analog Devices

RC Networks makes pizza-box sized DSLAMs, suitable for deployment in basement wiring closets. They cost as little as $3,000 and less in quantity, making it very inexpensive to serve the entire building from a single fiber line. Alcatel has announced a deal to resell their gear, offering yet another choice to serve smaller communities.

Samsung won a 600,000 line order in Korea, with a remarkable low bid of about $125 per line. Their next strategic target is China, but if they decide to expand elsewhere, they may drive prices even lower.

Siemens is the primary supplier to Deutsche Telekom 2 million+ line deployment, but they bought Efficient for $1.7 billion and ultimately have worldwide ambitions.

Sumitomo holds a major market share in Japan, but has not expanded outside.

Remote Terminals Reach the Far Neighborhoods

Remote terminals, fiber-fed *digital loop carriers*, or DLCs serve 25 percent of America whose lines no longer have a direct connection to the telco office. This is the most common reason you can't get DSL. The telcos first choose to install DSLAMs in offices serving tens of thousands of customers, and only now are getting around to DLCs, most of which serve hundreds. Some of the toughest regulatory battles are over DLCs, because they are physically small, making sharing them with competitors difficult and sometimes impractical. Since the mid-1990s, and in the wake of the 1996 Telecom Act, government strategy has been to replace regulation with competition. SBC is resisting competition in DLCs, however, and resisting regulation as well. The consumer is the loser.

Advanced Fiber has some of the most advanced units on the market, competing strongly with their competitor down the road, Alcatel. We spent two fascinating days visiting both in Petaluma, California, and they convinced us they can deliver excellent fast service 10 miles from the nearest telco office.

Adtran entered the market in 2001 with a small, inexpensive unit at an aggressive price. Low-priced units allow installing DLCs in small developments or neighborhoods.

Alcatel dominates this market, having purchased the pioneer maker of advanced DLCs, DSC. Their DSLAM division also has a small model, the Mini-Ram, that can fit in existing cabinets.

Figure 4.5   DLC remote terminals need to be replaced or upgraded to deliver DSL. Neighborhood gateway cabinets like this one serve much of the country, and need units like the Lucent Stinger RT installed for DSL.
Courtesy: Lucent

Catena Networks developed interesting chips that do both voice and data, and used them to create linecards for the older DLCs as a very inexpensive upgrade.

Lucent created the entire category, and many of the units in the field are older Lucent DLCs with limited capacity. Their prime offering today is a modified Stinger DSLAM, the RT, that is hardened against the environment in the field. Qwest is installing units like the one in Figure 4.5.

Zhone raised $450 million in the glory days, to develop a product line doing everything in networking. They used some of that cash to buy Nortel's DLC product line, and look to play a major role.

The Rest of the Gear

The network and services are typically controlled centrally, with major equipment in each metro at a control center, and generally a national network operations center (NOC). Users who know about this equipment can better understand what's possible: speed can be upgraded remotely in minutes, your connection can be secured, and your line tested to find problems and guarantee your performance.

Redback subscriber management systems are crucial network controllers. When you log on, they control your circuit, route your bits to the appropriate ISP or backbone router, and maintain a crucial interface between the unsorted data sent from the DSLAM and the actual Internet connections.

Nortel/Shasta was Redback's first big competitor, and the first to add central security to the network. The Shasta system can be configured to maintain a firewall and virus checker to protect all the users in that metro.

We cannot overemphasize the importance of testing, which has been short-circuited in many network designs. DSL Hell is real, with far too many problems in installation and sometimes after. You have a right to the service level advertised and sold, and we know it's possible to deliver it. When your line is slow or down, you're entitled to have it checked. The equipment is standard—the providers need to use it.

Harris is a traditional test supplier that has adapted its equipment to the challenge of DSL.

Spirent/Hekimian is a another traditional supplier to the Bells, and has delivered over 10,000 test units around the world. Their React 2001 system shows what's possible. It downloads a test applet to the end-user's computer. The applet runs a series of IP diagnostics from the test server to the customer, and back to the content provider. The technician may also focus on the connection to a particular Web site with which the user is having network performance difficulty. On test completion, the technician can also forward the test results directly to the customer's browser. That means you can locate the problem, whether it's in your network or outside on the Internet. This kind of information, should be available to every user.

Sunrise Telecom makes excellent handheld testers called *butt sets*, because traditionally they are carried attached to the back of an installer's belt. The latest models can detect DSL lines, but few folks in the field have them. The unfortunate but common result we call line stealing—the tech in the field assumes a line carrying DSL is not in use, because it has no dial tone and doesn't register on the test set. They then cut the line and use it for someone else's phone. Sounds funny now—but we were mad as hell when it happened to us.

Teradyne has a similar line-testing unit, and in field trials reduced trouble call time by 40 percent by letting the user and technician get results. British Telecom used Teradyne to check a million lines before offering DSL to the customers, and drastically reduced customer disappointments by cleaning the lines in advance, or not promising service if they couldn't cure the problem. We asked a U.S. telco exec why they didn't do the same, especially after BT confirmed to us that they saved a lot of money. The very off-the-record answer was "the @#$!(*& in finance took it out of our budget, and we're paying for it now." That's one more reason why in troubleshooting we suggest you stand up for better service—the problems are not just technology.

Turnstone was the first to specialize in DSL test equipment, creating the Copper CrossConnect that was installed in front of thousands of DSLAMs. Sitting in an operations center, tech support can check your line, and even switch it to another line card in the DSLAM if that's the cause of the problem.

The progress has been extraordinary, but some problems remain. We've devoted a chapter to your practical security choices, but the challenges are evolving rapidly. Following is some of the latest research, selections from Berkeley graduate student Nicholas Weaver's paper, alarming projections that scared us all in the summer of 2001.

In the early 1990s, the intensity revved up as Bell Atlantic saw the possibility of using ADSL to transmit pay movies to customers. BA invested several hundred million dollars in partnership with other telcos toward that goal. The technology worked, but the costs were too high—thousands per customer for DSL itself and the other components like video servers. Those costs have now come down, with a complete set of equipment, including modem and Internet connectivity, costing a telco about $300. Today's prices mean a telco can be profitable selling Internet service at about $30, as the Canadians, Germans, Japanese, and Koreans are proving. Once the system is in place for the Internet, the marginal cost of adding video is very low, and its time has therefore come.

For the Pros

*The most interesting work is done in the DSL Forum (www.adsl.com) and the T1E1.4 committee (www.t1.org/t1e1/_e14home.htm). They both have voluminous archives of the best technical contributions. That's where to find the real information. Cioffi and Starr's book (*Understanding Digital Subscriber Line Technology*—second edition due shortly) comes with a CD full of technical submissions, an incredible bargain.*

Warhol Worms: The Potential for Very Fast Internet Plagues

Nicholas C. Weaver

Microsoft IIS is an amazingly vulnerable target, even in the aftermath of Code Red I and II. IIS is installed by default with Windows 2000 server and it provides a highly homogeneous target. Furthermore, there is a continued negligence when it comes to maintaining patches, even on the part of Microsoft. The response following the initial breakout of Code Red demonstrated this clearly: a week after the first outbreak, the second outbreak corrupted nearly as many machines.

Microsoft Exchange is less prevalent than IIS, but it makes for a highly attractive second target for a multimode worm. Since e-mail needs to get into the corporation, this provides an excellent route for a worm to cut through firewalls. Once inside a firewall, a worm can cause considerable havoc since many internal networks are insecure.

Finally, holes in the current generation of messenger applications (AOL IM, MSN messenger) and peer to peer file sharing programs (Napster, Kazaa) make for excellent targets for worms. Although most machines running these programs have comparatively poor network connections, these applications have a great advantage for spreading a worm: Each machine already has information about other machines running the program.

Hitlist scanning isn't necessary for a worm attacking a peer to peer application, the worm simply propagates using the information built into the protocol and application before switching to subnet and permutation scanning as a way of shortcutting gaps and disconnects in the peer to peer structure. Windows XP will undoubtedly make this attack especially effective with its bundled messenger application.

The only problem with P2P applications is that they are kept updated by the users as older versions can't connect. Thus, a worm which attacks a P2P application will need to use an unpublished exploit.

Potential Defenses: *The most effective defenses: security by design, sensible defaults, and a diversity of targets, seem unlikely to happen until after a devastating worm is released. Although buffer overflow attacks have been understood for 2 decades, network services are still written in type-unsafe, bounds-unsafe languages. Security audits seem alien to developers while sensible defaults seem to be a myth. Until a major, highly damaging outbreak occurs, followed by the inevitable billion dollar lawsuits, software companies will probably continue their bad practices.*

Similarly, the Microsoft trend to use its monopoly powers to grow into new markets and force out competition has the side effect of producing homogeneous populations of computers. Homogeneous populations, whether in potatoes or computers, are always more vulnerable to diseases.

Reprinted by permission of Nicholas Weaver, whose full paper is at www.cs.berkeley .edu/~nweaver/warhol.html.

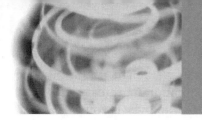

CHAPTER 5

Security: You Need It

"I virtually never find a system I can't get into."

PHIBER OPTIK

Our take on security is different than most. True security requires far more than just firewalls and encryption. We emphasize this because security vendors, and most books, make these comparatively minor issues their key focus. These are also the problems addressed by the products many merchants sell, often at inflated prices. Of course it's appropriate to have a firewall to protect the front door of your system. Encryption protects against someone on the net intercepting your messages—a comparatively rare problem, but one you can also protect against with virtual private network (VPN). However, network managers and security specialists tell us viruses, worms, Web server cracks, and denial-of-service attacks are more common problems. These can harm your system and make public, information you need to protect. They also can harm the net itself, and it is responsible and ethical to prevent your system from being used by a malicious hacker to attack others with a distributed denial-of-service attack.

We rank protection against viruses as the most important priority for securing your system because viruses are the most common way to penetrate your network and cause damage. We received as many as five copies a day of the Sircam virus during the height of the infection, indicating how many people were infected. Each included a random file from the user's e-mail, promising important information. Social engineering is the next important threat to security. This low-tech approach, which allows a hacker to bypass your expensive security system, is the tool of choice for most serious corporate break-ins. Insiders, a much greater threat than intruders and the source of most actual incidents. We urge you to protect yourself. Web site hosting is another bad security risk, it opens an unnecessary door into your system, and costs much more to secure than to outsource. Before you undertake to run your own server, consider Microsoft's experience. While they are among the most competent professionals, they are constantly failing under attack. Their in-house Hotmail servers were the latest victims of Code Red as we write this. Finally, we suggest you root out back-door vulnerabilities—an unprotected modem on the network, or a less secure network linked to yours can cause a serious breach in security. Microsoft hit the news once again their internal systems were infected by an employee hooking up a laptop.

Once those risks are addressed and an intrusion detection plan is in place, you will find it beneficial to follow our recommendations for firewalls and encryption. You will never have perfect security, but the steps we recommend can dramatically reduce your risk.

We take our lessons from the real world. Network managers changed our thinking by telling us they were seeing remarkably few damaging hacker attacks. Bruce Schneier's extraordinary book, *Secrets and Lies*, (John Wiley & Sons, Inc, 2000) crystallized our approach, pointing out that systems have many vulnerabilities, not just hackers coming in a weak front door. Schneier discovered in practice that even the best protection cannot defeat all hack attacks. His experience, and those of managers we interviewed, confirms that the bulk of the danger is elsewhere. Most dramatically, the director of an ISP responsible for over 200,000 broadband users said he had not seen a single incident of ordinary customers seriously damaged by hacking. We also asked the makers of three of the most popular firewall packages for examples of intrusions resulting in significant damage. They reported virtually none, not even from users without firewalls.

Of course, we recommend that you stick to your corporate standards, as we will discuss in Chapter 9, "Enterprise." Here we recommend that you make protecting yourself against the most common threats your highest priority. Then we explain the systems thinking that inspired our approach. We follow up with details on tools, including instructions for making your firewall more secure. Finally, we remind you that if you need serious security, outsourcing to a managed service provider or letting your ISP take some of the responsibility is sometimes your best option.

Warhol Worms, Distributed Denials, and Future Fears

"Everyone shares in a distributed responsibility for the Internet's health and proper operation," security expert Steve Gibson writes. He also says, "The users of machines are responsible for preventing the hosting of malicious Zombie attack Bots on their Internet-connected computers." We believe it is your obligation to protect your system and hence the Net itself.

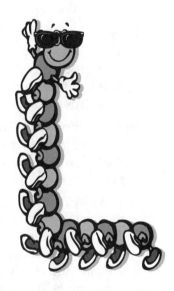

Many security fears are overblown, however, our research makes it clear that individuals are rarely harmed by front door attacks by hackers. As a result, the typical security measures adopted by many companies do little to protect them against the real threats to their systems. But we believe things will get worse in the future, and taking action to protect against attacks like the Code Red worm, which has been damaging servers across the Net is important even though the worm can probably never be completely eradicated. Nicholas Weaver of Berkeley has speculated about what he calls *Warhol worms* that can devastate the worldwide Net in 15 minutes. Script kiddies around the world are bringing down websites with distributed denial of service attacks (DDoS). Governments are spending billions developing tools for electronic warfare. The Net is endangered, and can only be protected if everyone co-operates.

Firewalls are the first line of defense, making it considerably more difficult for a hacker to commandeer your machine. The common fear, of hackers breaking in and causing damage, is widely overblown, because it happens so rarely. However, DDoS attacks on others, originating from your machine, have become increasingly common. DDoS attacks will happen on Windows XP. Worms like Code Red are also spreading, and need to be blocked as effectively as possible. Despite drastic warnings from Microsoft and others, Code Red on August 1 infected over 100,000 machines.

Unfortunately, typical measures will not stop these attacks. Unless the vast majority of computers (90 percent or much more) have strong protection, your firewall merely persuades the perpetrator to find another user less careful than you are, and they will.

Security Threats

To create an effective security strategy for your system you'll need to find a way to protect against the following threats:

Poor virus protection. This should be step one, because virus problems are frequent. Because we receive *a lot* of e-mail, we receive a virus every week or so. A good virus checker catches e-mail attachments, the easiest way to penetrate many networks. Make sure, however, that it is updated often. Out-of-date virus checkers are probably the leading weakness that lets outsiders in.

Social engineering. The art of persuading insiders to give you access, is the most common way in which systems are compromised. See more detail in the following section where we give some advice on how to train your people to avoid it.

Attacks by insiders. Your own people are far more likely to be your problem than any external hacker. According to accounting firm Deloitte and Touche, 73 percent of incidents come from inside. Every security measure against internal users is annoying and cuts productivity; security breaches are rare, and nearly every organization has people who decide to ignore them and help colleagues to get around the system.

Web hosting. You can host a Worldwide Web Server over a DSL connection, but it is almost always a mistake. Web sites are the most frequent target of malicious hacking. The results are visible and the chances of getting caught are low. The time and effort needed to properly secure a Web server will generally cost more than the entire fee for an equivalent commercial service. Hosting company fees are low (less than a penny for the average visitor) and reliability much higher. Unless you have special needs, we strongly urge against hosting your own Web site over a DSL line. Be cautious with other servers as well, including e-mail and FTP.

Poor follow-up after detecting an intruder. When someone is attacking you with vigor, there is a good chance they will get through. You need to respond quickly. If you fear they did breach, you must immediately look hard for any Trojan left behind that compromises your security. While we'll help you configure firewalls and encryption, we know they are far from perfect. Break-ins are typically a process, which begins by investigating your system, finding a weakness, and typically after getting in, installing a backdoor to ensure the ability to return. Intruders may use Trojan (horse) software like Back Orifice, or a Unix rootkit. You must detect and eliminate these tools used by intruders to facilitate return visits; otherwise, you are wide open even if you fix the initial vulnerability.

Backdoors. Microsoft had a network compromised this way, and so could you. A laptop was connected both to the Internet directly and to their corporate network. Miscellaneous modems and other parts of the system are often more vulnerable than the high-speed connection itself. So are remote users, whose machines, if commandeered, are given trusted access to your system, or even other branches of your own company, with security standards less rigorous than yours. Door locks are worthless if it's easy to climb in an open window on the side.

Poorly maintained firewalls. While sophisticated hackers can bypass even a strong firewall, most penetrations occur because your protection has not been rigorously maintained and updated. Nearly all routers have a basic firewall built in, which is your first line of defense, but not nearly sufficient. Telecommuters with modems can install a free version of ZoneAlarm product or any of several inexpensive ones like those produced by Norton and McAfee.

Blind faith in VPNs. Virtual private networks (VPNs) may not be the answer to your security needs. They are the automatic recommendation of DSL providers to business, but some are more effective in lining the provider's pocket than protecting against a real threat. In many cases, what's sold as a VPN is merely the regular service at twice the price, with the features built into your router and Windows turned on. The router you're already paying for has a built-in firewall, and the Windows operating system has PPTP encryption built in. Typical VPN offerings are not significantly more secure than what you would do yourself, and do not protect against most serious threats.

Figure 5.1 If you don't have a corporate standard, ZoneAlarm, free to individual end users, is an excellent choice for a firewall.

Courtesy: Zone Labs

A New Paradigm for Security

Before we explain the tools to address these threats, we introduce a perspective drawn from Bruce Schneier's superb book, *Secrets and Lies*. Schneier wrote the classic textbook on cryptography, but his subsequent experience led him to emphasize other aspects of security. This corresponds with what our hacker friends tell us, that even systems protected by high-tech firewalls and VPNs are vulnerable.

Describing many systems as "great in theory, but failures in practice," Schneier adds, "Research has concentrated on technologies like cryptography, firewalls, public key infrastructures, and tamper resistance. These technologies are much easier to understand and to discuss, and much easier to secure. This doesn't work."

Instead, Schneier suggests looking at every link of the chain of security, rather than just reinforcing the most obvious points. Only one hole is needed to breach your security. The good news is that few hackers are skilled enough to break through your basic security measures and many of those who can aren't interested in cracking your system, or doing damage if they get inside.

Examine all vulnerabilities carefully and take action to remove or reduce them, because you can lose your job if your system security is breached, or even if an auditor suggests that one is possible. We urge you to be very cautious. This chapter explains firewalls and other procedures, but those who need high level protection (banks, Web hosts, spooks) should not deceive themselves. Serious security takes much more than the commonly suggested remedies. If Microsoft can't maintain security, you shouldn't think you can unless you're a damn good pro. There are too many possible attacks. Following standard security recommendations, like improving your firewall, is false comfort. Fortunately, most users rarely encounter severe problems.

If you're serious about security, you'll need to go beyond this book and our explanation of securing the DSL line and develop a comprehensive overall security plan. We strongly recommend you read Bruce Schneier's *Secrets and Lies* and Scambray's *Hacking Exposed* (McGraw-Hill, 2000) for starters. John Chirillo's *Hack Attacks Revealed* (John Wiley, 2001) and *Hack Attacks Denied* (John Wiley, 2001) are two other books that do a good job explaining and configuring firewalls, although we emphasize that you would need to be a damned good pro to actually foil a competent and determined hacker. Be sensible: If you're a financial institution or natural target, people are more likely to come after you, and we strongly advise hiring first-rate professionals.

Two other principles should guide your decision. Most security precautions also create extra trouble for the regular user of the system. They get in the way of all the other work, from ordinary cooperation between two office workers to a professional system upgrade. Historically, small computer systems were designed to be easy to use and administer and ignored security. In many places, the trend has gone too far in the opposite direction with excessive security procedures cutting productivity.

Be realistic about how much cooperation you will get from your users. The near-universal experience is that after a few months with no obvious security breaches, people will become careless. They'll share passwords with their vacation replacement, forget to update their virus checker, and work around anything that slows their own work. A system that will fail if users slack off is doomed. If things break down because humans act like human beings, the system design is faulty. Don't blame the users for problems you can predict.

Strategies for Beefing Up Security

The one security precaution we urge everyone to take is virus protection. Your DSL installation may be the time to upgrade to network virus protection if you are still using software on each machine. The fatal flaw of most antivirus systems is that new viruses constantly appear, some spreading worldwide in days or hours. Even conscientious users don't update their virus checkers that often, and get hit. Network checkers can be updated regularly or automatically, protecting all users, so they are far more likely to be current. You needed virus protection before you had a DSL line, but DSL will probably encourage folks to use the Internet, and e-mail, even more. Inevitably, there will be more viruses.

Be Vigilant about Updating Virus Protection

Software alone won't protect your system against viruses; educating users is an absolute requirement. Most viruses are spread as e-mail attachments, and one of the best protections is to avoid opening them. This is a common mistake, because some of the more destructive viruses appear to be e-mail from their regular correspondents with ambiguous messages. An e-mail from a colleague with the tag line "I love you" proved to be irresistible to many.

Many people opened what they thought was a photo of tennis diva, Anna Kournikova, and systems went down around the world, because the *picture* was a virus in disguise. Pros know better than to open unexpected attachments, but we all get careless. Most of your users aren't pros, and many won't even understand that your warning about *attachments* refers to the underlined note they click on in the e-mail.

You can add another layer of protection, as we do by using Eudora for e-mail instead of Microsoft products. Most virus authors target the most popular products, especially Microsoft's. Microsoft's flaw is even more profound. They made a fatal design decision years ago to implement invisible, automatic features for ease of use. Experience since then with viruses and security has made it clear that this was a mistake; these features have been exploited again and again. Microsoft's vulnerability is not just because of bugs, but inherent in their products. The security leaks have been so frequent that Microsoft could easily be challenged under product liability law for selling a defective product.

Train Staff to Recognize and Thwart Social Engineering

Is your system more secure than the FBI's? Anthony Zboralski persuaded the FBI Washington office that he was from the U.S. Embassy in Paris, and convinced the FBI to give him access to the phone conferencing system. Bruce Schneier reports that Zboralski rang up $250,000 in phone calls over seven months.

If you're a secretary and your company's help desk calls say there have been security problems at the corporate server, and asks you to immediately change your password, you might hesitate before complying. However, when the voice on the other end of the phone line talks knowledgeably about the head of his department, adds some details about your corporate system, and mentions the name and the model number of the corporate server, you might relax. The voice is usually anxious (there's a big problem, remember), and urgently needs your help. You're a nice person and just want to help. You might cooperate, but if you don't, the next name in the corporate directory may prove easier to persuade.

You may have just been hacked, in a classic example of social engineering. A good hacker starts with research, and all the information described in the preceding example is often easy to come by. They speak quickly on the phone, sounding like a fellow employee desperately needing your help. One hacker demonstrated this technique live at a conference. While the audience watched, he dialed K-Mart and persuaded an employee to tell him the code that activated the public address system built into the store PBX. An expert on that system, he used the single code to hack in and announce "Attention K-Mart shoppers! There is a 15 minute 50 percent off sale in Aisle D." Crowds rushed over, to everyone's confusion.

Actual security problems are so rare that most people only know about them through headlines, not personal experience. Ordinary computer snafus, on the other hand, are common experiences to us all. What could be more natural than a fellow employee needing a hand to solve a problem? Good hackers are like skilled con artists—they can convince even intelligent people to do foolish things.

Social engineering is the hardest attack to stop, because even one unsuspecting employee can endanger the entire system. The only solution is to educate employees never to give out passwords or other information to anyone whose voice they don't recognize. Make a policy that employees must always call the caller back through the corporate switchboard to verify the identity of anyone calling to request assistance with the network or computers, no matter how persuasive the caller is. Establish a clear corporate rule that you will never ask employees for passwords or IDs, either by voice or e-mail, and make sure everyone in the company knows it.

Bad passwords are another mistake to warn against and design to foil. Far too many people use common words and names for passwords, enabling a *dictionary* attack that dramatically reduces your system protection. A similar mistake is to not change the default password on the router. These should always be changed, because they can easily be found on the Internet.

Beware the Thief Within

When you're talking about security, you have to ask, "Security from what?" People automatically think of the malicious outsider. An ex-FBI agent and private investigator with a specialty in data security corrects that notion. He says that 9 times out of 10, an insider is involved. Deloitte's recent survey of 1500 corporations confirms that 73 percent of security problems originate internally.

The most obvious problem is disgruntled ex-employees, many of whom swear revenge, or look for advantage in their next position. A good corporate security officer knows that it's important to immediately invalidate logins and passwords when someone leaves, but smaller companies may not

A Visit to the Hacker's Lair: Citicorp Center

It's the headquarters of one of the world's largest banks, but the downstairs atrium is a public lounge open to all. That's where hackers meet on the first Friday of every month. The informal group is organized by the editor of *2600, The Hacker's Quarterly Magazine,* and the New York meeting is just the flagship of a much larger organization. Thirty-five other meetings are held around the world on the same day.

The crowd is mixed; the star is the editor, and convener of the biannual Worldwide Hackers on Planet Earth Conference, Emmanuel Goldstein. Goldstein this night is fresh from the Federal Appeals Court where he unsuccessfully defended his right to publish links to information about playing DVDs under Linux. (The Motion Picture Association was suing, because the same information makes it possible to copy DVDs.) Others include a computer science student from Columbia University, the number-two technical person at a well-known financial site, several women, and many of the proverbial post-pubescent hackers in training. No obvious feds, but they do keep an eye on the group.

A half-dozen hackers read our chapter on security with interest, confirming that social engineering is the easiest way to hack into any system. Later I listened while they compared notes. Several could break through a professionally managed security system, if they chose. However, as they talked it became clear that while they are very proud of what they find and anxious to gather all the information they can, sometimes for the sheer joy of it, they are not out to harm your work, or destroy your company. The evidence is overwhelming; there are extremely few destructive incidents of hacking against corporations. However, experts warn that even a hacker who means no harm can inadvertently create havoc inside your system. It makes good sense to protect your network. If you're interested in meeting the enemy face to face on his own terms, the next Worldwide Hackers convention is scheduled for 2002.

respond automatically. Passwords provided for temporary assignments often still work months later. If the employee is knowledgeable enough about the computer system to pose a real threat, it's sometimes right to rework the whole apparatus.

The recommended way to protect against internal problems is to compartmentalize information, and only provide it on a need-to-know basis. A tight computer system works the same way, giving each user passwords and privileges to as few areas as possible. Root and supervisor access is tightly guarded. The corporate firewall is configured to monitor selected transmissions out as well as in. Remote monitoring of the computer system is tightly controlled, making it difficult to affect the system except from inside the secured building or department.

This approach dramatically interferes with ordinary production. A computer supervisor may want to log in and fix something from home on the weekend, or from a location across the continent where she is attending a conference. An accountant working in a branch office on another node may need to check something back on his own machine, and find access denied. Computer workers tend to trust each other, and leave backdoors and widely shared passwords accessible to the cognoscenti. This access often is incredibly useful in a crisis—but it makes a system vulnerable.

It's always hard to draw the line between efficiency and security. This is doubly true when you're designing a system to protect yourself from your own co-workers.

Don't Even Think about Hosting Your Own Web Site

Web servers by design allow remote interactions with your system, including CGI, Perl, and Java scripts. They are very difficult to protect, and make an attractive target for a hacker who wants to demonstrate her skills. If the server is on your network, then cracking the Web site also leaves your primary system vulnerable. You never want to receive an urgent bulletin like the one Microsoft put out after it discovered a bug affecting all versions of Windows 2000 running Microsoft's server. It would "run code of attacker's choice in system context"—allowing a hacker to do virtually anything she chose on your server. "Microsoft strongly urges all IIS 5.0 server administrators to install the patch immediately." Despite a forceful warning, thousands of sites did not protect themselves, and the worm that exploited the problem affected networks around the world.

"A lawyer who takes his own case has a fool for a client," and we issue a similar warning to you about hosting your own Web site. It will cost you more to do it yourself, and your system is far more likely to go down than the typical shared host's, with multiple Internet connections and a 24 × 7 trained staff. Web hosting can also be devastating for security.

Don't Leave the Back Door Open

You want to make sure that your entire system, not just the obvious connections, is neither easy nor attractive to hackers. When you upgrade a small or home office to DSL, you'll often effectively grant access privileges to everyone on that branch of the network. One classic mistake is to leave existing connections, including dial-up modems, vulnerable to attack, especially during the transition period. Any computer with access to your network must be protected by a firewall. This includes employees dialing in from home, and branch offices with dial-up connections. Anyone who remotes into your network represents a risk. Make sure that these secondhand connections are secure.

Under social engineering discussed earlier, we suggested that you insist on always changing the router's password, because they are easy to obtain. Also make sure the name of the system is not obvious from the router/network IDs. Never use the name of the company in this context, such as by naming machines sequentially with a corporate identifier. This can tell someone scanning who owns the computer, and a corporation is a more interesting target to crack than an anonymous machine.

Deal Aggressively with Intruders

Deep security assumes that your protections aren't perfect, and that your firewall might be breached. Everything we've learned over the years suggests that even the best security sometimes fails. You must be prepared to take action when your firewall is breached, if security is important to your business. Standard hacking procedure, once in, is to leave Trojan software behind that allows continued access even if you close the vulnerability that let someone in.

Schneier reminds us, "It's not enough to put up a firewall and be done with it; you need to detect attacks against the network. ... Good detection means finding intruders in something approaching real time, while they are still engaged in the attack." Once in, the hacker needs time to explore the system. You may even be able to trace the intruder, begin a counterattack, or even call the cops.

That's a world of feints and dives with honey pots to catch hackers who get in and keep them in a safe system, isolated from your production systems where harm might result. It may sound like science fiction, but it's the current state of the art.

Find the Right Firewall, and Create Good Policies to Make It More Effective

A firewall is hardware or software that protects your system from improper communication over the Internet. That covers an enormous range of systems, of differing strength and complexity. Few vendors are clear about just what their *firewall* protects against, and few authorities are sure what the real threats are. All offer some protection, but most need careful setup and maintenance to be effective. The best are darn tough to break—so the determined hacker will look for another way in.

Firewalls provide security by making ports (the logical channels through which data passes to and from the Net) invisible, effectively cloaking your machine. Some firewalls go much further than others, defining rules for specific ports and applications, rather than general settings. They monitor data that passes between your machine and the Internet, making sure that your machine accepts only the traffic you approve.

We know we made an unusual decision putting firewalls and encryption so low in our priority list, and we strongly suggest that every business at least turn on the firewall built into their router. On our home/office system, we run ZoneAlarm, software that's highly recommended and free for individual use. We emphasize, the kinds of problems prevented by firewalls are rare, fewer than 1 in 10 security incidents. This is especially true for residences and home offices where dynamic IP addresses make identifying the system more difficult, and attacks that cause harm fleetingly rare. We confirmed our experience by questioning the director of a 200,000-line broadband ISP, DSL, and a few cable modems, including a large group of smaller businesses. We asked how often hackers breaking in had harmed his customers and caused damage. He had "never heard of a serious actual instance." We also asked ZoneAlarm, Symantec, and McAfee how many residential or small business customers had seen serious damage before they installed the firewall products? In particular, we asked them to point us to actual examples, among the millions who have come to them for protection. They knew of almost none.

F or stateless protocols (such as UDP and RPC), the Inspection Module extracts data from a packet's application content and stores it in the state connections tables, providing context in cases where the application does not provide it. Again, the purpose is to allow approved packets, and intelligently block those not authorized, including malevolent items disguised to look like legitimate traffic.

We conclude that a firewall is important but not sufficient. If your security needs aren't critical, often all you need to do is turn on the protection built into your router. If you need additional software, ZoneAlarm is fine for most residential users; the firewall that accompanies the virus protection and other features of the Norton/Symantec or McAfee security suites is also fine for casual protection. Larger enterprises will almost always implement the corporate standard security system.

The simplest firewall is the network address translation built into your router to enable multiple users on the local network to share an IP address. This effectively makes the individual machines invisible to a simple outside scan. This is all the protection added by some inexpensive systems that claim to include firewalls. A better system blocks traffic in except on selected ports, thereby halting many attacks. Monitoring or blocking traffic out on unexpected ports can detect an intrusion. All the software packages mentioned previously have that capability.

The disadvantage of this approach is that you will often want to use those ports for legitimate functions, such as streaming video. While some corporations simply block streaming, Bloomberg, Yahoo Finance, and many other sites stream business video as well as general news. Corporate video—for conferencing, training, and education—is one of the best uses of the fast Net; you'll want to provide access.

The answer is more selective firewall filtering, called *stateful inspection* or *Layer 4-7 filtering*. The layers are defined by the standard OSI networking model. The first three (physical, data link, and network) handle the transportation of data, and general DSL systems do not go beyond them. By inspecting the packets of information at the higher layers (application, presentation, session, and transport), the firewall can allow selected information through (video from corporate headquarters, perhaps), while blocking unapproved uses of the same port. We believe the recent, more rapidly spreading worms will require all networks and operating systems to be designed differently, allowing inspection of incoming packets for particular patterns. It will likely become essential to incorporate features that can be remotely configured to protect an entire network from incoming damage. A sophisticated system, like today's Check Point, can examine incoming packets for the Code Red worm, and exclude them from the network.

The first limit of any firewall is that it is impossible to separate possible intrusion from common Internet activity. Firewalls don't work perfectly and are

Advanced Firewalls

Check Point, an Israeli company, is the dominant provider of corporate firewalls. Their *stateful inspection* technology is a preview of future protection, which will allow intelligent inspection of incoming packets, blocking specific content known to be dangerous like Code Red which spread massively in a single day, already too fast for many to update virus protection manually. Future malevolent software will spread even faster, requiring automatic updating.

Traditional firewalls block functions, such as utilization of port 80, and may inspect the headers of messages. Check Point FireWall-1 Inspection Module is more advanced. It analyzes all packet communication layers, and extracts the relevant communication and application state information. The Inspection Module adapts to individual protocols and applications. It works with the operating system kernel intercepting and analyzing all packets, verifying that each packet complies with the enterprise security policy.

The firewall looks at the *raw message*, not just the packet headers, and can examine data from all packet layers. It first examines IP addresses, port numbers, and any other information required in order to determine whether packets comply with the enterprise security policy. Then it matches the incoming packet against state and context information stored in dynamic connections tables, noting that the transmission comes from an approved source/appropriate application. This allows video, for example, to be accepted from an approved videoconferencing connection, but blocks other incoming video that might be a worm in disguise. These tables are continually updated, providing cumulative data against which FireWall-1 checks subsequent communications. FireWall-1 includes a security principle that blocks "any incoming traffic that deviates from its standards and generates a real-time security alert to the system manager."

often turned off, because what a firewall detects is not an intruder but any type of *possibly inappropriate* behavior. Repeated security alerts become a burden to an administrator who finds problems in the log, sees *possible intrusion*, laboriously checks them out, and concludes that it's something innocent. Eventually, like a car alarm that's gone off three times in one night, you turn it off. As a practical matter, having a firewall set for tight security is more likely to drive you batty than to do anything good. This is especially true for commuters and home systems.

In fact, one standard intrusion technique is to deliberately set off your firewall so many times that you conclude that it's defective, and shut it down. Then the real probe gets in. If you put the firewall alarms on, especially if you have a static IP, you detect activity often. Most of it is script kiddies testing everything around and looking to explore. An effective firewall will discourage hackers, let you know when you are under attack, and help to protect you against more serious intruders.

Firewalls can be either hardware units or software on the router or network system. Software firewalls will slow down a busy router, so if throughput is a concern, you will probably want to use a hardware router. Netopia, for example, has an add-in board for its router that dramatically improves firewall performance.

Virtual Private Networks and Encryption

A real private network connected actual wires between all points, a phone-like circuit between offices sometimes thousands of miles apart. The cost was high, typically thousands of dollars per connection. Today, encryption allows you to share the bandwidth of gigabit fiber-optic connections, without worrying about others intercepting your information. You have a *virtual*, not a *physical* network, and the encryption makes it effectively private. Traditional VPNs ran over dedicated networks, including AT&T's and MCI's, that effectively traveled at two or three times the speed of the Internet, well worth an additional cost. Today most vendors slap the term "VPN" on their ordinary service, and often double the price when all they do is turn on some features already built in to your router or Windows software. If you have any support skills, you can deliver the same service at lower cost, and refuse the VPN surcharge.

In particular, Windows 98 and later support PPTP, Point-to-Point Tunneling Protocol, an encryption standard that has rarely been defeated. Windows 2000 adds IPSec, an even more secure method. Windows 2000 or NT Server completes the loop, or other hosts (including Unixes) can provide the central service. Almost all current routers have a firewall built in. If that security isn't sufficient, the typical ISP VPN would also be inadequate—that's usually what they use. Go directly to a professional managed service provider (MSP) if you need stronger security and don't have the resources yourself.

Consider Managed Service

Many organizations choose to outsource, and a new breed of company, the *managed service provider* (MSP) has attracted $250M in startup venture capital amid forecasts that sales will grow to the billions. MSPs are either specialized ISPs with security features, or companies that work with your current ISP. They all work closely with security consultants, if they are not consultants as well.

The first company we'd consider is Counterpane, whose CTO is Bruce Schneier, from whose book we drew the perspective for this chapter. We'd also look to Scambray and McClure's company, Foundstone, also recommended by Bruce Schneier, which has an excellent training division. Large corporations often rely on the major accounting/consulting firms for security advice. This is a young field; the companies have only short track records, so choose carefully. Large corporations already have computer security departments; you'll always want to work with the experts and advisors your company has already chosen to implement added protections for DSL.

Centralize Security

Nortel Networks pioneered the latest technology emerging in this area. It pushes security to the edge of the network. Nortel sells the technology to ISPs who offer it, as a value-added service, to small and medium-sized businesses. Telocity and Qwest have announced that they will offer security as an inexpensive add-on service, activating a firewall and checking for viruses at the edge of the network, rather than at the customer premise. This promises to be an inexpensive service, perhaps $10/month per user. Encryption can be added as well. It has a theoretical weakness in that you're not protected against other users in your same network segment, but that's a much smaller risk.

The advantage of the centralized service is that professionals can update and maintain the system. New virus scans can be rapidly implemented, and a 24×7 staff can be maintained. Passing some of the burden to a large provider may prove to be an excellent system. Earlier we emphasized that this kind of outsourcing provides less than perfect security—and it won't address the many loopholes present in the rest of the system, leaving you vulnerable. Like your own firewall, this is only a partial solution; you must also attend to the other weaknesses we emphasized if you want strong security.

Parting Words on Security

If we can leave you with one thought about security, it is that securing your DSL connection is just one part of your overall security concern. Simply installing a firewall is only a small part of the solution. The crucial parts will be more difficult to implement because you are dealing with human beings. We urge you not to impose unnecessarily military standards that are almost sure to fail unless they are really necessary. Centralize to make everything as fail-safe as you can, and enlist your users in the effort to protect your network. Getting your users to buy in to the need for security may be the most important step you take. Fortunately, serious attacks are not common, unless you are an attractive target, like a bank or a Web host.

CHAPTER 6

Troubleshooting

We can't say it often enough or clearly enough. Your DSL will go down. Downtime is a DSL fact of life and a backup system is essential. Finding out what is wrong with your DSL and getting up and running can be challenging. The best advice we can give you when your DSL goes down is to take a deep breath and count to 10. It can take patience to find the problem causing your outage, and even more patience to get it fixed.

We're not being glib. As part of the Internet, DSL is a dynamic system, changing from moment to moment. The traceroute test described later in this chapter will verify the changing routes data takes on its path to your destination online. Increasingly providers are building "self healing" networks that identify trouble spots and blockages and signal the need for correction or simply correct them automatically. While we've come to expect near instantaneous response from the high speed Internet, the technology that makes this possible is complex and becoming more so every day.

In this chapter, we'll help you to isolate the problem that is disrupting your service, and to get up and running with a minimum of grief. We'll give you some help distinguishing the problems you can solve, from those you need your provider to fix. Finally, we offer some tips to help you get the support you need and, we hope, keep your sanity in the process.

And while understanding a problem doesn't always help you to fix it, we take a brief look at some of the problems that keep surfacing industry-wide, and at the changes some experts think will make things better.

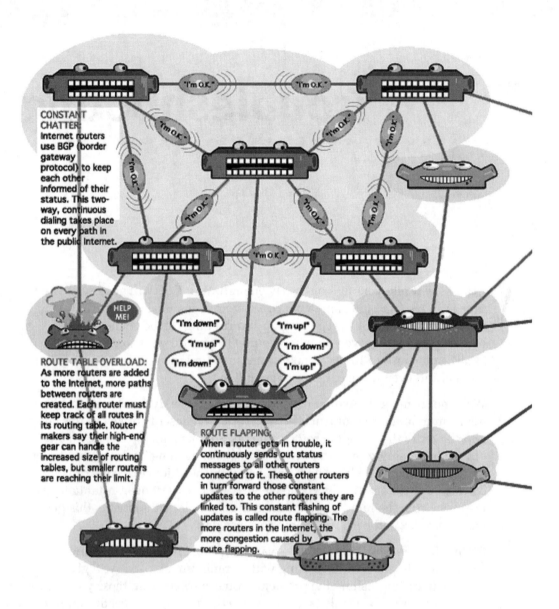

Figure 6.1   Inside the Internet is a mystery to most of us. This lively illustration shows some of the complexity of what goes on inside the Internet.

Courtesy: *The Net Economy*—Cynthia Jones

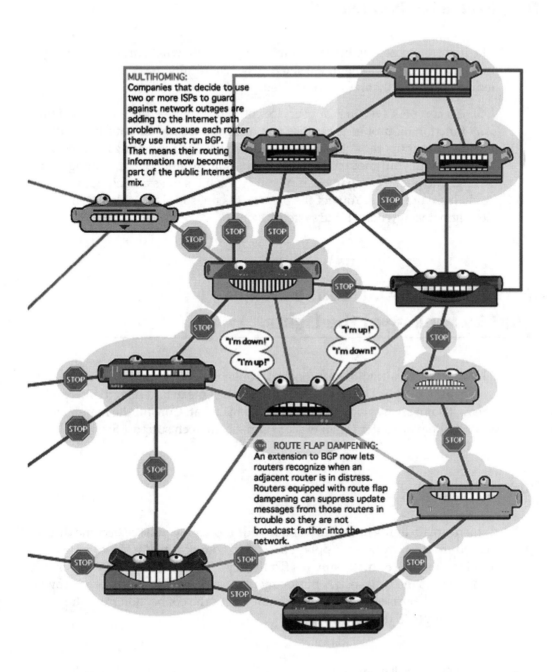

First, Isolate the Problem

The first step to getting up and running is to isolate what part of the DSL system is causing the problem. We suggest systematically bracketing the problem to pinpoint what needs to be fixed.

DSL is a complex system. Your service could be down because your modem isn't functioning properly, because you have bad wiring, or your line could be down. Your operating system might have deleted the settings needed to interface with your modem, or your stand-alone router could be configured wrong. The phone company equipment or the ISP's lines and equipment could have problems. You get the picture. It's not simple. Problems can and do originate anywhere in the system.

If You Have No DSL Connection, Start by Looking at the Lights

The tiny LEDs built into your modem/router can tell you a lot about what is going on with your DSL if you know what they mean and how to interpret them. It's not always clear which light means what. Consult the manual for your modem or router for an explanation, or call tech support for help.

Power Problem

If there are no lights lit on the front of your modem, you have become disconnected from your power supply. Check each connection. We like to plug and unplug the cable to make sure it's firmly in place. Your router may be directly connected to the wall socket, but many modems have a small external power supply. In that case, make sure to double-check the connection from the power supply to the modem as well.

CAUTION Your modem will probably have a reset button, do not press it. Your ISP may have physically changed settings inside your modem. If you reset the modem to the factory defaults, you might end up creating synchronization problems, and your system may not operate even after the original problem is repaired.

Every modem has a power light. When you plug your modem back in, or power is restored after an outage, the power light will flash red. Often, it will flash for a short time and then return to steady green.

If it does not, turn the modem off for about 10 seconds and back on again, or unplug it from the wall for about 10 seconds and then plug it back in. Give it a few moments to settle down. If your power light does not return to steady green, you may have a defective modem. Contact your provider and describe the problem for a replacement.

Sync Problem

Another light on your modem indicates that your modem/router is synchronized with the DSLAM equipment at the phone company office. DSL lines communicate in fractions of a microsecond, and if the sync light is steady green, it's almost certain that your equipment and the DSLAM are communicating effectively. The sync light may be labeled *DSL* or *sync*. On Netopia routers, it's called *WAN Ready*.

If you don't have sync, do a quick check on your wiring. A disconnection at either the modem or the wall is an easy problem to fix. One common problem happens because phone wires and Ethernet cables have similar connectors, and can be plugged into each other's sockets by mistake. It's also easy to confuse which Ethernet cable is which, and connect them incorrectly. These mistakes often happen in ordinary circumstances, such as when the unit is moved for cleaning, and ones we've made ourselves.

If the wiring is good, try turning off the entire system (including router and computer) one more time. Wait 10 seconds, and turn it back on. If that doesn't solve the problem, it's time to call tech support. The problem could be the DSLAM, the wiring, or the router, but it's unlikely to be something you can fix yourself. Before you call, make sure you have your operating system disk user name, passwords, and information about the date and time your system went down, on hand. Before you call, check out "What to Expect from Tech Support."

If Sync's Good, Which Side Is the Problem On?

If the router and DSLAM are communicating, the next step is to determine whether the problem is in your network or your provider's. At this point, most people call tech support, because it saves time and grief. If the problem is on the provider end, all you can do is report it and follow through. We speak from experience having spent a fruitless few hours checking our system one Sunday, trying to find the problem. When we finally called Earthlink, they explained that all of New York was down on their network, and they of course were working hard to fix the problem.

If you have reason to believe the problem could be on your end, you may want to do some checking before you call, especially if you've recently installed new software or had network problems. But before you do, we suggest you call tech support first and ask them to ping you to verify that their systems are up and functioning. Then, if the problem is on your end you can get to work trying to find it. The tools you'll need to troubleshoot computer problems are described in the sections that follow.

Fixing Problems Local to Your System

If you're working with tech support, their script will rule out the most common problems that can occur with their system and software. Even experts like the authors of this book sometimes miss something obvious, and you can, too. Don't be offended by how basic some of the questions are; just double-check and move on to the next step. Many questions are meant to rule out several problems. A common script question asks you to check the cord connecting the gateway and the computer. Checking the connection might also catch a very common error, plugging the Ethernet cable from the gateway into a phone modem connection on the computer. That's an easy mistake to make, because they look alike and the socket can take either wire. We've done it.

Scripts change constantly, as new problems prevail. Windows XP, for example, will cause a new wave of trouble. They're also different for each provider, and each piece of equipment. Most tech support scripts give priority to ruling out the common problems your provider has encountered with their software and hardware. We've created our own checklist to help you better understand the logic of isolating what part of your system (or your provider's) is causing the problem.

Your router, gateway, or modem may not be properly connected to the host computer, which may be either a physical or setup problem. A physical problem could be a loose cable, which you can check by plugging and unplugging both ends. Ethernet cables and phone wire look alike, so it's easy to plug the

What to Expect from Tech Support

When you call tech support, they'll ask you for the specifications on your system and other information. We've provided a form in the back of this book to help you to keep track of all the information you'll need to keep on hand. We strongly recommend you fill it out for every system and keep it close at hand. Keep a hard copy of this information in a file or attach it to procedures for implementing your backup system. Remember to keep these documents secure if you include passwords. Note the following:

- The exact wording of any error messages. Write them down if it's not possible to print the screen.

- The exact problem, including what you were doing on the machine when it first happened. It's often important to know whether the problem occurred while downloading mail, surfing the Web, or sending files to an FTP server.

- Has anyone added equipment or loaded new software, or had other problems with the machine? What was done on the machine shortly before the problem started? Knowing this will often help you to find conflicts or changed settings.

- The type of service you have (ADSL, SDSL, business/consumer) and the speed you contracted for.

- Operating System. Note which version of Windows, Mac, Linux, etc. you are using. The type of computer and processor, especially if it's an older system, may also be important. You should have the setup CD from your provider, because reinstalling some of the initial software is often the solution for the problem. Also have a system disk at hand, because the technician may ask you to reinstall Windows Dial-up Networking, a driver, or an extension.

- Your DSL router or modem brand and model.

- The Internet settings on your computer, described next. If the problem is on your computer, nearly always it is an incorrect setting.

- Whether you are using a protocol such as PPPoE or PPPoA. Most ADSL systems use PPPoE, which requires a different setup.

- The network settings of your computer.

- Software being used, Web browser, e-mail program, and the version number of the application.

- You need to have the login name and password for your account, and also the login and password for your router. You might want to keep passwords on the form that's easily accessible; however, remember that this represents a security risk. You'll then have to keep the form safe.

- Once you reach tech support, a *ping* test is the key way to determine if the problem is on your end or the provider's. The technician sends a simple set of packets from his or her machine to your router or computer, and gets back a response. If the ping is good, then your connection to your provider's network is working, and it's highly likely that the problem is within your equipment. If there's a problem with the ping, then the problem is probably in their network. Ping is described under *Tools* later in this chapter.

- Don't be surprised if the support technician begins by asking a scripted set of questions. If there are no reports of network problems, the technician often assumes that the problem is on your end. Like a visit to the doctor's office, the script is designed to rule out common problems. If the problem isn't solved within 10 or 15 minutes, make sure they ping your router or modem. It only takes a minute or two, and can save you hours of work if there is a problem on your provider's system.

- Pinging also verifies the integrity of the wiring, confirming what the green sync light implied. This saves you the trouble of tracing your DSL line to its origination point and testing all of its connections, another good reason to call tech support.

- If your provider has a network problem, or can't ping you, the problem is in their equipment and there's nothing you can do to fix it. Get a trouble ticket number, the name of the tech support person, and follow up to make sure the problem is fixed. After you're sure that your alternate connection to the Internet is working, we suggest you take a brief walk in the nearest park. If they don't solve the problem quickly, see *Getting the Help You Need* later in the chapter.

DSL Ethernet cable into a phone modem socket instead. It's also easy to confuse which cable is plugged into which computer, if you have several connected on the back of your router/gateway. You also could have a hardware problem if your Ethernet card failed or was loose in the computer.

It's possible that the router is misconfigured, which happened to us once. Getting the system back up required checking the setting in the router, until we discovered that it was not set to the PPPoE protocol used by our provider. This is not likely to be your problem, unless you've changed providers or equipment. To check router settings, you connect from your computer using either telnet or a Web-based interface, per the manual. We were very lucky, our router is from Netopia; their tech support helped to get us up and running very efficiently.

A systematic way to check this connection is to ping the router or gateway from your computer, rather than from the provider side. You simply need to know the IP address for the router, which will usually be in the manual. Follow the instructions under *Tools* later in this chapter. You can't ping a modem, they just don't have the smarts. If you can successfully ping your router, the problem is probably in the settings in your computer.

If you've checked all the equipment external to your CPU, your computer and its settings are the most likely problem. All operating systems require a half-dozen settings to connect, and if any one is not right, that could be the problem. Adding hardware or other software will often change settings, and we've all learned that occasionally Windows will foul up something like this without any apparent cause. You should also check other possible problems in your computer, such as a configuration problem on your Ethernet card.

Most installations today do not require the user to configure any of these settings manually; instead, they use a software program from the provider that sets them automatically. Often the best way to approach the problem is to reinstall the provider's startup software, which is what tech support may ask you to do. If this works, thank your favorite deity, write down the settings listed here in case you need them next time your system goes down, and get back to work.

 The crucial settings include:

➤ The IP address of your computer if you have a permanent one, known as a static IP. This may require a modifier, called a subnet mask. Both are typically four-part numbers separated by periods, such as 154.12.54.176. (Hint: Many times the subnet mask is irrelevant, in which case 255.255.255.255 or 0.0.0.0 is likely to work. Try them.) If you have a dynamic IP, changing each time you log in, in Windows 98 the proper setting is called "server assigned

IP address." It has a similar name in other systems. (Hint: Nearly all ADSL systems use dynamic addresses.)

➤ The Domain Name Server (DNS), which is the computer that translates an Internet name, such as wiley.com, to its actual address, usually a four-part sequence something like 135.23.121.45. You always have a primary and a secondary domain name server, whose numbers are given by your ISP.

➤ For networked computers especially, you may need the default gateway, and the local area network address and its subnet mask.

➤ In Windows, you must specify the proper server for your Internet connection, such as the PPP server we use on our Earthlink DSL. You also must install, in the network control panel, the appropriate adapter, such as your Ethernet card. Our system, using PPPoE, also has a special entry for the PPPoE software in the network control. The adapters installed in the network control panel, in turn, must be bound to TCP/IP.

➤ Configuring computers for the Internet, if not a black art, certainly can be confusing. You'll need all the right numbers, but it still might not work properly. Nearly all DSL installations are now done by software customized for your provider's network that makes all of this invisible. If just re-running the install software doesn't solve the problem, you have to dig into these (and sometimes other) settings.

Very rarely, you'll have to reinstall your operating system, but try everything else first. This is a time-consuming process that won't necessarily solve the problem. This should be a last resort, at least on Windows where you are likely to need to reinstall many other applications if you do. Unfortunately, when some tech support folks don't know how to solve the problem, they fall back on the instructions "reinstall Windows," which at least keeps the customer busy for a few days.

Follow Up to Make Sure the Repair Gets Done

If tech support can't fix the problem right away, your provider may send out a service rep to better diagnose or fix a problem. Known in the business as a *truck roll*, the service call adds at least 24 hours to the repair.

If you still can't connect to the Internet, your provider might have to get help from the phone company that owns your line. This may be a company they subcontract from, but even if it's another division of a telco, they won't always be able to tell you what the problem is or how long it will take to fix. Repair times vary by company. The support manager of a national ISP tells us a problem that takes two weeks to solve in the northeastern United States can be solved in a day by a more efficient telco provider in the southwest.

Some Problems Your Provider Might Hesitate to Tackle

➤ *Computer or software problems.* Many ISPs try to draw the line at helping you to configure your operating system. Their software isn't working properly until your computer recognizes your modem, but when it comes to sorting out which of the devices on your system may have caused a conflict, they may tell you that you're on your own. Don't hesitate to push for the support you need. Ask for a supervisor if you need to. Windows in particular is notoriously unstable, and unraveling what's gone wrong can take hours. Do whatever you have to do to get help.

➤ *Network configuration problems.* Most providers offer little advice beyond basic "home networking" through a gateway. Advanced firewalls and other security measures require expert help.

> Because tech support people genuinely want to help you, some will go the extra mile and try to help. Bell Canada, for example, routinely recommends tech support sites online where customers can get the information they need.

➤ *Interference from mysterious, unidentified causes.* One customer had difficulty each day around 5 P.M. It was later discovered that he lived next to a television station that used microwave to transmit video live shots around that time each day.

➤ *Line problems the telco won't identify and won't fix.* The problem may be a bridge tap, a load coil, or interference from another line in the binder group. Research is expensive and time consuming. If the line can be fixed, your provider may never know what the problem was, just that it has been repaired. On the other hand, telcos sometimes make a judgment call that it's not worth the time and trouble to find or fix the problem. One provider routinely denies service to customers with bridge taps or load coils, but relents if the customer pushes for service. Sometimes it pays to be pushy.

Getting the Help You Need

Always start by going through channels. Call tech support, describe your problem, and ask for help. Document your tech support call. Make sure you get a name, an e-mail address, and a phone number for follow-up. If you can, get a phone number that doesn't put you back in the queue. Ask if there is a trouble ticket number or another identifier for your case. Write it down. Make sure you understand what will be done before you hang up the phone.

If a support representative says "we'll call you," ask "when?" Ask for e-mail documenting your help request and the name and title of the person who will be calling to follow up. Ask about follow-up procedures. In particular, ask how long your repair should take, and who will be calling you to schedule any service calls needed. Ask what you should do and who to call if no one calls you back.

If You Connect Slowly or Unreliably

Not all problems involve downtime. You may find that your access to the Internet is so slow that it hampers your business. While no provider can guarantee the speed of the Internet, they can and should deliver the service promised on their own network.

Every DSL provider, in their ads, brochures, and president's speeches, describes DSL as an Internet service, and advertises speeds to the Internet. However, most really measure your speed only to the first part of their network, the DSLAM in your neighborhood. They then over-sell the connection from your neighborhood to their metro center, and from there to their connection to the Internet. It's called *over-subscription* and may be as high as 100 to 1. They also may have routers that are inadequate, DSLAMs without enough capacity, and many other inadequacies or operational problems on their network.

Figure 6.2　Cross-section of a cable showing wires in a cable binder group.
Courtesy: Paradyne

If your speed is advertised as 640K, and you frequently test at 200K, or you've been sold a symmetrical DSL line rated at 1.5MB and it can't maintain a 750K stream, there is probably something wrong with your provider's configuration of your service and they should work with you to solve the problem. Some providers will make it difficult for you to get help because troubleshooting performance problems is much more difficult than resolving total outages. But you're entitled to the service you are paying for and should fight for your rights.

We urge you to be careful and fair before you complain. You also should bend over backward to have your facts ready, and be gracious in your request if you want to get results. The majority of folks who think their service is slow actually are limited by the speed of the Web site to which they are connecting. Go to CNET, 2Wire, or many other sites that offer a speed test, and don't be surprised if your speed is often 20–30 percent lower than advertised. That's ordinary Internet overhead and variation.

Don't panic over occasional service problems. The Internet itself was designed to be resilient, not fast. If some part of the network is having problems, traffic is routed around the area of difficulty, and recovery is almost always quite fast. Similarly, the phone network was built with an extraordinary level of spare capacity and redundancy, and rarely does your call not go through. However, few providers built such redundancy into their DSL networks, meaning that when they have a problem in a particular router or connection, you suffer as well. One stock analyst who has dealt routinely with DSL problems says that when he encounters problems with his home DSL, he waits three hours and tries it again before employing any other strategy. Most times, he says, it works. In the meantime, he can get some work done. You may not have this luxury, but keeping a cool head always pays off. There's been some improvement, but the reliability of the networks remains so poor that Verizon, SBC, and the others refuse our repeated requests for the actual statistics.

 Your performance goes down the longer the wire between your modem and the CO. However, tests of thousands of actual lines suggest that you should be getting consistent downloads of over a megabit if you are within about a mile-and-a-half of the telco office or the DLC that serves you. If you aren't, insist that the provider check the line.

How you and your provider can find and fix the problem. Because the problem can be anywhere in the network, it can be tricky to isolate. There are several hardware and software tools your provider should have that can help. Common equipment, from Teradyne, Spirent/Hekimian, Virtual

Access, and others can very accurately measure the actual speed you're getting throughout your provider's network, and isolate bottlenecks. The problem can be a poor line to your DSLAM connection in the telco office, the DSLAM itself, the connection from the DSLAM to the metro center/megapop, the equipment there, or the link from there to the Internet hand-off. They may also have inadequate Internet connectivity, because the cost to the ISP of a good backbone connection can be high.

The problem is how to isolate the problem, which you can sometimes guess at by using traceroute. Described in the section *Tools*, traceroute programs send packets from your machine to any other site on the Web. The first connection or two are within your provider's network, and should be very fast. If not, or if you get error messages, you've found a problem. Your provider, however, has much better tools that can check each part of their network. In addition, they can check how your service is configured, and catch mistakes such as a 1.5 MB service being marked as 700K in their subscriber management system.

Problems in their network design, of course, will not be fixed just because one customer complains that he or she is part of the system. If you discover that's the problem, your options are to find another provider or complain so loudly that they do something. The latter is unlikely to work unless you start a public crusade.

However, if the problem is between you and the DSLAM, it may be solvable. A significant percentage of slow DSL connections are bad lines. Essentially, every provider now has powerful testing equipment that can be attached to your line to measure speed, packet loss, the actual resistance, and electrical characteristics of the line. The telcos are generally required to find and fix problems such as bridge taps, an extension on your wire that causes interference. DSL is very sensitive to interference from AM radio transmitters and certain microwave towers; however, interference from the other data services that share a binder group with your DSL line is more common. Each binder group has 25 or more wires, including your line. These are known problems, and years of work have minimized the impact of interference. The DSL standard reach of 18,000 feet is calculated to include a margin that covers the typical effects.

If a test of your line finds a bridge tap or other problem, then the telco can and should remove it. If the line is good, but performance poor, it will often be possible to improve things by switching your line. There are standard procedures for testing other lines running the same route, finding a good one, and switching you over. In practice, the telcos have been enormously reluctant to test and repair problems like this—we suggest that you insist if you have carefully checked other possible problems.

Other Problems

Mail and news configuration problems. When you switch to a DSL connection, your mail server will often change. If you use the provider's mail system, that's a simple change in your e-mail software. The operating system interacts with several e-mail programs invisibly to the user, however, and you may later need to check and re-enter the correct server. Mail servers are almost always named SMTP.ISPname or POP.ISPname; for example, SMTP.Mindspring.com, POP.Mindspring.com. If you continue to use an outside server, you may discover problems sending mail. If you want to send mail through an outside server, don't be surprised if you have a problem; many systems are designed to block spam. Check to see if they have a workaround, or do what we do. On our Mindspring account, we use their server for our outgoing mail, but the extraordinary reliable system at Panix for our large volume of incoming mail.

Username or password. These errors are surprisingly common among tech support calls. User names are often case sensitive, so make sure that the Caps Lock key is not on, and you've been careful about upper- and lowercase. It's easy to mistake an "I" for a number one, or a zero for a capital O. Make sure you use the format required by your ISP. On Earthlink, for example, the username should follow the format of username@domain.com (e.g., username@earthlink.net). If you forget it or lose it, you can always call your ISP, provide the agreed-upon clue, and they will e-mail it to you. They'll have a record, but you may have to wait in the queue to speak with them.

Line stealing. If your DSL line suddenly dies, it may have been cut by phone technicians, who in the real world are sometimes careless. Dedicated DSL lines have no dial tone on them, so a technician with an old model test set could mistake it for an unused line. It happened to us, when one day our DSL line went down. Apparently, the telco technician in the basement, looking to connect someone else's phone, needed a line. In time-honored tradition, the first *apparently* dead line was used. Unfortunately, that was our DSL line. Although never admitted "on the record," in the field we know that this is quite common.

Because a line with a working DSL connection is known to be good, they present an apparently irresistible solution to a field tech with problems. This is presumably rare, but we've heard complaints, at least one verified, where lines were switched in such circumstances, and the alternate line proved unreliable. Whatever the cause, line problems require the telco to test and fix them.

Third-party hardware. If you have a modem other than the one suggested by your provider, you may be out of luck. They'll know the ins and outs of making the suggested modem work, but may not be at all familiar with the right configurations for others.

Don't buy a modem from eBay in a rash attempt to save money. Each ISP recommends modems and gateways based on the DSLAM and software they use. In addition, they may change settings in the modem before they send it to you. The same modem purchased from a third party might not be properly configured and might not work. It's not worth the hassle. It also gives tech support an excuse not to help you. Most ISPs do not support third-party equipment; instead, they will direct you to the equipment's manufacturer.

The modem's manufacturer can tell you how the equipment is supposed to work, but not which settings your ISP uses. All in all, you'll spend more time than the money you save. We recommend in Chapter 3 that whenever possible, use the equipment specified by your ISP.

Tools

While tech support will help you with most of your needs, there are times when you'll want to tackle the problem yourself. You'll need the basic tools described next.

It Don't Mean a Thing If It Ain't Got That Ping

Step one for checking a Net connection is to send a *ping* to the other side. A *ping* program, such as the one included in the MSDOS part of Windows, sends a short message to the site you enter, sees whether it comes back, and how long it takes. These illustrations are from an excellent freeware package, TJPing. We tested from our machine to the publisher wiley.com. You can use ping to test any Web site, such as your provider's, and even a particular router whose address you know. Here's the tracking from one such ping:

That ping showed that the connection was healthy. The software sent three packets and wiley.com returned them all, with an average roundtrip of 31 milliseconds. A good connection not too far away will show times of

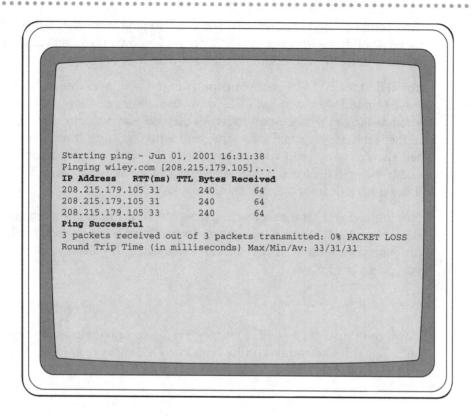

```
Starting ping - Jun 01, 2001 16:31:38
Pinging wiley.com [208.215.179.105]....
IP Address    RTT(ms) TTL Bytes Received
208.215.179.105 31      240       64
208.215.179.105 31      240       64
208.215.179.105 33      240       64
Ping Successful
3 packets received out of 3 packets transmitted: 0% PACKET LOSS
Round Trip Time (in milliseconds) Max/Min/Av: 33/31/31
```

20–60 milliseconds, while a connection across continents can be fine with a 150-millisecond delay.

Asking your ISP to *ping* your router is the simplest step to see if the connection is good. If the technician on the service desk can send an Internet packet to you as a ping, and it comes back clean and reasonably quickly, you can be 95-percent sure that that end of the connection is fine, and proceed to troubleshoot your end. If the problem is in their system, they should get errors or delay in the ping.

If most sites respond, but a few can't be pinged, don't be surprised. That's exactly what you'd expect from a site that is slightly overloaded.

Pinging is one way to isolate connection problems. Ping tests network connectivity and measures whether packets are getting from one host to another and how fast by sending a 32-byte packet of data to a device. The device responds with an acknowledgment that your signal was received loud and clear. The way it works is special IP control messages, called Internet Control Message Protocol (ICMP) Echo Request packets, send network information between your computer and another host. You can also ping your router; this tells you there is nothing wrong with the TCP/IP stacks on your computer, and the cable running from computer to router is working properly.

You'll find the IP address of your router in the written materials the installer leaves behind when you get DSL, or in your self-installation kit. However, if you have to call tech support to retrieve it, you may want to take advantage of the fact that they can do the same tests with less angst from their end. They can also access and test your connection to the local phone company office and between the telco and their megapop (the point where your ISP consolidates the traffic from one metropolitan area).

Pinging verifies that the connection between your router and your computer is good, and helps you to rule out router and local wiring problems. If you can ping your router but you still can't connect, or if you don't have a router, you ping your ISP.

```
DOS C: ping yahoo.com
```

If you can't reach a site with a *ping*, or the connection is slow, you can find out why with traceroute, a utility built into DOS other operating systems.

Traceroute

Ping measures how long a packet takes to get from one host to another, and traceroute shows you the route that a packet takes. This will tell you whether the slowdown occurs within your provider's network or at some point on the Internet. Traceroute, called tracert in Microsoft operating systems, traces the network path to a Web site or gateway. The printout lists the intermediary nodes between you and the destination, showing you how long, in milliseconds, the packet took to get there.

Traceroute works by addressing a packet to a UDP port on the destination machine. It sends three packets with expiration dates to the router, and the feedback from the packets expiring as they travel to the remote host creates a map of the route.

Traceroute sends back a message from every router in the path from you to the site you're testing, with a measure of the delay at each. Again, routers on the other side of the world should have delays in the low hundreds; closer to home in the low dozens. Anything else—or when the traceroute gets to a router but can't connect and returns an error message—suggests where on the network to

```
Starting trace - Jun 01, 2001 16:31:41
Tracing to wiley.com [208.215.179.105]....
Hops  IP Address    RTT(ms)
1     192.168.1.1    1
2     165.247.58.1   20
3     209.86.66.65   20
4     4.24.187.53    28
5     4.24.8.89          28
6     4.24.10.209    26
7     4.24.10.82     26
8     4.24.6.230     27
9     4.0.6.142          25
10    152.63.18.222  27
11    152.63.23.142  35
12    152.63.17.241  30
13    208.215.179.105 33
Host reached
```

look for the problem. If the problem is within the provider's net, they should attend to it. If it's outside on the Internet, there's little you can do.

Consistent slowdowns in one area may mean that your provider's network is oversubscribed or some adjustment needs to be made in the path your signal takes. Documenting the problem will help you communicate with the support team working to solve it.

Bandwidth Meters

You can also keep track of your speeds by accessing a bandwidth meter online. Your provider may have a bandwidth meter on their site, although not all have proven accurate. DSL Reports has an excellent tool, while CNET and others offer alternatives. Do not trust a test solely within your provider's system, as it will not discover problems in your subscriber's connection to the Internet itself. On the other hand, don't be surprised if occasionally the

Be Prepared—Downtime Is a DSL Reality

Your backup system can be as simple as leaving a dial-up modem in place for small offices where volume and speed are not issues, or as complex as a backup ISDN line or ordering a second DSL line from another carrier.

Those of you who don't have backup will likely be inspired to install one after your first experience going down. No major network in the United States is doing the network build-out and re-routing that could effectively prevent that. Furthermore, they have little incentive to insure your DSL service when they can sell you quality-of-service guarantees for frame relay, ISDN, and T-1 service. The key to is to prepare a strategy for dealing with downtime when you implement DSL.

Identifying the source of your problem is hard enough without kicking yourself through the whole process because you weren't prepared. If your backup is working, your damage should be minimal. The best system won't serve you if you don't have a plan in place for switching over and personnel trained to do it. Hardware, planning, *and* training are needed to make a backup system work. You can find more information about creating and installing a backup system in Chapter 3. One way to determine the necessity for and the extent of your backup system is to ask how long your business can afford to be down? If you can't afford a three- or four-hour outage, DSL may not be right for you.

Net itself slows down; that's the nature of the beast. If your bandwidth is consistently low, check above. You may need to negotiate with your provider, upgrade your service, or change providers.

Service is Good Business

We firmly believe good service saves money. Hundreds of millions of dollars of marketing cannot reverse the customer anger that has resulted from DSL Hell. Hundreds of millions more are being spent on resolving service problems that could have been prevented with proper testing. There is nothing in DSL technology that makes it inherently unreliable; these are all problems of service, support, and inadequate network design. There will always be a need for troubleshooting, but the volume of problems today, during installation and after, is a stain on the reputation of the companies involved.

The COO of Qwest makes a convincing argument for the bottom line results of better service. Reporting to Wall Street, he said a key factor in the company's growth was the progress they were making in solving the service problems of the former US West (sometimes called *U.S. Worst* by angry customers). The first result was directly increased revenues, as people were moved from angry members of waiting lists to paying customers. He also saw lower costs in customer service and repair, as they reduced problems in the field. Everyone at the top knows the telcos will fall behind the cable companies if they don't improve performance.

Some problems were inevitable, delivering a new service to millions. But after three years, reliability is overdue. Be patient and gracious dealing with your provider, but you're entitled to decent service and support. Insist on it.

For the Pros

If you're taking the time to read a book like this, you probably will know more than 95 percent of the folks calling for help, and be frustrated as they go through the basics. Courtesy and patience is almost always the best response, but don't hesitate to ask for second and third level support when you need it. The best of business providers have dedicated, quality corporate support teams that can save you much time.

CHAPTER 7

Voice over DSL

Voice over DSL (VoDSL) can deliver as many as 24 separate telephone lines over a single copper wire. The savings can be significant. "50% off basic charges" is what New York's Broadview Networks offers business customers. Florida's Network Telephone includes a free DSL 160K connection for its voice customers, paid for by its savings on the voice connection. Mpower, Network Plus, and half a dozen more are also growing. Focal and other competitive telcos have jumped in, and VoDSL service is available in most major cities.

Telephony is being transformed by a simple principle: switch to digital, and you can carry as many as 20 calls on a single line. New companies are jumping in, renting a single line to a business, and taking clients from the incumbent telcos. This brings competition to a crucial sector that represents over 100 billion dollars of revenue worldwide.

The technology underlying VoDSL is simple: A DSL line has the capacity to carry megabits of data. The average voice call can be transmitted using 64K of bandwidth or less, VoDSL uses an integrated access device (IAD) usually housed in a digital VoDSL phone to translate your call into a data stream, and dozens of calls can be carried on the same line. Your DSL line carries this data to a gateway, which translates the data and delivers it to a telephone switch. Signals that indicate, for example, that you picked up the phone or have another call waiting are similarly carried as data and translated at both ends.

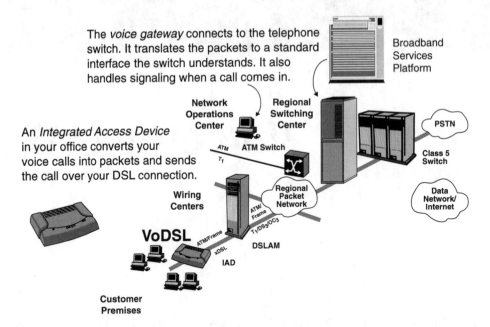

The *voice gateway* connects to the telephone switch. It translates the packets to a standard interface the switch understands. It also handles signaling when a call comes in.

Broadband Services Platform

An *Integrated Access Device* in your office converts your voice calls into packets and sends the call over your DSL connection.

Network Operations Center

Regional Switching Center

ATM Switch

PSTN

Class 5 Switch

Wiring Centers

Regional Packet Network

Data Network/ Internet

VoDSL

DSLAM

IAD

Customer Premises

Figure 7.1   Voice over DSL will probably be delivered as illustrated in this diagram from Jetsream. Your phones plug into an IAD in your office, which translates calls into packets. A voice gateway further down the network translates them and delivers them to a phone switch.

Consumers may be waiting for quite some time to reap the advantages of VoDSL, three or four phones lines for little more than the cost of a single line. Telcos are backing away from the service, however, part of their worldwide move to cut spending after the Internet boom. SBC planned residential VoDSL in 2000, Verizon in 2001, in an effort to compete with the cable companies, who had similar plans. The telcos were motivated to move quickly, because AT&T Broadband scared them by offering a bundle of four phone lines, broadband, long distance, and video at an attractive price. However, AT&T backed off, amidst financial and technical struggles, and most cable companies also slowed deployment of their telephone service. As competition lessened, the telcos also backed away. Another factor is that equipment costs remain high, with home gateways still costing over $300—a very large amount to earn back with a service selling for a few dollars. Before the cutbacks, telcos were telling us they would move strongly as soon as the equipment costs came down below $200; equipment vendors expected to reach that price point in late 2001 or early 2002. Since then, telcos have dropped over $10 billion from their capital spending, which will make finding the funds for VoDSL very difficult.

European companies are planning large-scale deployment of VoDSL in 2003 or 2004. Equipment sales tell the story. France Telecom, for example, has requested information from vendors about deploying over 2 million lines. Volume production of advanced cable modems, designed for voice-over-IP, should encourage cable companies to move aggressively. Sprint and AT&T have invested heavily in facilities in telephone offices in 2001, which should lead to nationwide deployments in 2002. Sprint has installed Lucent Stingers (DSLAMs) in 2000 offices. AT&T bought 1700 equipment collocations from NorthPoint's bankruptcy auction for $130 million, and will be equipping them for merged voice plus data. That will give them reach to 40 percent or more of U.S. businesses. As we write, Sprint is re-thinking the entire project; AT&T is looking to move ahead in the middle of 2002, amid major corporate changes.

The basic technology is old and proven. Traditional T-1 lines have delivered 24 voice circuits in just such a fashion for many years, and have been the mainstay of competition to larger businesses. The principle is simple: At the customer's premises, a gateway or integrated access device (IAD) changes a voice signal into bits, requiring 64K of bandwidth (or less) per circuit. That data travels over the DSL line (which can carry from 4 to 24 such channels) to a network gateway, which converts and passes the data to the telephone network. Because a T-1 circuit costs a carrier from $80 to over $300 per month, it's uneconomical for businesses needing fewer than a dozen lines. The lines for VoDSL cost about $20 per month, saving the provider $120 to $200 per line per year. The difference in the customer's retail price is even larger.

The slow deployment is a shadow of what we, and most industry experts expected in 1999, when CopperCom, Jetstream, and Tollbridge were the toast of SUPERCOMM, the industry's biggest show. We all flocked to Atlanta's Sundial for a celebratory dinner and revolving over Atlanta we toasted what everyone believed would be "the next big thing." Catherine Hapka, whose Rhythms Network was expanding nationwide was saying "VoDSL is here. It works. We're going to do it. Soon!" So were Rhythms' competitors North-Point and Covad, in partnership with dozens of ISPs. PSINet claimed dramatically that, "Voice is just another form of data, and requires so little bandwidth we'll be giving it away free." Investors responded: Early VoDSL companies (CopperCom, Jetstream, Tollbridge, Accelerated) were valued in the billions, and we all envied those with options.

Early reports were enthusiastic—the technology works. However, running a phone network is much more difficult than just switching a few circuits. Customers must be found, equipment installed, working lines provisioned, supported, and quickly restored to service when (not if) problems arise. Billing can be a nightmare, as many of us have learned from our long-distance companies. Support becomes essential—no customer expects to spend hours on hold trying to get a static-y line fixed or a mistaken bill corrected.

So, we have clear advice for you: Choose a provider that's a telephone pro, whether major telco or competitor. Plan a system that works for the business, even if problems arise. Broadview, for example, delivers the first line through a regular telco connection they resell, so that service is still there if the rest of the lines, delivered as VoDSL, develop a problem. Be careful before jumping at the savings—the cost of an office unable to work because the phones are down can be enormous, and far greater than any discount on the bill. The new providers that are succeeding offer personalized service, and the best of them probably deliver service at least as good as a mega-telco. Make sure that the folks you deal with have that level of skill; otherwise, you may find that when the phones don't work, they can't fix them for days. Less dramatically, a bad provider will cost you more money reconciling billing errors and dealing with ordinary service issues than they save.

Technology

Your plain old telephone has a microphone in the handset that translates your voice into an analog signal, but as soon as it gets to the switch, your voice is transformed into a digital signal. Behind the switch, a fiber-optic network carries your voice calls around the world in the form of a digital signal. Essentially the entire network, other than your phone and the line connecting it, is already digital. Delivering your voice call over DSL requires a device on your end to translate your voice into a digital signal. The IAD or a digital phone serves this purpose. On the other end, a *gateway* must translate those digital pulses into the format of the telephone switch. The two-way communication required to carry digital voice calls is quite sophisticated, sending signals back and forth that a receiver has been lifted, or a call-waiting beep that another call is coming in. The full range of features includes signaling for coin telephones and much more.

The gateway connected to the telephone switch can receive digital data either as ATM (asynchronous transfer mode) packets or IP (Internet Protocol) packets. The switch follows standard protocols, GR303 or TR008 in the United States, and V5.2 (which has many variations) in most of the rest of the world. The newer packet telephony systems are designed to use the MGCP Media Gateway Control Protocol, although that equipment is barely out of the labs. Normally, the gateway is at the central network point, where it communicates with a switch; it can also be located on a card in the DSLAM.

One key technology decision for VoDSL is whether to use IP or ATM to handle the traffic. Tollbridge uses IP, because using the IP makes it easier to use the same equipment on other platforms. There are arguments for both technologies. Martin Taylor, CTO of Coppercom, wrote this for us about the advantages of using ATM.

> "The Internet Protocol is, indisputably, the universal language of the data communications world. IP provides a common foundation for data exchange over every kind of physical communications medium that is in widespread use today, enabling end-to-end networking solutions that are constructed from many disparate transport technologies. What's more, the universality of IP promises to revolutionize the way we build telephone networks.

> But is IP really ready for local telephony? In the world of derived voice services over DSL, the clear consensus seems to be no. The phone companies made a wise choice when they decided to roll out DSL infrastructures based on ATM technology. They could see beyond the short-term applications of DSL for pure data access, and anticipated the role of DSL as a multi-service delivery platform—a role for which ATM was originally conceived and is ideally suited.

> Every ADSL and G.lite line, and a growing proportion of SDSL lines, brings an ATM connection to the end user—whether a small business or a residential customer. These ATM connections of course support IP for Internet access. But there is nothing to stop other applications such as voice from exploiting the native ATM protocol on those connections. Native ATM is good for voice quality because it can guarantee controlled speed end-to-end, and good for bandwidth efficiency because it can transport the small packets that voice requires with relatively little protocol overhead."

The alternate view, recommending IP, comes from Asher Waldfogel, CTO of Tollbridge .

> "Because of the diversity of current and planned network implementations, and the well-established trends toward IP-based voice in the network core (Qwest and Level 3 are the leaders) and IP-based services on the customer premise (Nortel, Lucent, and Cisco have all announced IP-based telephony), IP is the most flexible solution. ATM drum beating to the contrary, voice trunking over ATM reduces to a simple technical question: Is the ubiquitous Internet Protocol the right choice?"

The DSL providers have generally chosen ATM gateways, despite their plans to migrate to IP eventually. The decision is a hard one, with at least one large telco pausing in its deployment to determine whether IP is ready.

Channelized Voice is a presumably lower-cost technique championed by chip designers Centillium, Infineon, and Aware. While standard VoDSL transforms the voice call into ATM or IP packets, which then require a gateway on the other end to decode them, channelized voice simply uses more of the DSL bandwidth to deliver extra voice lines. The advantage is simplicity, eliminating the gateway at each end and the problems in the local network. For a telco that typically has a switch in each office, this may be the least expensive way to deliver four voice lines to a home, although end users will sacrifice some data bandwidth. All others, however, need to transport the call past the local office to their centralized gateway. They therefore need the coding and decoding in any case. That means channelized voice is a technology for the telcos, not their competitors.

Players

VoDSL, the hottest technology of 1999, seemed a path to riches in 2000 as Accelerated Networks went public to the tune of 1 billion dollars, despite lagging behind CopperCom, Jetstream, and Tollbridge in the marketplace. The *VoDSL three* all had partnerships with nearly every other company in the business. All three were rumored to have turned down offers in the billions. That wasn't implausible in the days when Cisco was paying $7 billion for Cerent, barely more than a startup, but seems wild fantasy after the bust. The equipment manufacturers were still struggling to find customers in 2001. The telcos all had advanced trials in 2000, but none resulted in products on the market. Actual sales, so far, have been limited, and almost exclusively for business service.

Sprint has the most advanced trial in the world, although they may be dropping the entire project. Thousands of customers receive high-speed data and either two or four voice lines for a competitive rate, packaged as *Sprint ION* service. Beneath overwhelming marketing hype, ION is a voice and data service delivered over DSL, fixed wireless, or other high-speed data connections. Sprint, preparing for mass sales in 2002, has located Lucent Stinger DSLAMs in 2000 telephone offices serving half the United States. With an Internet backbone around the world, and a wireless division with which they can bundle services, Sprint is banking on VoDSL to replace declining long-distance revenue. They've reported technical problems, especially with the Telcordia gateways, but similar have been solved by other providers. The real problem is Wall Street after Sprint's failed merger with MCI. Wall Street is looking for a quick sale of the company, and long range projects like ION are seen as obstacles. If Sprint were to stand alone, ION is clearly their most promising future. ION however is a deterrent to a purchase by a company like Verizon or BellSouth, that already has facilities in place.

AT&T has a similar strategy and plans to offer bundled voice and data. They acquired 1700 equipped offices in the NorthPoint bankruptcy. Even before spinning off of the cable companies as AT&T Broadband, they had major plans to use DSL in areas where they did not own cable. Now, it will presumably be their lead technology across the nation, with major plans for 2002 and 2003. However, AT&T has reversed strategy so many times, amid purchases and spin-offs, that no plans are firm.

CopperCom was a company with drive, personified by its hard-charging CEO, Cynthia Ringo. After they purchased DTI, a softswitch maker, the entire operation moved to Florida, and Ringo resigned as CEO. The result is a much quieter company, conserving capital until the market develops. The early customers are all small competitors, but they hope that the advanced trials with the major telcos (including Verizon and SBC) will yield some elephantine customers.

Jetstream uses a similar but incompatible ATM technology, with dozens of trials worldwide and great prospects. The customers, however, have been slow to move. AT&T is the key customer, with Jetstream expecting orders for hundreds of thousands of lines when AT&T moves forward.

Tollbridge is the other triad member, due to adroit market positioning. Their technology is different, based on IP packets rather than ATM. This gives them flexibility to work with cable companies as well as DSL companies, at a theoretical cost of lower efficiency. Founder Asher Waldfogel developed some of the original Internet technology 20 years ago when working at BBN.

Accelerated made a major splash when MCI and others chose their gateways, which were among the first to use the more adaptable SVCs (switched virtual circuits) to connect over the network. Compared to PVCs (permanent virtual circuits), they require less setup and provisioning. However, they have been hurt by pullbacks at MCI and bankruptcy at customers Winstar and @Link. Siemens is a major investor.

TdSoft is an Israeli company delivering product that meets the V5.2 standard prevalent in Europe and much of the world. Being first to market has won them partners, including Alcatel (trials in Singapore), Lucent, Next Level, and Fujitsu. CTO and cofounder Eytan Radian has moved to the United States to open an office and expand their market.

General Bandwidth aimed right at the telcos for customers, and gained instant credibility when SBC invested. They emphasize residential capability, including lifeline support, and are active with Intel in the VoBB initiative.

Texas Instruments' Telogy division is the world leader in software for voice compression, which reduces the bandwidth required for each connection to 16K and possibly down to 8K. The more sophisticated compression algorithms require more processing power, but are practical with today's signal processing chips. The result: even more voice lines over the same wire, while allowing higher rates for data.

Polycom was probably the first with volume shipments of the customer equipment, and intends to win a strong position. They are the leaders in video-conferencing, for which they've developed expertise in voice processing.

Efficient's Flowpoint supplied the equipment for most of the first trials, and now as part of Siemens has a strong manufacturing capability.

Alcatel's dominant position in DSLAMs (over half the world market) means that the VoDSL gateway option they offer for their 7300 DSLAM is likely to take a major share of future contracts.

Panasonic entered the market mid-2001 with a splash, a VoDSL gateway with a key marketing advantage: it looks like a phone, and supports four lines with inexpensive cordless phone units.

Figure 7.2   Panasonic's VoDSL gateway supports four cordless phones.
Courtesy: Jetstream

CHAPTER 8

Fast Enough to Watch

T he *Third Internet* is fast enough to watch, and the technology is ready to deliver it today. A generation ago, television replaced print for most people's information and entertainment, and the Internet is sure to follow the same path. One meg service—well within the capabilities of most DSL connections—delivers a fine pre-encoded video. The logjams are the provider networks and the closed doors at their edges. The technical problems are mostly solved, but the telcos in the U.S. are too blind, or too greedy, to deliver the Internet at video speed. We are fighting hard, including testifying at the F.C.C., to break down those barriers. Meanwhile, here are some applications that are practical today.

You've heard the hype, all the cool things you can do with DSL: teleconferencing instead of racking up miles as a road warrior, collaborating with your team online, outsourcing applications from word processing to project management, telecommuting, training watching video and attending conferences, all in front of your computer monitor. The truth is, everything you can do with DSL was possible before with ISDN and T-1 lines. DSL simply makes the applications that require speed cheaper, and those that were irritatingly slow with a dial-up modem more convenient. However, with these bandwidth-hungry applications, everything we've been saying about reliability becomes crucial.

Videoconferencing

Videoconferencing is already a billion-dollar business, but its use has been limited by the cost of high-speed Internet connections, the equipment required, installation problems, and reliability issues. New equipment has come down dramatically in price. A $600 desktop unit, like Polycom's ViaVideo, is being used by some professionals to provide a level of quality that cost tens of thousands of dollars only a few years ago.

Polycom's high-end ViewStation, and competitive units like it, include a remote-controlled camera and echo-cancelled audio, making them ideal units for use in conference rooms and other settings for face-to-face meetings at a distance between individuals or groups. Software that works with both the desktop and room units allows concurrent collaboration between the participants, including shared whiteboards and exchanges of documents. Additional uses include sales presentations, conferences and training, tele-medicine, and distance learning.

New high-quality desktop videoconferencing hardware and videoconferencing over IP make the technology widely used by large corporations, colleges, and universities accessible to even small and home-based businesses. Typically, desktop units include a small fixed camera and microphone that plug into the sound card on users' computers.

Figure 8.1 Polycom's ViaVideo desktop system, quality good enough to conference with the pros.
Courtesy: Polycom

Figure 8.2   High-end systems like Polycom's ViewStation yield better quality images and full duplex sound.
Courtesy: Polycom

Videoconferencing requires speed. Uncompressed broadcast-quality video requires 184 Mbps per second. Today's hardware and software codecs dramatically reduce that enormous number, but substantial bandwidth is still needed to provide a life-like moving image. What is needed is not the "up to the advertised speed" offered by most telcos that can bottom out at a mere fraction of the offered speed, but consistent symmetrical bandwidth of at least 175–200 Kbps up and downstream. Business-oriented providers like Covad and Concentric have been more consistent in providing the needed bandwidths than telco providers have.

While much videoconferencing is still being done on 128K ISDN lines, 128 Kbps of DSL bandwidth isn't enough for high-quality full-screen videoconferencing. Even if your DSL speed is rock solid, the information carried by ISDN's "control track" requires an additional 20 percent of DSL bandwidth. With today's compression algorithms and the raw bandwidth available over DSL, videoconferencing is perfectly practical. While Internet browsing and many other DSL applications are asymmetrical, video needs to travel at the same high speed in both directions. A "business quality" videoconference requires 384 Kbps (or above) of symmetrical DSL.

 The H.320 protocol for videoconferencing over ISDN and the newer H.323 protocol for conferencing over IP are not compatible. Communication between H.320 and H.323 units requires expensive bridging hardware or use of a service that provides it.

For example, using Polycom's ViaVideo desktop equipment at 384 Kbps symmetrical, you can get good-quality audio and a 320 × 240 video image that looks almost as good as TV, but is bit less sharp and a little more jerky because of the high compression required. Corporate room-based videoconferencing systems blow up whatever image you send to full, so 320 × 240 is the lowest quality you can afford to send corporate recipients. Dedicated videoconferencing facilities housed in large conference rooms include multiple high-end cameras, special lighting, and big screen projection displays. While desktop systems can't compete, they are entirely adequate for sales calls, one-on-one meetings, and many other purposes. They're also easier to use and will save you money.

A low-end *room system* starts at about $5,000 without monitor. What you get for that money is a higher-quality video image, better audio, and more sophisticated compression of your video signal. However, quality depends, in part, on the same level of technology existing on the other end.

High-end room systems like Polycom's ViewStation FX can cost $15,000 or more. These systems use state-of-the art multiprocessor hardware compression and decompression technology providing the highest-quality videoconference. A high-quality desktop system uses single-processor hardware compression and software decompression. Because video compression is far more compute-intensive than decompression, this configuration still yields a substantially high-quality videoconference than low-end systems. Low-quality desktop systems use software compression and decompression, creating the lower-quality video and burdening the PC's CPU heavily. This limits effective concurrent use of CAD/CAM or other applications that might otherwise have been valuable to use in the conference.

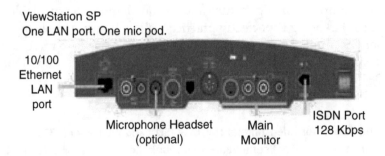

Figure 8.3   Rear view of Polycom's ViewStation showing connectors.

Courtesy: Polycom

For social or noncritical videoconferencing, you could use a low-end $50–100 video camera plugged into your PC connected to Microsoft NetMeeting, a free product shipped with the latest versions of Microsoft Windows. However, don't try to fool the pros. Although low-end manufacturers promise that you'll have many of the same functions as the more expensive dedicated systems ... you won't. Cheap cameras and unsophisticated codecs create lower-quality images that defeat the purpose of videoconferencing. If you just want to let your new baby make faces at grandma, the postage-stamp-sized video-conference created by Web cams might be sufficient. However, for doing business, a clear image, quality, good sound, and a reliable codec are essentials.

A low-cost alternative to video if you can't afford a low-end $600 professional system is using *Web Conferencing* collaboration software along with a voice call. The same white-board software and document-sharing applications that add value and functionality to high-end videoconferencing systems can be used independent of them. This lower-tech alternative yields better communication and better results than a poor-quality jerky, blurry video call. Low-quality video is distracting and does more to create antagonism than it does to get work done. See the section in this chapter titled *Swimming with the Sharks* for an introduction to videoconferencing.

The key thing to consider is the standard used by most offices. If you are a telecommuter setting up video collaborations with your company's home office, desktop videoconferencing using DSL can help to keep your hardware and connection costs affordable—but only if their hardware and software support the H.323 standard for videoconferencing over IP.

Traditional videoconferencing over ISDN lines uses the H.320 standard, which is different from the H.323 standard required for the newer IP video-conferencing over DSL and cable modems. To make the video connection, both the sender and the receiver must use the same standard, or use bridging hardware or a third-party bridging service to connect. Most higher-end room-based video conferencing systems sold today can support both standards, but the unit you call must in fact have an unblocked IP connection for you to use DSL to connect to it.

ISDN, IP, and proprietary systems each have their own standards. Specialized service providers can link the callers with incompatible hardware through an offsite gateway. All participants call into the gateway to connect with one another. However, if your meeting is confidential, remember that a technician at the gateway will be monitoring the call to make sure the signal is consistent and all parties remain connected.

Reliability is a key issue to be considered. ISDN, T-1, and T-3 lines guarantee rock-solid bandwidth, providing stability for videoconferencing. DSL speeds fluctuate. While the H.323 standard defines what kind of signal can be used for IP videoconferencing, each manufacturer is free to use its own methods for achieving that standard. Some equipment manufacturers, like Polycom, create a *superset* of the standard compression algorithm. They use proprietary compression software that compensates "on the fly" for changes in bandwidth and improves image and sound quality. When two units of the same series from the same vendor communicate, they use the extended standards. When they communicate with competitive units, they fall back to the basic H.323 standard.

The audio segment of a videoconference takes priority when bandwidth fluctuates because people are more sensitive to interruptions in the audio segment of the conference than to breaks in video. If the bandwidth suddenly drops during a conference, the video might freeze or distort for a few seconds and then return to normal, while the audio continues uninterrupted. This can lead to some potentially embarrassing freeze frames, but the continuity of the conference continues.

High-end videoconferencing requires a lot of bandwidth. You need at least 384 Kbps for what is commonly called "business quality," but 512 Kbps will yield a much higher-quality conference, particularly if motion, such as a pacing presenter or an equipment demonstration, is involved. If your DSL is connected across a local area network, you'll need to install a *switching hub* to ensure that the computer you're conferencing from has enough bandwidth.

A switched Ethernet network protects the bandwidth you need for videoconferencing and limits access to specified computers. Videoconferencing signals can, however, be blocked by firewalls. Sometimes the only solution is to put videoconference hardware in the DMZ between the firewall and the DSL connection. The security risk is minimal. Calls cannot be easily monitored, because the compressed video signals are changing rapidly to accommodate signals from other conference participants, making them difficult to tap into. To videoconference, the signal encoded by the codec needs to be able to get through firewalls on both ends. Using the UDP protocol you can configure your firewall to specify a limited number of ports for the video signal. When you set up a conference, you'll have to work out security issues with the network manager on the other end. Most corporations impose IPSec standards (See Chapter 5, "Security: You Need It"), which automatically screen out unfamiliar activity (like the compressed video data) coming into the network. Although it is technically possible for a hacker to tap into the bit stream and eavesdrop on a video call, the use of complex compression and with handshaking between the codecs makes this of little practical concern to most users. However, the U.S. Military and highly competitive industries do use available third-party encryption and decryption hardware in certain applications.

One consideration when you're choosing videoconferencing technology is whether the system can be configured remotely by a network administrator offsite, or whether it must be configured at the location where the videoconference takes place. Large companies use tools such as Polycom's Global Management System for this purpose. Small business users will want to take the same care to make sure the system you choose is easy to configure and easy to use.

Jim Harper, CEO of HarperMedia (www.harpermedia.com) says, "Technology should enhance, not get in the way of your meetings. Participants in a meeting should spend their time interacting with each other, not trying to make the system work." When choosing videoconferencing technology he stresses, it's important not to lose track of your business objective, which is to create, maintain, and strengthen relationships between people—between team members across various parts of the organization as well as with customers, suppliers, investors, and others. We asked Harper to share with you what it takes to produce a professional Videoconference. As you will see below, the formula includes two parts technology and one part chuztpa. He's also adamant that technology should be easy to use. "Look for appliance-type ease of installation. Plug it in, turn it on, use it." We asked our expert at HarperMedia to help explain the best way to videoconference over DSL. First, we look at the technology you'll need and use, and then at where you can cut corners and where quality counts.

Swimming with the Sharks: A Technology Primer for Videoconferencing

> A good-quality videoconferencing system can enable a home office user to have a professional appearance indistinguishable from that of a Fortune 500 user—even though the home user may be wearing gym shorts and bunny slippers under the desk during the call.
>
> Jim Harper

Videoconferencing is a two-way communications technology that translates moving pictures and sound into computer data and sends it over telecommunications links such as ISDN, T-1, T-3, and the Internet to facilitate face-to-face meetings, distance learning, and online collaboration.

A critical component of videoconferencing is the powerful software that compresses and decompresses the images and sound into a form that can be transmitted through available networks. This software includes compression and decompression hardware or software called a codec. The quality of the codec combined with the quality of cameras, microphones, speakers, and other peripherals is only one part of what determines the quality of the videoconference. Network capacity, system reliability, and transmission delays also affect quality. In many cases, the greatest improvements in quality can be achieved simply through better, brighter lighting, zooming the camera in for tight "head and shoulders shots," and making sure that the users are close to the microphone—techniques that were known to professional videographers long before the popularity of videoconferencing.

Traditionally, videoconference calls were carried at 128 Kbps to 384 Kbps (by using inverse multiplexors) over ISDN networks or at higher speeds over T-1 lines. Today, there is a strong trend toward videoconferencing over the Internet Protocol (IP). DSL provides the bandwidth to carry higher-quality calls (which require increased bandwidth). However, because stability of bandwidth from DSL is limited, more than enough bandwidth is required. Business-quality talking-head video has traditionally required 384 Kbps of bandwidth. This provides a 320×240 pixel image at 15 frames (30 fields) per second (fps). This is in comparison to Standard Definition Digital Television, which is 704×480 pixels at 30 frames (60 fields) per second.

Multiparty calls of three or more participants in different locations require a conference bridge. This can be a hardware component built into one of the endpoints, or can be remotely accessed by calling a third-party company that has hardware to connect each participant's call. The standards for videoconferencing over ISDN and over IP are different and incompatible unless bridged by videoconferencing gateways.

In high-quality professional equipment, the codec is contained on a chipset inside a *set-top box* required for videoconferencing. Because videoconferencing uses a different protocol from the Hypertext Transfer Protocol (HTTP) used to transmit Web pages, both the sender's and receiver's networks must be configured to pass the UDP protocol through firewalls.

Web cams attempt to do in software what professional systems do in highly sophisticated signal-processing hardware, and they will not yield an acceptable quality image for professional videoconferencing or provide full-duplex sound. Software-based videoconferencing also lacks advanced features that accommodate drops in bandwidth, full-duplex audio, far-end camera control, and other important features. These are necessary and important if you plan to use videoconferencing for professional meetings. Because images and sounds are compressed, starting with high-quality media improves the end result. Use the best-quality cameras and microphones you can afford. Pay attention to lighting, camera angle, and zoom, shut out background noise, and have an uncluttered background and preplan your presentations to maximize the impact of your video calls.

Do It with Style

Videoconferencing is all about appearances, about capturing that 60-percent plus of human communication that scientists tell us is nonverbal. When you're using the technology to make a sales call or meet with a client, you want to give the appearance of being larger than life. Sophisticated users in major corporations will recognize poor quality. Bad equipment can also create images so poor that they defeat the purpose of the conference. If you can't look someone in the eye and read his or her body language, you are far better off using the telephone.

It's quite possible for a small office or home office user to give the appearance of being on the level of a General Motors, but you have to pay attention to the equipment you use. An okay-quality camera with good lighting can yield acceptable results. Lighting is a key element that many people fail to consider. Paying attention to what is in the background is also important.

What constitutes "good video?" For most people, the answer is "TV." Today, everyone is an expert on television because we all watch TV. Trying to videoconference without the necessary bandwidth is a big mistake. You may look great in the preview window on your computer, but the other end can be gruesome. Don't make this mistake. Another pitfall is reducing frame rate to limit bandwidth demands. TV runs at 30 fps, movies at 24 fps; at lower frame rates, your eyes and brain don't effectively translate fields of video into moving pictures. Videoconferencing frame rates are measured in fields per second. There are two fields to each frame. Low to midrange videoconferencing systems transmit only every other frame. If you don't want to give the people you're meeting with a headache or blurred vision, stick with a rate of at least 15 fps or 30 fields per second.

While we're on the topic, unreliable bandwidth can be embarrassing. The image can and will freeze, for example, when you have your tongue stuck out. In time, you'll learn to use the technology to your advantage. I've done a lot of international videoconferencing. At one company, we liked to joke that the British, with their stiff upper lips, have mastered it. It's a little more difficult for Italians, who are much more animated.

When you're setting up a videoconference, you want the same kind of functionality that you'd have at a meeting: you can see the people, read their body language, hear them, and share documents. You might even collaborate to draw up a list or create a diagram or map. You need the same capabilities for videoconferencing.

To achieve this you'll need additional software to share documents and collaborate. There are two kinds of software in wide use, both under the general

Visual Collaboration Tools

Whiteboard is a component of Microsoft's NetMeeting and other Web-conferencing software that lets you collaborate in real time with others using graphic information. With the Whiteboard, you can review, create, and update graphic information, manipulate contents by dragging and dropping information on the whiteboard with the mouse, and cut, copy, and paste information from any Windows-based application into the whiteboard. The technology allows you to use different colored markers to differentiate participants' annotations and comments. It is widely used to provide collaboration as a part of videoconferencing, and is integrated into some videoconferencing packages.

WebEx and *PlaceWare* are hosted Web-conferencing services that can be accessed through an ordinary Web browser, eliminating the need for investment in hardware and software installation, and reducing the need for training and maintenance. The software provides a high-resolution full-screen interface for meeting participants to share presentations in real time. Features include document sharing, Web browser sharing, and sharing applications. Some collaboration software includes a tiny video window to show participants, but the quality is poor. Stick to presentations with voice calls for the best quality (www.webex.com and www.placeware.com).

heading of "Web conferencing." The first is *document conferencing*. Shared whiteboards allow all parties to see whatever text, image, or annotation each participant puts on his or her whiteboard. *Application sharing* allows one party to take charge of the mouse and keyboard (kind of like, "let me drive for the moment") of another, remote party. WebEx and PlaceWare (see *Visual Collaboration Tools*) are two good packages targeted at delivery of presentations to remote viewers across the Web. Some high-end videoconferencing systems integrate Microsoft's Net Meeting to collaborate, but many of my business customers feel that it is overcomplicated, so it's not widely used.

Professional videoconferencing equipment connects effectively to a range of established systems, and thus will be more compatible with more systems. However, it's at its best when it's talking with another of its own make and model. Vendors who produce equipment with the H.323 standards also build in additional functionality—called a "superset" providing multiple advantages—when talking to another of their own systems. If you're an auto parts manufacturer planning on videoconferencing with General Motors, for example, find out what kind of system they use; it may be to your advantage.

Videoconferencing is getting better and better. One emerging technology is MPEG 4, which allows you to sit—like the TV weather person—in front of a blue screen and key in any background you want ... but it's a little ways off.

Applications Service Providers: An Idea Whose Time Has Gone

DSL lines are fast enough to run many applications from a central server, which could be managed by another company on the other side of the country. Every study of the cost of supporting computer users finds that it is enormously expensive—thousands of dollars per person per year. Large companies seeking to drive down that cost often outsource much of their IT divisions to specialists like IBM. Bell South, for example, neither manages nor purchases its own microcomputers for their multi-billion-dollar organization. Instead, they outsource with Electronic Data Systems, Ross Perot's old company, to provide hardware, software, and support for the whole system.

Many believe that outsourcing provides major savings, even if the typical contract includes hiring the existing support staff and leaving them physically in place, but on a new payroll under different management.

Several billion dollars of financing, mostly from venture capitalists, went into creating a business of application service providers (ASPs) who would remotely manage the computer needs of small and medium-sized companies. Microsoft developed a special division of Office designed to run remotely, and every ISP and service provider, including Verizon and Earthlink, hoped to jump on that bandwagon and increase their revenues.

Nearly all were disappointed. The cost of sales, convincing small businesses to change their applications, was prohibitively high. The initial investment including setup costs was so high that companies would not break even for many years. Few customers signed up for the service, possibly because the pricing, at around $150 a month for software they could buy for $500 and support themselves, was less than attractive. Costs were high because ASPs had no miraculous pool of superb, well-trained support people who would work for low wages and answer everyone's questions successfully over the telephone.

ASPs also found that they didn't get the easy, inexpensive-to-serve customer with few problems; those who could already take care of themselves. Many of the customers who did sign up needed extra support. The ASP either delivered that support and lost money, or disappointed customers.

As we write in 2001, essentially none of these companies has shown a profit. As the easy financing of the dotcom era has disappeared, many are going out of business. The projections are clearly not going to be met, and even Microsoft has backed away from promoting its Office suite for outsourcing.

ASPs work where the nature of the software is specialized and expensive, making it logical to look to dedicated support. For example, Virage leases video-encoding software to CNN. However, for all but the largest customers it makes sense to outsource encoding to Virage because it is difficult and expensive to find and train the expert staff to support the software. Even though it is costly—$2,500 setup and $500 per hour for encoding—many sign on to Virage's service that delivers the software remotely and uses Virage's own support staff.

ASPs are particularly appropriate in a fast growing field. Applications that require constant updates make the ASP equation work because it makes more sense to pay for service and support than to make a large capital and training investment in software that will soon need updating.

Nightfire software is a classic example. They provide billing and provisioning software for DSL companies, including large ones like Covad. The software requires constant updating because one of its key features is interfacing with the telcos' constantly changing systems for ordering lines and entering trouble tickets. Many of their smaller customers need the updates and support directly from Nightfire, who sells it as a complete service and application package.

We believe that the ASPs that failed were the ones that planned to sell software that doesn't require specialized expertise to a mass market. Those with a good prospect of succeeding have a specialized knowledge of the particular software and the subject matter that allows them to add enough value to make it profitable. These are typically the manufacturers of the software itself or service providers with a close relationship to the software manufacturer.

ASPs fail when the software involved is just as easy to acquire and use as a stand-alone application. They succeed (we demonstrate in the following section, *Video*) when the software is so expensive that all but the largest corporations need to lease it. It also works when the application requires dedicated or specialized hardware to function, and the cost of leasing the service includes maintenance and support of that equipment as well as updates of the software.

Video

Video is the great promise of broadband, and DSL provides the bandwidth for streaming as well as video on demand. It makes possible business applications from Morgan Stanley's *Morning Call* to set the day's agenda for brokers nationwide, to video news releases, product releases, training, and even video tech support.

Streaming high-quality video over DSL requires a combination of expertise, technology, and bandwidth. Let's start with bandwidth. The optimum for full-screen video at about VCR quality is about one megabit per second (1 Mbps). Television-quality video is possible over bandwidth as low as 300 kilobits per second (300 Kbps), but it must be carefully compressed. More often, 300 Kbps buys you one-third of a computer screen. The tradeoff for low bandwidth is quality. Video must be highly compressed for transmission over the Internet, resulting in a lot of artifacts and glitches in the image.

High-quality samples created by Microsoft and others promoting Web-based video are carefully selected and meticulously encoded, which is time consuming and expensive. Video compression and decompression algorithms (codecs) reduce the bandwidth required to stream video by reducing the color spectrum, the frame rate, and the overall quality of the image. Images that stay the same over time, like talking heads and interviews, compress much more easily than images with lots of movement, like sports. Highly compressed images tend to be dark and lack contrast.

Encoding video "on the fly" for a simultaneous Webcast of a conference or a speech results in larger files requiring higher bandwidth, a minimum of about 750 Kbps for reasonable quality. Satellite- or DVD-quality images by comparison require about four megabits per second (4 Mbps) bandwidth. One way to reduce files sizes and the time it takes streamed video to buffer is to reduce the image size. Hence, the *CNN solution*, postage-stamp-sized video clips that download fast and depend largely on audio for understandability.

Video over the Internet is not television; video news over the Internet is also very different from its television counterpart. For one thing, it's smaller, much smaller. Postage-stamp-sized windows have become ubiquitous. The villain in this story is bandwidth. Because much of the audience is still on dial-up connections, news sites—including CNN, NBC, ABC, and FOX—keep file sizes small. Video clips designed for broadband, typically at 100 or 300 Kbps, are a little larger, but don't even approach what is technically possible over DSL.

Looking at the major news sites, you might think these small video clips are the state of the art for broadband video. While they *are* the most common presentation format for video, much more is possible, particularly over broadband. Virage Video created the codecs and software used to bring all of the major news organizations' footage to the Web. The codec is fully capable of translating the professional-quality video generated by television news departments into high-quality Webcasts. However, to squeeze that video down the pipe to dial-up and low-bandwidth DSL Web users, companies using Virage technology dumb down their video to the least common denominator.

The classic format for streaming video news clips over the Web gives users a choice between dial-up speed 28/56 Kbps and broadband 100–150 Kbps in one or more formats. Microsoft Windows Media Player and Real Player are the most common. Clips are broken up into program segments to reduce file size. However, even the 300 Kbps is delivered as a small format window designed to download quickly—and the difference in quality, while visible, in negligible.

One reason they can get away with this in a market where consumers regularly watch DVD-quality images and high-definition TV is the additional value added during encoding in a process. Virage calls its process "smart encoding." Audio tracks take precedence over video, resulting in high-quality audio signals. Even when the image degrades as bandwidth twists and dives, it's possible to follow news stories and interviews by listening. In addition, while video is being encoded it is automatically logged and transcribed. The software can even recognize and identify newsmakers using a unique face identification feature. These transcripts make the video clips easily searchable.

Searchable video is easier to syndicate and repurpose for other uses, so smart encoding adds value.

A good example of this is CNN's *Moneyline*. Dave was recently interviewed on *Moneyline*. We missed the broadcast, but a day later a full transcript and a teeny tiny video clip appeared on CNN's Web site.

One of the most exciting uses of this technology to date is CSpan's *Campaign 2000* searchable database of the presidential campaign speeches. The archive includes every major speech made by the presidential candidates. The encoded video was syndicated to 40 Web sites including Yahoo Politics, iVillage, and NBC.

Encoding video for Webcasting doesn't come cheap. Some companies like Virage's largest customer CNN, license the smart encoding process for 50 separate encoders. Forty of those are used to capture footage from headline news alone. Many smaller companies pay Virage a $25,000 setup fee and $500 an hour to encode their footage. The service includes one file format, either Real or Windows Media Player, and two bit rates, usually 56 Kbps and 300 Kbps. Although expensive, the service still represents a savings over training staff, and maintaining and running the equipment required for encoding.

CNET, for example, shoots five and a half hours of news programs weekly, sends it to Virage for encoding, and then syndicates the programs to AOL. The beauty of this technical ASP model is that CNET added broadband capability without buying any equipment or hiring any staff. The encoded footage is also being used as a research tool to create new shows.

News and public affairs programming are only the tip of the iceberg. Corporate business provides many opportunities for streaming video. Bear Stearns, for example, links several dozen offices to its *Morning Call* meeting via broadband. Video news releases, catalogs, and training videos are also being streamed.

Ivy League Streaming

Both Harvard University and MIT (Massachusetts Institute of Technology) are selectively streaming video content of classes and serving up video on demand. MIT's Singapore-MIT Alliance (SMA) project creates a virtual classroom in which students from the National University of Singapore, Nanyang Technological University, and MIT study together, although they are 12 time zones apart. Students share a virtual classroom through a collage of streamed video of the professor lecturing, PowerPoint slides, and whiteboard software. Cameras and microphones in the classrooms facilitate student participation.

While MIT is using the 2nd Internet, a high-speed alternative to the commercial Internet, to deliver the service, it could just as easily be delivered over VDSL (very high speed DSL). The sample shows a video image of the professor supported by an audio track, and interjects PowerPoint slides and information from the professor's whiteboard.

The technical specs for the project include not one but five backup plans to compensate for the unreliability of the 2nd Internet. An excerpt from a white paper describing the project's technology explains the need for backup. Although this project is not delivered over DSL, it illustrates effectively what it takes to deliver video over unreliable Internet connections.

"The normal mode of synchronous delivery relies on *Internet2*. ISDN and satellite were considered too expensive to consider for routine connections. *Internet2*, however, is a research network, which is not guaranteed to function with the same reliability or availability as commodity connections. (Intermediate routers could be down or misconfigured or overloaded by other experimental applications. Any portion of the 10,000+-mile link could be compromised.) Because this was a basic assumption, a fundamental part of the implementation included a contingency plan, which has matured into its current multitiered structure."

That structure described includes four contingency plans. You have to love any engineer this prepared for the realities of Internet problems. Only as a last resort does MIT cancel class. Encoded versions of all the lectures are archived and loaded into a database along with course materials, homework assignments, lecture notes, and readings. MIT makes the video encoded in the Windows Media Player and Real Video formats available to students by streaming them from video servers collocated for better access. To ensure adequate bandwidth over the university backbone, video servers required special configurations.

Harvard Business School now has cameras in many of its classrooms. They're keeping a rolling archive of the most interesting lecturers and making it all available to faculty, staff, and alumni over the public Internet.

Another MIT initiative delivers video on demand to the campus and alumni. Dubbed *MIT World*, the content includes talks open to the public and videotaped for transmission to campus and alumni over the Web. The project also streams televised events in real time. At some point in the future, MIT anticipates public access, but the much-publicized initiative to *put MIT online* includes only text-based course material, not video.

Major League baseball contracted with Virage to encode and stream every league game for the 2001 season. This project was offered to the public as a season pass to all the games, or by subscription to a team's Web site. Some hundreds of hours of footage were encoded and Webcast. The searchable archive gives viewers the option of programming their own fantasy league, or simply looking at self-generated highlight reels of whatever interests them, whether that's hours of foul balls or a whole program of stealing bases.

Ten highlights will be featured on Major League Baseball's home page. Akamai is providing the video servers for this massive effort, but the encoding technology is so effective, according to Virage, that video won't have to be co-located on servers in major cities to arrive seamlessly to viewers.

Cost is the primary factor holding back webcasting. Server networks, especially the more efficient edge serving systems such as Akamai, charge upwards of $1 per hour per stream, even in large volume. That means all but limited special programming is too expensive to webcast. Declining server and backbone prices have the potential to dramatically drop the cost to the pennies per hour cost of broadcast networks. That will require massive volume, and co-operation between providers, open peering, and removal of toll barriers at the edge of the network. Instead, we see each company trying to develop a monopoly position in their market, and charge substantial fees to access their network.

We go to press with Verizon, SBC, Sony, Disney and other massive companies promising to deliver Video on Demand, but none willing to go beyond trials. This will be a premium service, at $4–5 per movie, which should mean there is room for profit for all. The companies can't agree, however, with every participant looking to increase their revenue. A quiet war has broken out between Hollywood, who wants more for the films, and the telcos/cable companies, who want a steep fee to carry it. The costs will be high until volume is high, so they are fighting for (relative) crumbs. Neither side has shown a willingness to solve the problems equitably.

Broadband entertainment companies have faired poorly in the past year. Digital Entertainment Network (DEN), Dreamworks' Pop.com, and Pseudo all failed. While everyone seems to want video on demand, few companies have found a way to make quality that people want to watch cheap enough to deliver.

One option to reduce bandwidth demands is to bring video servers closer to users by colocating them in office buildings, apartment buildings, and telco DSLAMs. Verizon plans to locate video servers near the DSLAMs in their central offices, caching several hundred of the most popular movies on servers closer to their customers. Their newer DSLAMs, including the Alcatel 7300, have enough capacity to simultaneously transmit a movie to nearly every subscriber. The older model DSLAM is more problematic, but it can certainly support streaming video to the 5–15 percent likely to want it if they only offer expensive movies.

VDSL Explained

Configurations now in use include 26 Mbps downstream and 1 Mbps upstream, and synchronous service 13 Mbps down and 13 up. One limitation of VDSL technology is its reach, only 4000 feet. However, it is an effective way to deliver the high-speed Internet to office buildings, campuses, and other bandwidth-hungry institutions. Fiber to the basement is translated into DSL lines that can deliver up to 52 Mbps of bandwidth to anyone within reach.

Because VDSL chipsets are less complicated than their ADSL cousins, they should be cheaper, but to date only one company delivers the high-speed alternative. Broadcom, a specialist in business networks, has developed a VDSL chip that also supports ADSL and SDSL. It can also be reconfigured to support Fiber-to-the-Node (FTTN), Fiber-to-the-Curb (FTTC), and conventional central office network configurations. The low-power chip is designed to allow DSL providers to deliver digital services, including movie-quality videos, CD-quality sound, 120 channels of entertainment and information programs, "pay-per-view" movies and events, "onscreen" integration of popular telephone features, and high-speed Internet access. You can read more about Broadcom and VDSL at www.broadcom.com.

Server costs have come down along with hard drive prices. A small server large enough to hold 200 top movies now requires less than $2,000 of disk drive capacity. This too makes video on demand practical. One thing holding up the wide-scale distribution of movies and other video on demand is Hollywood's reluctance to release the rights to films for DSL distribution. Currently, movies are seldom available until all other sources of revenue, including airplane sales, are exhausted. Microsoft's digital rights management software is designed to better protect copyrighted content, paving the way for more attractive entertainment offerings by DSL providers. However, to date, Hollywood and DSL providers are *just talking*.

One reason for the all-out effort to make video on demand over DSL work is the competition with cable broadband providers. While cable's inherent limitations for business users rules it out as an option for most, that's changing, and the ease of getting cable broadband has seduced many consumers.

Distinguishing their service by offering "any movie ever made anytime," is the goal of many providers, and an advertising claim made by Qwest has demonstrated its ability to make good on that claim by rolling out video projects in Phoenix and Cincinnati.

ZoomTown (www.zoomtown.com/) brings video on demand to 40,000 homes in Cincinnati over ADSL. It offers subscribers movies on demand, games on demand, and e-commerce. Video is delivered via DSL directly to customers' televisions, using a set-top box and Microsoft's Windows Media Player. The content includes over 500 hours of programming, including full-length movies, music videos, TV shows, music shows, and children's programs. The required speed, 640 Kbps, is still higher than what most consumers get consistently with ADSL.

Intertainer (www.intertainer.com) provides video content. Full-screen, high-quality video on a pay-per-view model isn't just a promise from Intertainer, it's a reality. Partnering with Colorado-based telcos, Qwest in Phoenix, and ZoomTown in Cincinnati, Intertainer is delivering video on demand over DSL. Intertainer has proven that TV-quality movies can be delivered at 1 Mbps and below. They use Microsoft's version of MPEG4 encoding, a new standard currently used in satellite and digital cable systems that is more efficient than the MPEG 1 and MPEG 2. They've encoded several thousand movies at 750K, with decent results that customers are paying for in Cincinnati and other cities. Older coding schemes and live events encoded in real time may require up to 4 Mbps, still less than the 7 Mbps downloads SBC plans for 60 percent of their clients.

The model for the world is Phoenix, where 50,000 homes are connected to Qwest Choice TV, one of the most successful rollouts of video to date. By using existing fiber in the neighborhood, Qwest reaches within 4000 feet of a customer's location, which allows it to deliver speeds of 26 Mbps downstream and 3 Mbps upstream using VDSL. At the neighborhood, signals are converted and sent via ATM and MPEG2 technology through the existing telephone copper-wire network to homes.

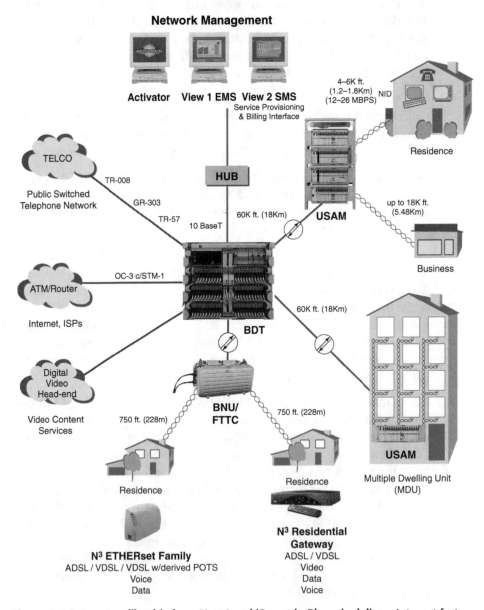

Figure 8.4   A system like this from Next Level/Qwest in Phoenix delivers Internet fast enough to watch.

Courtesy: Next Level Communications

Figure 8.5   These boxes throughout Phoenix deliver the Internet at over 20M. Why isn't your telco doing as well?
Courtesy: Next Level Communications

Choice TV allows viewers to click on ads on screen and be linked directly to a Web site. This facilitates e-commerce, as well as providing supplementary information like suggested reading to complement educational programming.

Next-Generation Applications

As we emphasized at the beginning of this chapter, none of these applications and business models for DSL will work if customers cannot rely on consistent bandwidth. Video-grade networks are practical and affordable for telcos to deploy, and claims to the contrary are misinformed or disingenuous. Movies and video encoded in advance require less than a megabit of bandwidth, deliverable by DSL to at least 60 percent of a telco's customers. ZoomTown is doing it in Cincinnati, Qwest in Denver, and other telcos are in trials. The telcos are very scared, because they heard this story before in 1994 when they first planned DSL to deliver movies. The technology was still too expensive, and veterans of that era remember the hundreds of millions of dollars in losses. Today, however, the DSL networks are in place, supported by Internet usage. The cost of the necessary hardware has plummeted, and continues to go down.

The projects and businesses detailed in this chapter are pioneers, early adopters willing to go the extra mile to work with the existing technology to deliver video and use other applications. However, competition from cable providers and others will increase. As we write this book, a cable television company's service truck labeled *fiber optic lab* is parked outside our window provisioning our 400-unit apartment building with broadband and digital cable. The package offered includes telephone and long-distance services. Which technology do *you* think will win customers in the end?

For the Pros

Hire a video pro to get you started. Management will expect smooth, high quality operation from the start, so don't be afraid to ask for help. Video is great when it works, but we've all seen how often it can fail at the most embarrassing moments, such as a CEO speech. Failure on a project like that is unacceptable.

CHAPTER 9

Enterprise

I f a DSL system goes down, threatening corporate productivity or causing a serious security breach, your job as a network administrator or the manager responsible could be at risk. This isn't so far fetched; undue dependence on DSL lines that frequently go down is an easy mistake to make. An auditor could also declare the system a dangerous security leak. For your sake, and the firm's, you need to plan a network that's supportable, effective, and well documented.

This is not a new problem. Over three decades, computer professionals have learned the special concerns of systems with hundreds or thousands of users, often spread throughout the world. That's a very different problem than taking care of a system in one location, where an individual can take personal responsibility. Computer support is always a difficult and expensive task. A *Total Cost of Ownership* (TCO) study produced by the Gartner Group calculated annual support costs at over $3,000 per computer—much more than the cost of hardware or software.

The enormous cost of enterprise support means that managers of large networks can't look at any project in isolation. The traditional systems approach of *define the problem, find the best solution for that problem* is not sufficient. What might be the best solution for the given problem might be a mistake for the organization as a whole, which needs to adhere to standards.

This means that some of the advice in our other chapters will not apply in the largest of organizations. For example, in Chapter 2, "Choosing a DSL Provider," we point out that many regional providers, like Panix in New York, have done a consistently better job than any of the national sources. That would suggest using several of the better *regionals* for the local offices of a national network. However, a large enterprise might find it much more efficient to work with a single national provider, building a close relationship with their support branch and negotiating a favorable contract across the enterprise.

Every decision must be made to coordinate with established company standards. If the company is using Check Point, IPSec, or IBM's NetVista Management tool, a router that doesn't support that system will probably be a mistake, even if it is superior or less expensive for your DSL network. Even the use of DSL could be a mistake, if the company has an efficient frame relay or T-1 network in place. A few individual offices might save money by switching to DSL, a much cheaper service, but the cost of retraining the central staff might be greater than the savings to a few offices.

When you use DSL to extend your network to serve employees working in branch offices, in the field, and at home, you must develop a sustainable support plan. You'll need to implement standards, build relationships with your providers, and have backup Internet access ready to go when you need it. *The system is only right if it works without you.* While you, the network manager, are indispensable, the enterprise is ill served if it is totally dependent on one person. Creating a system that stands on its own allows you to take a vacation in Kauai without a cell phone, and more to the point, means that the system can run well if you're promoted or leave the company. We've been in many places where the answer to a problem is "just call Hank" or "Carol would know about that," and when Hank or Carol leaves, catastrophe looms.

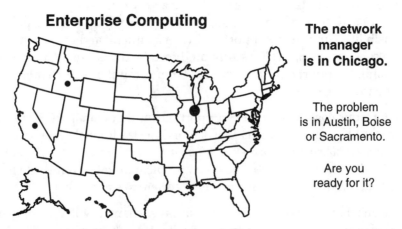

Enterprise Computing

The network manager is in Chicago.

The problem is in Austin, Boise or Sacramento.

Are you ready for it?

Figure 9.1 Outline map. If you are managing your network in Chicago and there is a problem elsewhere, are you ready to take care of it?

To ensure the system's future, always document your work. Standards should be written, contacts recorded, machine information logged, and tech knowledge updated in memos, FAQs, or a support database. Anything too complicated to handle through the regular system is a problem to avoid if practical, and documented clearly when necessary. You or your successor will be very grateful.

Always ask yourself, "can somebody else take care of this system?" If not, you have a problem that needs solving.

Standards Are the First Step

You can reduce support costs by working with a limited set of suppliers, using a limited selection of products, and setting some basic procedures for your users. Inevitably, that means you won't always choose the "best" solution, because sometimes it will be more efficient to go with what's in use throughout the organization. Because that approach is antithetical to the way we would prefer to design computer networks, we'd like to acknowledge that this lesson was painfully learned. We learned the hard way, despite old hands warning us against our approach. We're sure the same lesson will apply to DSL-focused networks, and urge you to anticipate that users will need support. Familiar systems and those currently in place and working are almost always the best foundation to building out a network. Frankly, we hate this limit—it stifles creativity in the industry, making it much harder for innovative new companies to succeed—but it works best.

Guidelines

Use the existing standards for the company. The company has probably already chosen a product for virus protection, security, inventory, and remote management of the computer systems. Your job is to integrate DSL into an existing organization, so nearly always you will support the same products. You can't change your entire corporate network to deal with DSL. On consulting assignments we've learned that if the company has a system, there is probably a reason for it to exist. That, of course, is not always true, as Dilbert cartoons make very clear. Dilbert was created by Scott Adams who learned the futility of corporate systems working for SBC/Pacific Bell, one of the key DSL companies. We advise you to be very careful when sweeping away what appear to be corporate cobwebs, in particular:

➤ Most security systems, especially the popular Check Point and Cisco systems, claim to support standards and be interoperable with other vendors. However, experience in the field has been that problems often arise, and it's usually better to stick with a single vendor. Check Point, in particular, has been the driving force behind the IPSec security protocol, but the supposedly *vendor-neutral* management features have often proven incompatible. If you are using a CheckPoint IPSec system, use routers tested and approved by Check Point, such as the Nokia Ramp units.

➤ You've probably already implemented network virus protection, typically provided by Trend, Symantec, or McAffee. Network versions of the software contain tools to make updating easier, as well as centralized management, including updates. These are very similar products, with copycat features and few significant differences, so there will rarely be a reason to choose a different product for your DSL users. If the network version is inappropriate, each of these vendors has versions for individual machines, again the obvious choice. You receive volume discounts on the purchase, and as a corporate customer should receive priority support.

➤ SNMP—the Simple Network Management Protocol—allows software to remotely check and update the unit. It's widely supported, and a key feature to look for in routers.

➤ The enterprise will need to keep track of remote inventory, typically including the hardware and software on each machine. The most popular tools are IBM's Tivoli and Computer Associates' UniCenter, both of which provide a full set of tools for the network manager. If your company supports either, that will be the best way to organize DSL support.

➤ Use as few providers as practical. Many companies will look to a single provider nationally, to negotiate for a volume price and build a strong knowledge base and support relationship. Our experience is that the better DSL specialists have been more effective than the bigger telcos, but you certainly should consider an offer from your corporate telecom supplier. All the major companies (AT&T, MCI, Sprint, and the Bells) have offerings, but among the Bells, only Qwest is building its own network out of region. The others are essentially resellers. Later in this chapter, we discuss building a vendor relationship—you should at minimum expect a national accounts-level salesperson and a dedicated or high-level support contact.

➤ Extend corporate standards, gingerly, to telecommuters' machines. If the corporation uses Lotus rather than Excel, for example, make that available for home use as well.

➤ If you work internationally, remember that American standards may not be effective abroad. In particular, the most common business DSL configuration in the U.S. is SDSL, from vendors like Covad. However, SDSL is not supported widely outside the United States, where a newer technology, G.SHDSL, will be common. By standardizing on G.SHDSL, (which is becoming more available in the U.S. as well), you can maintain wider compatibility.

➤ If you supply machines for your telecommuters, use a fixed configuration and include a standard group of software. Creating a master machine and then cloning it with software like Norton's Ghost can conveniently do this.

➤ Protect against machine failure by automatically backing up crucial work. Consider network backup, whereby a backup to a remote drive is automatically scheduled. DSL is fast enough that your can do the backup remotely, just as you would on the office network. In most uses, an incremental backup (just of the files that have changed) only takes a few minutes, and can be done unobtrusively, typically in the wee hours of the morning or automatically on shutdown.

➤ Remember that it will be expensive to do any field service on computers used remotely, or to provide direct hands-on supervision for telecommuters or other remote users. Procedures should work with minimal, if any, support required. That's why we emphasize remote management tools, allowing updates and troubleshooting. When that's not practical, consider an elaborate automatic startup routine, including items like an automatic logon to update virus protection.

Making the Standards Work for Users

Some organizations enforce standards with military-style discipline, extensive training, and an active program of review. That's certainly appropriate, for example, if you're responsible for security standards at a bank. However, the far more common reality is that remote offices and telecommuters will not follow difficult or involved procedures. Your users are human, and have their own needs and work to worry about. The needs of the network manager, possibly thousands of miles away, are the least of their concerns.

Keep it simple, net manager, or they'll just ignore your rules.

The rules have to work, which means that they must be clear and put a minimal burden on your users. There is always a dynamic tension between the network managers' needs, and the extra work they make for users. Part of the solution is to automate as much as possible, which is why we recommend automatic updates and configurations. Preinstalling standard corporate software removes the impetus for a user to load whatever he or she can get easily. Using centrally updated anti-virus and firewall programs eliminates the need to train your users in those functions.

Check ahead of time with the folks who will be working with your rules, and incorporate ways to allow them to work the way they are accustomed to, if at all possible. All projects work better if people sign on and believe they were consulted. See how they already work, and make changes at your peril.

Procedures that conflict with what folks are likely to do with the unit are the rules to avoid. In branch offices, for example, folks will add additional users to the network. While you may hope to keep an accurate inventory of all hookups, the local users will resent it if they have to check centrally first. Create a way for them to add users without breaching security protocols. Similarly, telecommuters will add and update software on the machine they work with if they need it to get work done.

Notoriously, rules that corporate machines can only be used for company purposes are often ignored. People will manage football pools at work, send personal e-mail, and browse unapproved Web sites. At home, if the kids *need the computer for homework, just this once*, few parents will say no. Corporate resistance to such behavior, if not totally futile, takes far more effort than it is worth.

Security can be maintained with less heavy-handed measures. In particular, maintain a separate login to the corporate network rather than automatically signing in the telecommuter on machine start. That way, kids can use the machine without gaining access automatically to the corporate net.

Inhouse Support

Step one is to establish a mailing and contact list, to rapidly reach your users in an emergency. In May 2001, for example, Speakeasy.net, a national ISP, had a fire in their headquarters, raising fear that the network would go down. If that happened to your provider, the first thing you'd want to do, if the network was still up, was to blast an e-mail to all of your users with a warning. The previous month, a security alert went out about the widely used Alcatel modems, and Alcatel put out an advisory that anyone using the default password should change it promptly. Remember, your users are human and easily bored. If you send too many e-mails, they will stop reading them. Excessive use of this access will result in users mentally or literally filtering your notes. Don't send too many e-mails, and put important items in the subject line to get your users' attention. When writing *action notes*, borrow a strategy from journalists and put the important information in the first sentence, so that even a casual glance gets the message across.

A second suggestion we make nearly universally is to create a FAQ (Frequently Asked Questions). The FAQ will often allow your users to solve problems without calling support, and the effort is repaid very quickly. This can be as simple as a one-page memo with basic contact information, or a thoroughly detailed reference for all related problems. There is a standard FAQ at http://condor.depaul.edu/~jkristof/xdsl-faq.txt from which you can take information, and your provider almost surely has one that you can use. None of the typical published sources, however, has much practical troubleshooting information, so you'll probably need to develop that yourself.

Your firm might support an expensive network management tool that can query the network nodes, and maintain maps and databases of their performance. Popular ones include IBM's Tivoli, Hewlett-Packard's OpenView, Peregrine Systems' InfraTools, and Computer Associates' Unicenter. A help desk tool like TSD Magic provides a good supplement and enters all requests into a database. This generates trouble tickets and follow-up reminders. It also creates a knowledge base you can search in case the problem recurs elsewhere. If these tools are in place, use them; if not, consider implementing them.

If you don't have these major tools, we recommend creating a simple database that records each problem and when and how it was solved. This information is necessary to manage the process, and also builds a *corporate memory* of solutions. If others are likely to face a similar problem, add the answer to your DSL FAQ so your users can find it directly. The company needs that information for the day you're not there—so may you, a year or two later. We often don't remember ourselves how we solved a problem, and records refresh our memory. Good records also cover you in case of unfair criticism.

Ipswitch Software's *What's Up Gold* is an ideal network monitor if you don't already maintain one. Priced under $1,000, it builds a sophisticated network map by SNMP querying the nodes on your network, records performance of your routers, and triggers a notification to you (or your pager) if a unit goes down, or sends an error message. Microsoft Visio Enterprise Edition, about the same price, also has a node discovery and mapping tool, as well as sophisticated drawing tools. Mapping isn't foolproof, especially with remote nodes and those behind address translation, but it is an excellent way to visualize and report on your system.

Remember, if the DSL lines are down, users may not be able to send requests by e-mail or logging in to the corporate intranet. Plan phone or other alternatives to gather information. In either case, it's often helpful to work like the providers, with a standard script of questions to rule out common problems.

Sometimes the problem is the provider's network, and you should call on tech support after trying the basics in Chapter 6, "Troubleshooting."

Far more often, the difficulty is software configuration or user confusion. In either case, reviewing first the most common problems will often lead to a solution. Most users will have a guess about the problem, and if that directs you straight to a solution, fine. However, the universal word from the tech support folks is that if you don't have an immediate answer, spending 10 minutes on the routine is time well spent.

Most corporations have developed an informal support network as well as the official one, because skilled users are usually proud to help their peers. Most offices have an Allan or a Sue, whom others call on for help. If corporate policy allows, consider bringing them together by creating a voluntary mailing list or a special section of your corporate intranet. Let the folks with an interest communicate with each other, perhaps by a second mailing list on the topic or other features of your intranet. Encourage this informal mentor system by thanking folks and giving them visible credit for their help.

Enterprise-level Support

An enterprise customer should expect suppliers to take care of business and help you when you need it. Your time is valuable, your company needs priority, and your volume of business is significant enough to demand service. Begin by building personal contact. The right salesperson can facilitate repairs, resolve conflicts, and give you extra support when needed from your provider. You should also request a dedicated support person to call when you need help. Spend some time, on the phone or on e-mail, getting to know these people before you have a crisis. Nearly everyone responds well to occasionally being asked a question in his or her area of expertise, and it pays to build the relationship.

You don't want to be *the one who cried wolf*, immediately escalating a problem and demanding priority, but you should be ready for true emergencies and tech support failures. Create a procedure for escalating support from your provider when you have a crisis. Know the names and the contacts of the people you need to call ahead of time, and ask that your support be guaranteed contractually before you sign a contract. Ideally, have your sales rep identify a manager you can call on if all else fails.

Every large service provider has a team and a process to take care of severe problems and very important customers. We discovered the difference once

Must You Support Home Users?

What support should you offer your home-based users? We surprised ourselves writing this chapter when we realized that some companies could properly say *virtually none*. Most executives today know enough about computers to take care of their laptops and home systems, especially if you choose a better provider. The provider can often answer most of your users' support needs better than you can, with trained help desks running 24×7. You still need to consider security, and have to expect occasional demands for help that you can't turn down. However, you are not obligated to take on an extensive support burden just because the company provides a connection or even a computer. Supporting a variety of home users on different systems can be expensive; and in many cases, just isn't necessary.

when our DSL line went down. Tech support couldn't solve the problem, so they dispatched a repairman who determined that the problem was with the telco line in our basement. He said he had to refer it through channels to arrange with the Phone Company to check the problem, and warned us it could take weeks.

We took advantage of being professionals in the field and called a senior contact who assigned us to a *priority support team*. The next day, two separate crews appeared, one from the telco and one from the DSL provider; they worked together and got us right back up. Senior people have access to solutions that the person you call in a support center in Idaho won't—sometimes, that helps.

Switchover

System down! Red Alert! Nobody in our office can do any work, and it's your fault, system manager! Solve it!

You'll be in that position often with a DSL network, and a quick solution is—step one—to keep your users happy. This can be very rudimentary for a small shop, which can work temporarily with a dial-up system. That's how we have our system configured. All that's required when the DSL goes down is to plug a phone line into the computer's modem, open up Window's dial-up network, and click on the icon to use the dial-up connection instead of the DSL line. The Netopia 7131 router makes falling back to a backup ISDN line almost as simple, with an ISDN modem built in. ISDN lines are well more

How Often Will You Go Down, and How Long Will It Take for Repair?

We emphasize the importance of switchover, because we know far too well how severe the problems have been. "My DSL service is great. I've only been down five times in two years," was the perfectly serious comment from one network manager about his personal system. That's totally unacceptable to us, and would be prohibitively expensive for a corporation that required a professional to get involved each time there was a problem. Telco equipment is traditionally designed for 99.999-percent reliability, or 15 minutes of downtime in three years, and a mature DSL system should come close to that.

Even if the DSL networks improve, you still have to expect a maintenance burden. If you assume one outage in two years, and support 100 nodes, that means you will have four problems per month. We doubt that any system currently deployed is that reliable. There is nothing inherent in the technology that causes the problem; rather, it is that the companies have grown much too fast, and haven't invested in testing and network management. In fact, the generally more reliable, but expensive, T-1 service is today essentially another flavor of DSL, HDSL, with more careful network design and faster repair time.

If repairs were quick, that would be much less of a problem, and a high-quality T-1 system is designed for repair within four hours, with redundant equipment and adequate staff and testing. However, DSL repair is often delayed. Typical telco response time is quoted as three days on a data line, and if the problem is complicated can be more. The experience we had—being told it might be weeks—has happened to many. You must be prepared.

A Switchover that Didn't Work

A printer that specializes in newspapers needs absolute reliability. Even a short delay can throw off the schedule and, of course, "you can't sell yesterday's newspaper." A very large one we know prints a dozen papers a day, many of which are FTP'd over the net, some locally and some from 6000 miles away (the American editions of Russian, Israeli, and Jordanian newspapers). When a new systems manager took over, he decided to rely on a single connection, a supposedly reliable T-1 line that cost over $1,000 per month.

When that line failed, there was no contingency plan or machine configured and ready to go. In another part of the building, fortunately, there was a DSL line in another department. However, there was no network connection in place, and in fact every workstation had been hard coded with a static IP that only worked with the (now useless) network server. The manager had neither documented the system nor trained anyone else to cope in emergencies, and when this problem happened, he was in another state. No one knew what to do, and one employee, for several shifts, had to sit at the one good connection, receiving files, and sneaker net them to the prepress department where they were needed. Everything came together, with pain and expense, but simply being ready to reconfigure for the outage would have been easy. The extra expense would more than have covered the cost of a full backup as well.

than twice as fast as dial-up, and in most areas inexpensive to use for short-term backup, although each telco has a different rate. Verizon is typical, charging about $25 for the ISDN line, with additional per-minute charges when it's used, which shouldn't be very often.

The key to making the switch smooth, at whatever level, is to have the alternative preconfigured and tested. Our backup dial-up has the ISP phone number, DNS server, and other settings already configured, which means we can switch in a minute or two. If it weren't set up, and we had to determine all the right settings in a crisis, it would be a major delay if we hit a problem. Therefore, we strongly recommend that when the system is installed, the backup is installed and tested, and brief instructions are written up—they will thank you one day.

If an ISDN backup is insufficient, or you need more capacity anyway, consider a second, perhaps less expensive, DSL line. Many providers, including the telcos, have a budget business offering that costs less than $100 per month. That's inexpensive insurance for a busy office. One particularly convenient way to use both connections is with a Dual WAN router, such as the Nexland Pro800 Turbo, a $400 unit that bonds two connections for greater speed, and automatically cuts over when one is down. The switchover is so automatic that your users might not even know they have a problem with a line; but fortunately, the unit can send an SNMP message back to your network monitor.

Security

Recognize what the real security threats are, and protect against them in a manageable way. Automatically update virus protection and prevent *social engineering* by making it absolutely clear to users that it is imperative to call a named corporate security officer immediately if anyone claims to be from the company and needs action or info that breaches security. Your firewall should also be updated automatically, rather than counting on users to perform routine maintenance.

Remote users are presumably more vulnerable, being away from corporate supervision and training, so you should carefully consider their security privileges. A trusted user may be allowed wide access at headquarters, but should probably be given a separate login with more limited rights from home.

Chapter 5, "Security: You Need It," suggests that most systems pay too little attention to the more common problems, such as Trojans attached to e-mails and social engineering. While we urge you to deal with those problems first, we don't dispute that firewalls are necessary as well. Your corporate auditor will probably follow the routine procedures, which means looking intensely at firewall and encryption vulnerabilities. Recognize that the auditor will be looking for problems, and make sure your security, if examined, is considered sufficient. You might be right in your approach, and the auditor might have a mistaken emphasis, but you never want the question to be raised. An audit problem is often magnified, and can ruin a career.

Train users to never give out machine names, logins, passwords, or even their own personal information, because that can be used to impersonate them. Thwart social engineering with clear procedures. A good example is America Online's oft-repeated assertion, "We will never ask you for your password." If the user doesn't personally know the voice on the other end of the phone, she should never release information. At minimum, the user should immediately hang up the phone and call back the switchboard. Social engineering is remarkably effective, even if the vast majority of your employees don't fall for it. Its's easy for a hacker to make 20 phone calls to find the one employee who violates security because she doesn't understand what's going on.

Nobody working at home will efficiently back up their system, no matter how many times you tell them to, especially now that they have 20GB hard drives and no way to do that quickly. If somebody's work at home is crucial and can't be lost, the advantage of a fast DSL line is that its practical to back up all critical files to the network server late at night. If you have a backup system in place on the network, with a faster DSL line you might be able to offer it to selected users whose work you want to protect. Alternatively, you can sign up your employees to commercial services that offer backup over remote connections such as xDrive (www.xdrive.com) or Connected (www.connected.com).

Have a second line of defense that makes sure that what is really critical is unlikely to be affected if some of your users act like human beings.

CHAPTER 10

Small Office Home Office Telecommuters

D SL is fast enough to support multiple users. Depending on how they use the Internet and what they do, that might be a handful or several dozen. Using DSL to provide Internet access for your small business has its own set of peculiar problems. Since you are less likely to have an IT professional on staff, we start by shepherding you through the installation process. The basics of networking a DSL line make up the guts of this chapter, which also addresses security issues for both small business users and telecommuters linking to corporate systems with rigorous standards.

Sharing DSL means you'll probably need more bandwidth than you anticipate. Heavy users of video and audio files and large graphics tie up the system, more than people who check their e-mail. Therefore, it's impossible to predict what the average use will be. To complicate things, when people get faster connections, they not only do things they didn't do before, they do more of them.

It's not critical to predict the demand on your DSL line in advance because it's relatively easy to upgrade service to a higher bandwidth. The standard modems and routers usually support faster service. You can often scale up service from your current provider in a few days with an e-mail or a phone call. However, not all providers offer higher-speed service; one of the things to find out when you are choosing a provider.

DSL Installation

Because installation is the source of so many of the woes experienced with DSL, we thought we'd do a little hand-holding in this chapter. One reason installation remains a continuing source of frustration and anxiety for customers is the lack of coordination between the DSL provider, the telco providing the lines, and sometimes an independent ISP. Curiously, telcos that own both their own lines and the ISP still seem to suffer from these coordination problems.

Scheduling problems and delays top the list of complaints. Always confirm the date and time for the installation of a line by a telco and the installation of DSL. ADSL lines typically are customer self-installed; they just send you a kit, and give you help over the phone. 80–90 percent of customers succeed with self-install, with configuring Windows more likely to be a problem than the DSL line itself. If the telco is installing a separate line, typical of an SDSL setup, there will be two separate appointments. Typically, a DSL installation is scheduled for some time after the line is installed, because delays and missed appointments for lines are common. We suggest you call the telco the day before the date your line is scheduled to be installed. Often, they will claim they can't verify installation because the provider has booked the installation. Push to get confirmation. Verify the address where the installation will take place, particularly if you're ordering service for a new location from your previous one. You may have to work through your provider, but it's worth the extra effort. Appointments are often rescheduled without notice, delaying DSL installation. On the day of your appointment, don't wait until 4 P.M. to verify whether they're coming; if installers haven't arrived by 2 P.M., call while dispatchers can still do something about it.

If an installer is coming to your premises, take an active role in your installation to avoid waiting for another service call to fix problems. Here are some of the details you should monitor.

ADSL installations require a micro-filter between each phone and device on the line and your wall jack. This includes burglar alarm systems, answering machines, and cordless phones. There should be no micro-filter on the line going into your computer. If there is, your DSL connection will not function properly. Installing the microfilter backwards is a common mistake, sometimes hard to diagnose when you try to troubleshoot.

While the technician is there, check your service to make sure it's working. It's a good idea to check both the browsers and e-mail applications you'll be using to make sure they are configured properly. We also suggest that you run a speed test. If you are not getting at least 80 percent of the bandwidth your provider advertised, raise the issue immediately. Dramatically lower performance can signal a bad line or other problems. Many things like load coils and bridge taps can reduce bandwidth. Your line could also be misconfigured. The provider could have sold you one speed and loaded the *Redback* (provider hardware controlling your login) with another. Don't rely on a single reading, however; a slowdown at the site you're testing or a particular Internet path can be the cause. Check again a few minutes later, and go to the bandwidth meters at both DSL Reports and CNET.

Each computer on your network must be configured to receive DSL (see *Easy Networking*). While the installer is there, fill out the checklist you'll find in "Resources." Do it now because the installer may be able to answer your questions. Wait until later, and it will probably never get done—and when you have a problem you may be hard pressed to come up with the settings you need.

Although DSL theoretically creates a security risk, break-ins to ordinary small office and home office systems are exceedingly rare. Still, we urge you to protect yourself in sensible ways, starting with virus protection. You needn't panic; ZoneAlarm, free to individual users and available for small businesses to purchase, is an adequate firewall for most purposes. If you are using Norton or McAfee for virus protection, it may be easier to get the whole suite of tools, including a firewall. Small businesses should also be comforted by the rarity of break-ins that cause problems, but you definitely need virus protection and a basic firewall.

Telecommuters linking to a corporate network that has serious security concerns must be more cautious, because if your machine is taken over it can be used to subvert the corporate machine to which you have access. The corporate security officer may insist on tight integration with the company's network, and might insist that you access that network through a managed security system based on the high-end security standard IPSec. Corporate users will find everyone's job is easier if standards are extended to include those who have access to the network for remote use.

Security, of course, should follow the corporate rules, but you will also find it much easier if you maintain your home system with the same version of e-mail, word processor, and even operating system as other machines on the network. This comes in handy when you need help. The corporate support staff is much better equipped to assist you on the equipment and software they know.

Most corporations are slow to upgrade their software because they've found that the new features rarely justify the added effort. Using last year's version of Microsoft Word doesn't make you a Luddite (one who is opposed to technological change), and it can sometimes make it easier to work on files from office computers at home.

If you are a telecommuter, find out where you can get support. Some companies direct all telecommuters to their regular corporate support staff, but others point them to the DSL provider, whether chosen by the corporation or the user, for primary support. Make sure you know who to call and how to get help for your home use. If you work for a large corporation, you may be eligible for priority support.

One corporate standard we urge you to adopt for home or small office is backing up your system regularly. Hard drives fail, and although sometimes miracles can be done to retrieve data, they are expensive (around $1,000) and don't always work. Today's 20GB and larger hard drives are much bigger than any fast inexpensive backup systems can easily handle. So far, too many users become careless and learn to back up their systems the hard way. The discipline of backing up every week during the typical two years or more before you'll need it is challenging. If you have a problem, you'll be glad you did.

Often, the most convenient, fastest, and least expensive backup is to a second hard drive, which can be turned to in an emergency. Many corporate backup systems have evolved, including backing up your local hard drive to a central corporate server, which in turn is periodically mirrored to tape.

Because your DSL line is always on, it may be practical to do your backups overnight when you are not using your machine, and DSL is fast enough to make that practical. Another choice is offsite backup, which many people find convenient.

Easy Networking

Many small offices don't have a full-time IT professional to maintain their networks. The cost of outsourcing the job can be $125 an hour or enough to buy a new computer. Therefore, doing it yourself makes sense. To help you understand the basics, we've included, on page 179, "Basics for Your Home Network," advice from Danny Briere, one of the authors of *Smart Homes for Dummies*, a book we highly recommend.

If you don't have a network, you'll need to create one to share DSL among several computers. Macintosh pioneered easy peer-to-peer networking more than a decade ago, and a simple network of Windows machines is now almost as easy to set up. With or without wires, a simple network can share the DSL connection through a router, either supplied by your provider or added by you and connected to the provider's modem.

Figure 10.1   Ethernet routers are the traditional way to connect a network.

Routers now often incorporate modems, and modems often have routing functionality. Some vendors confuse the issue even more by calling many of their devices *gateways*. The most common office connection will be a business-class router, typically Netopia or Efficient, which contains a built-in DSL modem. Some models include connections for multiple computers, and others have only a single Ethernet connection , which must be connected to the other computers through a hub. If your DSL service is delivered through a modem, you will need to add your own router to build the network, or run routing software (such as Microsoft's Internet Connection Sharing) on the PC connected to the modem.

The router manages the Internet connection, typically using Network Address Translation (NAT) software, and assigns each machine an address using Dynamic Host Configuration Protocol (DHCP). All the computers connected through NAT are hidden from the public Internet, offering some security. However, this basic firewall may not meet the corporate standards required to connect with your office network.

Figure 10.2   Home gateway's like 2Wire's are powerful enough to network a small office.
Courtesy: 2Wire

The midrange commercial-grade routers (Netopia or Efficient models cost from $400–$700) are our preferred way to connect an office, and most providers continue to use them. The added reliability is more than worth the cost, and built-in test and reporting can be invaluable for troubleshooting. Less expensive units can work fine, however, and are becoming more common. If your DSL connection comes through a modem, typical of residential service and some of the less expensive business offerings, you can inexpensively add a router from Linksys, D-Link, or Netgear. These are excellent units, with a price around $100, but require that you configure and support them yourself. Wireless units from these manufacturers are also coming to market, for a few hundred dollars more. You must know what you are doing if you add your own router, because your DSL provider almost certainly will not support it.

Rarely would we recommend using PCs running software like Vicomsoft, Win Gate, or Microsoft Internet Connection Sharing (ICS) to save so little money. Software networking also creates a more complicated, less reliable system, and requires that the host computer remain on for networking to take place.

Wired Networks

The tried and true way of networking computers is Ethernet. There is an enormous range of Ethernet equipment on the market costing between $30–$100 per computer, and Ethernet is built in to many computers, including the iMac. This was the near-universal choice until the recent drop in wireless costs. When the total length of a network is less than a few hundred meters, Ethernet cable is highly reliable; it is also easily extended with hubs and repeaters if you need to network over a longer distance. Here are some basics we've learned when installing networks:

Use standard category 5 twisted pair cable. It looks like phone wire but is much more reliable. Generic Cat 5 is cheap and available at any computer store or Radio Shack, name brands (we like Belden) cost a little more. Use fire-resistant Teflon shielded cable or conduit inside ceiling panels or other high-risk areas. Follow the fire code to avoid problems.

The new generation of *home* gateways is designed to be easy to use, and attractively priced. Don't let the name fool you; they are really small routers, with enough throughput to serve a small office of up to 10 or 12 computers. One of these powerful units, full of features, is often the best choice for an office without an in-house network professional.

Make it easy to see which cable is which with color and labels. If you are running multiple connections, buying cables in different colors will help you to keep on top of what is connected to what. The red cable may go to accounting, green to the sales office, etc.

It is almost as effective to put an adhesive tag securely on both sides of a given cable, and use a Sharpie or similar marker. Simply writing the same number on each end of a cable can save you hours of work when you need to troubleshoot or reconfigure your network.

Professionals, especially those managing larger networks, draw a map. Visio software is an excellent tool for creating network maps. Even if your network is currently very simple, you may want to keep a visual record of the way it's set up.

The speed of your Ethernet connection is determined by the adapter card in your computer and to a lesser extent by the hubs and switches. The slowest Ethernet adapter at 10 Mbps is faster than most DSL connections, even after allowing for network overhead. If the only reason for your network is to share the DSL connection, it would be adequate. 10/100 cards with a maximum speed of up to 100 Mbps are virtually the same price today, so you'll probably choose to buy the faster cards, anticipating future needs.

For maximum speed, install a switch rather than a hub. Ethernet creates a shared network, which means that everyone's service can slow if there are several heavy users. That is rarely a problem in smaller networks, but we learned the limits of Ethernet working in a shop where many large graphics files were being transferred. If your situation is similar, make sure you connect your network to a switch that gives the full bandwidth to each user instead of a hub, which shares bandwidth among all users. All manufacturers make both.

Instead of Ethernet, you can use the Home Phoneline Networking Alliance (HomePNA). It uses existing phone wiring. If you do not now have wiring in place, use Ethernet, because the industrial-strength wiring is faster and more reliable. If your location is already wired, HomePNA will work fine over legacy phone wiring.

To create a network with HomePNA, you'll need an HPNA network adapter (in the form of an internal PCI card or a USB adapter) for each computer. Plug a cable into the network adapter and the phone jack, and then install vendor-provided software. The initial version of HPNA (HPNA 1.0) provided just 1 Mbps. HPNA 2.0 offers 10 Mbps, or essentially the same speed as Ethernet. The distances are more limited, but usually are fine for home or small office.

Keep your eye on powerline networking, which works well in the lab and may soon be practical in your office. Digital signals can be carried over the electric power lines you have in place. Power lines have been used for home automation for two decades. To date, only low-speed applications have been practical. However, power-line networking can be dramatically improved using today's digital signal processing chips, which can transfer megabit data streams over the wires. HomePlug, a new industry consortium, has promised 10 Mbps products for early 2002.

Wireless Networking

When Steve Jobs introduced the Macintosh Airport system in 1999, wireless technology was new and unproven. In 2001, it's available from dozens of sources. Wireless networking is starting to take off as an increasing number of manufacturers offer competitively priced equipment. Switching to a wireless version of your gateway will usually add less than $200 to your costs, while the cards for individual machines are under $150 and falling. Wireless units that perform decently are now much more affordable and a heck of a lot easier than running wires. Lucent and Intersil deliver the chips, and plan to keep lowering the price. Dozens of manufacturers, including all the gateway manufacturers, are offering or planning wireless models.

A wireless network allows computers to communicate with each other via radio signals, providing flexibility and convenience. The attraction of a wireless network will be very clear to anyone who has received bids for wiring an office that are higher than hardware costs. However, wireless networking *is* more expensive than an Ethernet-based or HPNA-based network.

To create a wireless network, install a wireless network adapter on each computer to be networked. Typically, the adapter is a PCI card for desktops or a PCMCIA card for laptops. Alternatively, an external USB adapter can be plugged into a desktop's or laptop's USB port.

Figure 10.3   Wireless gateways save the cost of wiring.
Courtesy: D-Link

For small office and home office networking, there are currently two major types of wireless products available: Wireless Fidelity (WI-FI) and HomeRF. Although there are several technologies for wireless networking, the 802.11 or WI-FI standard seems to be the most pervasive.

WI-FI (IEEE 802.11b) is a standard created by the Wireless Ethernet Compatibility Alliance (WECA). Using the 2.4 GHz frequency band and direct sequence spread spectrum (DSSS) technology, WI-FI-compliant products provide up to 11 Mbps throughput.

Equipment configured for the 802.11 wireless standard is now available from every gateway manufacturer. Its speed is comparable to low-end Ethernet, about 10 Mbps, enough to share a DSL signal. In practice, it is reasonably reliable and able to go a few hundred feet including through most walls. 802.11a is also coming to market, with speeds up to 54 meg, but will not be widely deployed until 2003 or so.

HomeRF uses the Shared Wireless Access Protocol (SWAP). SWAP also operates in the 2.4 GHz frequency band, but it uses frequency hopping spread spectrum (FHSS) technology, instead of DSSS. The initial version of HomeRF provides only up to 1.5 Mbps throughput, but second-generation HomeRF products offer 10 Mbps. HomeRF-based networks are typically peer-to-peer networks.

Basics for Your Home Network

We asked Danny Briere (one of the authors of *Smart Homes for Dummies*) what you should know to create a network for your small office or home office. If you're planning to use your DSL connection to connect your home or office LAN to the Internet, here are some tips and a few things to consider.

First, if you're building a new network from scratch, consider some of the new wireless alternatives to standard wired CAT-5 Ethernet networks. Systems based on the 802.11b wireless standard are the most popular as of the middle of 2001, with vendors like 3com, Cisco, Apple, Compaq, and others offering systems for both home and small office applications. These offerings grew out of the business environment where 802.11b has been used for years. New follow-on standards 802.11g and 802.11a will expand the speed and breadth of this wireless standard.

You might also want to consider the latest offerings from makers of the competing HomeRF system, like Proxim and Intel, which can be less expensive and more functional, but are not compatible with the 802.11b connections.

In some cases, you can actually get a DSL modem/router with built-in wireless LAN capabilities from companies like Nokia, Cayman, and 2Wire. Be sure to ask what standard they support, because it does make a lot of in-home, down-the-road decisions for you.

Regardless of which standard you choose, you'll need a base station (usually called an access point) that connects via Ethernet to your DSL modem, and then a card for each PC you want to connect to the network. The card can fit into the PC card slot of a laptop, and for desktop computers, you can buy internal PCI bus cards or external cards that use a USB connection. The access point can be configured as a NAT router, so you can share a single IP address among multiple computers, and most systems will support fixed IP addresses (if your provider does) as well as PPPoE.

If you already have a wired Ethernet LAN, or if you decide to build one, connecting your DSL connection to it is usually quite easy. In most cases, the only physical connection you need to make is to connect the DSL modem/router to the uplink port of your Ethernet hub or switch.

The next step is to make sure that each of your computers has, or can obtain, an IP address. For a business-class DSL connection, with multiple fixed IP addresses assigned, all you'll usually need to complete the connection is to configure the network settings of each PC with the proper IP address and server addresses (e.g., DNS servers). Other service providers might give you multiple IP addresses, but require you to use the DHCP protocol to obtain them dynamically (this is more typical than fixed IP addresses for lower priced ADSL connections), and this can be easily configured in your PC's networking control panels.

If you've got a consumer-class DSL connection (typical if you've obtained your DSL from the local telco), you'll likely have just one IP address. So you'll have to consider how you'll share the single IP address among multiple computers. For most small networks, the best approach we've found is to use a NAT gateway router like those offered by Linksys and Netgear. These devices plug in between your DSL modem and Ethernet hub (or incorporate the hub for up to four computers within their own chassis), and distribute data between the Internet connection and computers on your LAN. Many of these devices also offer some firewall protection for your network, both through the NAT process and also by offering some more advanced *stateful* firewall functionality. Many ADSL connections use dynamic IP addresses and PPPoE, which requires careful attention to the setup software.

Once you have your network "online" and all of your PCs accessing the Internet, you should not forget security! Some DSL CPEs (typically the more sophisticated business class routers) offer built-in firewall protection, as do many of the gateway routers mentioned earlier. If you're not behind an equipment-based firewall like this, you should definitely consider the following:

➤ Use passwords for any printer or file sharing, and change them often.

➤ Don't bind printer and file sharing to the TCP/IP protocol if not required.

➤ Consider installing personal firewall software, like Zone Labs' ZoneAlarm or Norton Internet Security, on your computers.

➤ Keep your anti-virus software up to date, and use it regularly!

Finally, the great thing about a home network is that once it is installed, you can use it for so many things. Think about putting a computer monitor by your treadmill to kill off your e-mail, or installing a bank of kid's computers so they can not only do homework but also play games against one another. With wireless connections, you can think about putting other things online, like some of the neat new wireless tablets for surfing the Web, or e-books to read in bed. While these may seem either futuristic or not your style, these and other aplications are easy to do once you have that home networking backbone—wire line or wireless or both—in place.

CHAPTER 11

The Future

W e could call the future of DSL very dull, because it will become invisible to most users. It will be built into your computer, you'll be connected to the Internet, and only the true geeks will know that something called DSL is making the connection.

Even invisible, however, the technology will have enormous impact. UBS Warburg forecasts 150,000,000 users worldwide by 2005, an explosive growth rate for the industry. That's not implausible; the developed world would just have to catch up to South Korea, where in 2001 one in four homes has a broadband connection.

The truth is we can't predict the future, and the failure of past forecasts proves that anyone who answers the question with certainty is a fool. Shakespeare's Lear reminds us, however, that "Jesters do oft prove prophets." Hence we let the fools lead the way, with some provocative speculation, and we follow with some calmer projections of trends. We end the chapter with the best source we know for anticipating the future: an award-winning science fiction writer.

Voice will be free

Bill Schrader, founder of international Internet backbone PSINet

> "Voice is just another form of data, and requires less than 5 percent of the bandwidth of our fiber. Telephony, worldwide, will be free."

Investors who watched Schrader's company fall from a multibillion-dollar value to bankruptcy are no longer amused by his dreams, and when we first wrote this, we disagreed as well. Then Danny Briere of Telechoice described some fascinating business reasons why this might come true, at least for customers of the same network. See Why Voice May Be Free.

Video will offer thousands of choices

Mike Powell, Chairman of the U.S. Communications Commission

> "In five years, the Internet will run fast enough to deliver an extraordinary selection of video, and we all will have a choice of far more than today's channels."

We hope so—but the providers and Hollywood moviemakers with their own revenue models, may block that for shortsighted reasons.

Everyone on the Net will have broadband

Fred D'Allessio, group president at Verizon

> "A third of our subscribers will very quickly sign on for DSL."

We hope he's right, but it clearly won't happen as soon as he thought in 2000. Verizon and the other telcos have to bring their prices down dramatically, and solve the operations problems that hold back their growth.

Most of broadband will be DSL

Pete Castleton of Verizon

> "We're going to beat cable!"

This 1999 quote from the New York Times *made Castleton the posterboy for the expected war between the telcos and the cable companies. The practical problems we covered as DSL Hell held them back, and then a decision at the top to cut investment and raise prices means that Pete's fighting with one hand tied behind his back. That's our opinion, not his.*

Broadband will follow you everywhere

Gavin Young, who did pioneering work on DSL while at British Telecom

> "You'll have a fast connection anywhere you take your portable computer. At home, you'll connect to the network via a wireless network, probably 802.11b, to the DSL gateway, at speeds of multiple megabits. Outside the house, the same unit will connect to the 3G wireless networks being designed today, which will deliver throughput in the hundreds of kilobits or more, depending on how the bandwidth is shared."

As chips become more capable, this is almost a sure bet, although it's a few years away.

Infinite bandwidth will be too cheap to meter

Arun Netravali, president, Bell Labs

> "A mega network of networks will enfold the earth in a communications 'skin' with ubiquitous connectivity. By 2010, bandwidth will be too cheap to meter. We'll see a new Age of Virtuality that will transform the way people live and conduct their business—with virtual enterprises and with virtual travel, virtual business conferences, virtual offices, virtual universities, and a host of other virtual experiences."

We've heard about too cheap to meter *for nuclear power. Didn't happen, of course. The incremental cost of adding bandwidth on a fiber network is remarkably low, however, so Netravali may prove a prophet. When we look at SBC's network, a 10–15 percent increased investment yields a 4–10 fold improvement in performance.*

Telcos that fall behind might go bankrupt

Paul Johnson, Columbia University professor and investment banker

> "One of America's great telcos will go broke, unable to cope with the transition of the network to IP. Not just merged, but bankrupt."

We disagree.

DSL will have a rich, long life

Ray Smith, president of Bell Atlantic.

> "Folks say DSL will only be an interim technology on the way to fiber. They're right, it will probably be an interim technology for the next 40 years."

Fiber really is the future, but the telcos have neither the vision nor the resources to deliver it. In 1989, they held back on fiber because "It's impractical, and would take more than 15 years to deliver it." Twelve years later, they give the same explanation, and probably will back away for another decade.

Simple, sober projections include DSL spreading widely around the world, at lower costs. It will deliver pay movies, office-quality videoconferencing, remote learning, and your e-mail faster. Folks with professional incomes (we hope that's you) will have home gateways to multiple computers, and they'll often be wireless. Before we cover those almost guaranteed trends, let's look at some possible ones we hope we'll see.

Better, Cheaper Voice with DSL

DSL will deliver 10 times more bandwidth to most homes, which if dedicated partly to voice can supply four phone lines for little more than the cost of one today. The equipment for that, in 2001, costs about $400 per home, but is rapidly dropping. That's easily predicted, because the telcos already are requesting prices for millions of lines.

Wonderfully better voice quality is easy to deliver, and hard to merchandise. You can get much clearer *CD quality voice* by dedicating additional bandwidth to voice calls. Standard telco voice quality is poor compared to what's possible. Forget about *hearing a pin drop* over your phone line, and imagine in the background the *wind in the willows* or the subtleties of Philly Jo Jones, the drummer who "played like the wind." The quality will be great for remote radio broadcasts, delightful music, or the clear voice of the teacher when you can't be in the classroom. This is particularly attractive if you listen at length, as in remote learning or business meetings, because it dramatically lowers the fatigue. Within a well-designed network, such as MCI/UUNet, and on a corporate dedicated network, with the right, high-quality phone and encoder, the sound can be magnificent. Cisco has demonstrated just such a phone, for dedicated corporate networks; the better DSL nets can do the same.

The problem is not technology, but deployment. It can only work if both ends are upgraded, and the network is good. The hope is that a standard will emerge, and be adopted first on special-purpose networks for business and education. The enhanced phone, of course, works as a normal phone for those without special equipment on the other end.

Voice calls can be free *and* high quality, at least within one network. Large networks, especially America Online, have strong economic incentive—and the right technology—to offer high-quality free phone calls to members. Currently, free calls, computer to computer, can be easily made between any two people with the right software, but the quality is unreliable. Higher-quality calling requires bypassing the public Internet, where latency delays, lost packets, and transmission inconsistencies (like jitter) cause problems. Using a reliable private connection for most of the call journey solves this problem, as exchange carrier ITXC has proven. Nearly every telco in North America uses ITXC for some of their international calls, all of which are transmitted via IP.

A few struggling dotcoms are subsidizing this service (bypassing circuits and telco charges to connect with someone's phone, rather than with their computer), hoping to recoup the cost through advertising or sale of other products. However, that business is failing with the end of the easy-money Internet boom. That leaves a natural opportunity for America Online or other large networks to step in, and offer truly free phone calls *among their members*. The voice traffic would be within their network, and could be carried (with higher priority if needed) at minimal cost. Soon, AOL or Microsoft could sell an IP phone to you at a consumer price ($79 is planned in one trial), and charge nothing within their network, or a highly competitive rate, combined on your monthly charge, off-network. This would, of course, be a major incentive for someone to stay with the service and persuade *family and friends* to sign up as well.

The Third Internet—Fast Enough to Watch

People watch television far more than they read, and the *third Internet*, including VDSL, is fast enough to watch. Any program, anywhere in the country, any time, is both technically and economically feasible; if not in 2001, then within the next five years.

All video, not just pay movies, is the true killer app for broadband.

Without a great selection of programming, broadband brings in your e-mail faster, and has plenty of niches. The mass audience doesn't have a good reason to pay much more than the $20 or so they currently spend on the Internet. If the telcos don't want to price much lower, then they need the compelling programming that will be available if they can carry it. One meg video, pre-encoded, gives a picture as fine as most TVs. SBC committed to serving 60 percent of their territory at reliably delivered speeds of 1.5 MB or 6 MB by 2002, and if they actually delivered that (they won't), that's sufficient bandwidth for video. The other barrier is the cost of video serving, but technology is driving that down very fast, both hardware and fiber transmission. Video equipment is now a fraction of its former price, and plummeting. A $10,000 Avid system can do professional work, and remarkable things can be done on inexpensive PCs and Macintoshes. The result is that any small college, large church, ski resort, sports team, political group, or dedicated team of amateurs will be able to produce video. So, of course, can thousands of TV stations around the world. New content is already blooming, just looking for distribution.

There are also tens of millions of hours of the finest professional programming already available, the vast bulk of it very inexpensive. We predict the rise of special interest networks similar to We (Women's Entertainment Network), MTV, and others created for cable TV using existing movies and TV programming. A few popular items will continue to command premium prices, like the best of the Hollywood movies, but the cost of production has already been met, so selling at nearly any price is welcome revenue. Tens of billions of dollars' worth of programming is in warehouses around the world, whose costs are sunk. Included are television shows that found audiences of tens of millions, but aren't *revival favorites*, as well as the vast majority of movies out of country. Extraordinary films from Hong Kong, Hollywood, France, and Sweden have essentially no market in the United States, and could be acquired cheaply. Professional videos of world-class orchestras, dance, and opera that rarely find a distributor could also find a home on DSL video networks. Encoding is coming down in cost; an encoded library of 1000 feature films can be stored on less than $10,000 worth of hard drives. IBM and other disk drive manufacturers predict that cost will drop 90 percent in five years, allowing immense cached servers distributed throughout the network.

That's our dream, shared by most technologists. We—and the former management of US West who built the Phoenix network—believe it is practical and economical now. One of the smartest men in the business, the CEO of Qwest, believes that video is on the cusp of becoming practical economically, and is keeping his options open. The CTO of Telenor believes that 40 percent of Norway can economically be served video today, and that the deployment will be so successful they will need to expand. Others whom we respect believe that three to seven more years of progress in reducing costs is required.

If you don't live in Telenor's Oslo or Qwest's Phoenix, business decisions by the dominant companies may deny this fast Internet to you. The DSL and cable providers are considering whether restricting your programming can increase their profits. The cable networks have traditionally maintained their *walled garden*, whereby they select the programming for you. The fewer choices you have, the more likely you are to subscribe to their paid services, such as Home Box Office (HBO), or other services that pay a fee for carriage. We, and everyone interested in open political discourse, find this repugnant, and believe reducing content is bad business practice. In a competitive market, it might prove a fatal defect, but of course these are not competitive markets.

The first issue is whether the networks will provide enough capacity to deliver the services they advertise. The difference in cost between a network that reliably carries the promised megabit speeds and one less adequate is typically a small fraction of the system cost, and less than the marketing budget. More capable remote terminals, for example, cost only 5 percent more, but SBC refused to buy them, perhaps to limit competitors. Many of the nets have resisted that investment, building for past demand and cutting off their prospects for the future. A telco network planner explained his approach to us: "We build for the demand we know, plus a reserve. We don't believe in installing capacity until the demand is proven. Our 45 meg DS-3s aren't overloaded, in most places, so why should we spend even a small amount on a fiber-fed, upgradeable OC-3/OC-12 that we're not sure we'll need?"

Not building for the future might be appropriate for phone line capacity, which generally grew slowly, but we believe the telcos are making a bad mistake by not anticipating the growth of the fast Internet. One of our analytic axioms is that *people will use the Internet more*, and we're convinced that will hold true, if the doubling rate is closer to a year than the oft-cited every 120 days. We know limits are starting to pinch. We've already heard from marketing people planning new services, "we couldn't do that, we don't have enough capacity."

Will DSL providers accept content at their network edge without levying a *tax on the Internet*? That's another, unanswered question. We believe it is false advertising to claim you're delivering 1.5 Mbps Internet service you can't deliver. Providers must have some way to accept traffic at the edge of their networks where the programmers can deliver the content to them, to deliver those rates. It's reasonable to expect programmers to share the cost, as is routinely done with Internet peering points, but charging a toll at the edge could effectively put content providers out of business. We believe that smart DSL providers will not exact such as fee, but @Home cable and BellSouth are already actively charging if you want to stream on their networks.

Video e-mail can deliver a message from the CEO or the broker's morning call, at high quality. My computer (and yours, probably) is ready today to receive a video download of e-mail, which on a fast connection running in the background is reasonably painless. *Granny mail* with home videos of the kids is the popular thought; a message from the company president to inspire the ranks is also perfectly possible, with the faster connections provided by DSL. The technology is already here; our hesitation comes from the fact that no one has proven that this is a corporate essential, despite an excess of hype.

Get Quality Video Instantly

Video ready to go (cached) is the least expensive way to distribute high-quality video. Video on demand is practical, as Intertainer has demonstrated, but requires a strong infrastructure and plentiful bandwidth. One alternative that may prove effective for corporate news and training materials is the set-top box. Hard drive prices have come down so much that Microsoft is including gigabytes of hard drive storage in the xBox gaming console, and capacity for 20 hours or more of quality video is inexpensive to add to a set-top box or DSL gateway. This could then be preloaded with a selection of the video, instantly available to the user without any network delays.

When network traffic is low, as it typically is overnight, hours of video can be downloaded to each customer. The telcos are considering a plan to use this strategy to offer video on demand; making a half dozen encrypted movies instantly available, and thousands more available if you download in advance. A brokerage firm might archive locally the presentations of their analysts and other research, ready to play back on any desk at superb full-screen quality. A real estate broker with multiple offices could economically show each of the houses he or she currently represents. Ten-minute walk-throughs of a thousand houses and apartments can be instantly available, after being downloaded in advance.

Speed Thrills

They've gone about as far as they can go might have been the thought in Kansas City in 1905, but 60 years into the atomic era, we should have learned not to stand in the way of progress. People will want faster net speeds, certainly for high-definition TV within the decade. If you've ever seen an HDTV live, you'll understand why you'll want it when the price is right. Manufacturers are confident that will happen before mid-decade, and certainly soon after.

We think the telcos are foolish not to move rapidly to VDSL or fiber, because unless they have a superior service, the only way to compete with cable is on price. Right now, cable and DSL are comparable offerings, and neither has strong advantages for most users. The real difference is in the quality of the provider; on both sides, some are good and some are poor. Cable is easier and less expensive to install, while DSL has better penetration in business districts. Some businesses need more upstream bandwidth than cable can deliver, but they are the exception. Most who want upstream bandwidth intend to run servers, which we believe is totally inappropriate with today's reliability. It's also cheaper to use an outside host.

VDSL: Five Times the Speed Is Better

Phoenix is the most effectively wired city in the world, with 50,000 inhabitants connected to Qwest at speeds over 20 Mbps. Within a building, or over short distances, VDSL can deliver up to 53 MB downstream or 13 MB symmetrically. This is not a trial, but rather a full deployment of the type of network every community in America deserves. That's delivering 200 channels of video, in direct competition with the local cable franchise, as well as voice and data. Because VDSL only works to about 4000 feet, Qwest runs fiber to neighborhood gateways, and then copper to each home. The giant telcos should be embarrassed that a slew of small carriers is so far ahead. Companies including Blue Earth Phone, Eckles Phone, Chester Phone Company, and West Carolina Rural Phone Cooperative offer their customers a finer product than SBC or Verizon does.

VDSL is not inherently more expensive to deliver than ADSL, except for the requirement for the intermediate gateway. In Phoenix, that meant they had to install small broadband network units throughout the city, connected by fiber. In Toronto, the units are in the basements of apartment buildings. VDSL chips actually are less complicated and draw less power than the

ADSL chips. The faster DSLAMs and OC-12 fiber connections add only a small factor to the equipment cost, if (like a telco) you already have fiber in place. The Internet backbone requires a richer pipe, but the cost for that too is dropping dramatically.

Next Level, now controlled by Motorola, produced the equipment for Phoenix, using Broadcom chips and Tektronix VideoTele servers. They have a two-year lead on competitors, and dominate the market. However, multiple competitors entering the market, including Lucent and Alcatel, will drive the costs down. With Lucent, Infineon, and others, Next Level supports the VDSL Coalition promoting a standard based on the QAM line code. An alternate technique, using DMT coding similar to ADSL, is supported by Alcatel and Lucent through the VDSL Alliance, but is much slower coming to market. They've fought a royal battle over standards; one reason why telcos have been reluctant to sign on.

By the time we are writing the second edition of this book, we hope that VDSL will have entered the mainstream, and we can move this discussion to the "Technology" chapter. For now, in most of the world VDSL may be possible in the future, but it's not a current reality. For more on the technology and issues, see the articles by Krista Jacobsen and Martin Schenk at www.dsl-prime.com/News_Articles/a/VDSL/vdsl.html.

Safe Predictions

We don't have a crystal ball; neither does Yankee, Gartner, UBS Warburg, Telechoice, or the literally hundreds of others we consulted for these basic predictions. We absolutely guarantee that some of this will prove wrong, but we would bet money on almost all of it. Improved speeds and pay movies are already moving out of the lab into the field. We should remind you that these are our judgments, unless we credit someone else.

Technology

Reach and performance will improve 15–25 percent over the next few years. This prediction is based on what folks are demonstrating in the lab. The current DSL chips are remarkable engineering achievements, hundreds of thousands of transistors each. Literally thousands of engineers, working at dozens of companies, have moved this technology close to the theoretical limits suggested by Claude Shannon in his seminal work on the technology that became DSL a half century ago. Improved versions of current technologies are already percolating out of the labs, and the next two generations of chips will show a small, but definite, improvement in reach/speed/reliability. Speeds of 10 megabits will be achieved at the shorter distances, and megabit speeds will be more securely achieved over 12,000 feet. ADSL was designed to work well to 18,000 feet, but most providers set a 14,000 or 15,000 cutoff in practice. Reach will extend toward 20,000–25,000 feet. Researchers are excited by reduced noise, improved error correction, echo cancellation, and the improvements possible with more complicated coding of signals. That is very close to the theoretical maximum possible without breaking the laws of physics, based on the current models of the real-world networks.

The only breakthrough in sight will come from better control of interference created by the multiple phone wires carried in the same binder group. Current models assume Gaussian noise, an essentially random pattern. By using multiple wires, noise can theoretically be more carefully measured and controlled. Adaptive techniques based on the actual, as opposed to theoretical, environment can also be employed to improve signal quality.

DSL modems will be built into many computers. Dell is supplying a special model with DSL built in for BellSouth, and Compaq is producing a similar model for Pacific Bell. Built-in DSL will become much more common as coverage becomes near ubiquitous and prices drop. Our confidence is based on long talks with the computer manufacturers themselves. Nearly every computer in the store has a built-in 56K modem, because the costs have come down so far that the manufacturers add them as a standard feature. DSL modems are not at that price point yet, adding $30–50 to the manufacturing cost, but that cost is dropping rapidly. Texas Instruments predicts that the chipset price will drop to $10–15 in 2002, while DSL soft modems will drop that lower.

Many modems will rely on the computer's CPU rather than a DSL chipset. There is no *modem board* in the majority of today's modem-equipped computers, and most of the chips have been eliminated by using part of the power of the main CPU instead. PCTel and Motorola are close to market with a similar design for a DSL *soft modem* that would use about 200 megahertz of a Pentium's processing power. The chips being replaced cost $20–35 today, so tying up so much processing power seems like a bad bargain. With 1.3GB Pentiums already at a modest price, and every indication that processor speeds will continue to ramp, *soft modems* become practical and even likely. We don't know whether the volume shift will be around 2004 or 2007, but in either case, watch for a dramatic decline in DSL modem chip sales.

Pay movies, if not a full range of video, will be a common service. This is not the 500-channel universe, or the "any program, any time, anywhere" promise from Qwest that will require a major commitment from the carriers, but a video-on-demand service financed by the $4 or so they intend to charge you for each movie. Because only 5 or 10 percent of the subscribers are likely to want to buy pay programming at any one time, this can mostly be carried on current networks with multiple servers. The limit is that if more than a small fraction of users want video, the networks, until upgraded, won't be able to handle it.

Cincinnati's ZoomTown service and Intertainer are already offering the service, and nCube has an order in hand for a 6000-stream video server. The enthusiasm is high, although the key problems still need to be solved. The technical issues are close to resolution, practically and economically, as we described. The business issues may prove tougher, as every party fights over sharing the revenue. Enron and Blockbuster had a 20-year deal with Verizon and SBC to deliver $billions of video on demand, which fell apart because the studios didn't want to allow a middleman such a large cut. The studios are setting up their own distribution, while Verizon is planning its own network, but as we write, the big deals are being blocked. The telcos believe they have to keep most of the charge, perhaps $2–3 of a $4 movie rental, to make money on the service. The studios believe that because they have the movies, they deserve most of the customer dollar. They want the telcos to carry the transmission costs and make their money on the DSL service. The telcos are investing in DSL with the expectation that their profits will come from add-ons, like video.

The technologists and the regulators are arguing things out, but the real battle is between the giants carving up the revenue. Unfortunately, they'll probably reach a deal that results in higher prices for the consumer. That produces a short-term maximized profit, perhaps, but is a long-term mistake. The big money is from a large volume market, which will drive down costs. Volume will only come if prices are low.

Everyone's ahead if the logjam can be broken—low price, huge volume, and a wonderful service for all. The engineers can deliver that dream; shortsighted business decisions can kill it.

Many homes will have gateways and multiple computers. Steve Jobs and a million hackers proclaimed "one person, one computer" more than a decade ago, and that's becoming a reality in the average business office. With perfectly fine home computers costing $500 or less, many middle-class families can afford one for every member. Research firm Parks Associates predicts that one in three American homes will be networked by 2005, over 40 million households. We predict that a majority of networked homes will connect to the Internet through DSL.

Game machines will be a common alternative to PCs. Microsoft's xBox has an Ethernet connection to hook to DSL or cable, and nearly all the game machines are matching that capability. The game industry is bigger, for example, than the movie business. DSL providers hope to ride that wave, which will also drive home networking. Sony's chairman Idei Nobuyuki, knows what's up; he says "Sony will become a personal broadband network company by developing gateways. The era of stand-alone TV products is over."

Industry

The investigative journalist's axiom, *follow the money*, is a necessary perspective for any look into DSL's future.

DSL will grow much faster outside the United States. North America was the first to deploy, and the half-million lines deployed at the end of 1999 were far more than the rest of the world combined. By early 2001, however, the balance had shifted, with plans for millions of lines from Germany's DT and Japan's NTT, and with Korea already over two million. By the end of 2001, two-thirds of the 13–15M lines will be outside the United States. UBS estimates that the U.S. share will drop to 20–25 percent by 2005. This means that all equipment providers will need to become international to compete effectively. Germany's Siemens, Korea's Samsung, Japan's Sumitomo, and NEC will likely expand from their home bases.

Costs to provider level will continue to decline. They may or may not pass the savings on to customers, depending on competition. Moore's Law applies—chips get better and faster at a dramatic rate, typically doubling performance or halving price every 18 months. The equipment prices are dropping dramatically, with a DSLAM and modem costing a larger provider under $200 in 2001 compared with $400+ in 1999. The fiber glut is driving down prices for Internet backbone connectivity 40 to 60 percent each year, a big savings because backbone currently costs $5–15 per month per subscriber. The switches, routers, and metropolitan area connections needed for the providers' networks are among the most competitive of telecom products, and prices today and in the future should reflect that.

Until SBC got greedy, the telcos expected to drop consumer prices from $40 to $30 sometime in 2002, and stabilize at that level for several years. Low-end business offerings, without guarantees, would cost little more. Business offerings with service commitments, from reputable suppliers like Covad, currently are priced from $100–400, and these rates should go down.

Early equipment will still be in use, limiting the services on many networks. The DSLAM that Alcatel makes in 2001 has 10 times the throughput of the unit sold by the thousands in 1999, resulting in much more substantial capacity for applications including video. Progress will continue on density, speed, and throughput. The potential result will be service much closer to the promised 6 Mbps speeds, fewer problems with congestion, and expanded offerings including voice and video.

Reality will bite, however. The telcos will not rip out the old equipment and reconnect customers to the new. Besides not wanting to write off their investment, it would require a fortune for the reinstallation and cutover. Unless forced by competition or law, telcos will try to maximize their current investment, and hence move slowly on improved services that render obsolete the equipment they have.

The limits of the equipment in place will discourage improved services. For example, the older DSLAMs will bottleneck if more than 10 or 20 percent of subscribers want to watch video at once. If they could replace the equipment every three years, like consumers are forced to with personal computers, it wouldn't be an issue. However, what's installed in 2000 will be holding back the company; if not in 2002, then certainly a few years later.

Fixed wireless will be a big competitor. Put a little antenna on the outside of your house, and who needs a wire for high-speed connectivity? Sprint is delivering that service now, in a dozen cities with more on the way. AT&T's Project Angel is also promising wireless broadband with a heavy consumer penetration. The deployments to date have had teething problems like most new technology, but are working to commercial standards—much more to come.

Fiber, probably as Gigabit Ethernet, will be the primary competitor in many cities. In New York City in 2001, it's cheaper to rent fiber, with capacities in the gigabits, than to pay for a $1,500 T-1 line that delivers a fraction of the speed. There still is a large cost for hookup, including as much as $75,000 if the sidewalk to your building must be torn up to connect you, but 11 separate companies are running fiber. MFN alone has conduit with 768 fibers spanning down six major avenues in Manhattan, and Time Warner, RCN, the Con Ed Power company, and others are almost as ambitious. Yipes, Telseon, GiantLoop, and IntelliSpace are the early innovators, but AT&T, Verizon, and SBC are looking hard at jumping in.

Gig-e brings fiber capacity with the simple connectivity of Ethernet. That's been a key factor in why cable modems have been easier to deploy than DSL, and the bandwidth possible with gig-e means that you can offer 50+MB service to dozens of offices without running into congestion problems.

How We Forecast

We all know how far off some forecasts have been, so we wanted to give you some information to help you judge what's presented here. We're constantly asked for numbers, for marketing plans, magazine articles, and books. Some forecasts are clearly well researched, intelligently argued, but totally in contradiction to other forecasts equally well considered. A few sound like they were improvised because The *New York Times* or *Telephony* was on the phone, and an analyst took a wild guess because her career and even salary are dependent on being publicly noticed. They ask for a number, and it's hard to say, "I don't know," especially since very rarely will anyone notice three years later if you're wrong. Clearly, much of what we see in print, and even some analyst's reports, are not carefully researched. The folks we respect are diligent and hard-working, and right more often than they are wrong. Matt Davis, who comments later in the chapter, was right on in 2000, predicting year-end DSL subs in the United States at very close to the actual 2.3M, while the telcos themselves were promising over 3M. It's amazing that the telcos were not merely bad forecasters, but didn't have the resources to realize their plans. That failure forced their CEOs to explain to Wall Street why they couldn't deliver, and heads rolled.

The world changes and some things are unpredictable. Therefore, a careful look at certain factors, as Davis describes, sometimes is not enough. Another approach, taken by Bank of America in a persuasive article about DSL's prospects against cable, is to look at the underlying cost factors, and assume, over time, the corporate structures will adopt, and demand will be created. Pointing out that DSL has been more expensive to deliver, he believes that cable will always be ahead. (If the difference continues to be as big, we'd agree, but the latest data from SBC says that DSL costs are going way down.) The UBS Warburg team looks at economic growth in several countries, the plans of the dominant telcos, and whether competition will drive prices down and stimulate demand. A recent Morgan study emphasized the importance of price as well, with dramatically different projections depending on how aggressively the telcos price. The telcos themselves have all done extensive market research, asking prospective users whether they would be interested; it was all professionally done, but their actual customer demand has been far lower than projected.

Our Approach: Almost Axiomatic

We try to understand the business long term, by making some assumptions we think we can defend, and then looking at the consequences. There's an implicit model in our work, which has evolved as we've learned more. These are not as rigid as Euclid's axioms, nor as clearly demonstrated as the laws of thermodynamics, but have yielded some very surprising results. Some are commonly accepted or appeal to common sense; others come from our own research.

The power of reasoning from first principles was illustrated by our worst mistake. We had persuasive sources showing that "Internet traffic was doubling every 120 days." They included the presidents of AT&T and MCI/UUNet, the largest backbone providers, the chair of the FCC, and the president of Level 3, a company valued at $40 billion because investors in 2000 believed this expectation of Net growth. We used that assumption, with appropriate adjustments, to compute how much bandwidth each user would require if the trend held until 2003. That exponential growth would require a nonblocking 2 Mbps per home, enough to deliver video. This was dramatically different from what the DSL networks were being designed for, and we used the conclusion to urge more robust network building during a June, 2000 *DSL Forum* speech.

We were dead wrong in that conclusion, because the actual Internet traffic was growing at a much lower rate. Andrew Odlyzko of AT&T Labs had been writing for a year that *all the experts*, including his own CEO, were simply wrong, because they were working from bad and misunderstood data. By that fall, we had discovered and confirmed his work. Recognizing the slower growth in 2000, ironically, left us far ahead of the pack; Wall Street didn't get the message until the following May. Level 3's stock fell 95 percent, and their peers were battered as well.

Moore's Law: Chips get twice as fast every 18 months. Corollaries include the expectations that prices for similar chips will drop by half, that any given chip design can have features added, and that more functions will be packed into smaller spaces. Gordon Moore of Intel has found that this has held consistently true during the last 15 years, and there is a clear engineering track to bring chip feature sizes down to 0.07 microns by late decade, following past trends.

Metcalfe's Law suggests that the value and use of a network rises with the square of the number of people connected. As more people have fast Net connections, individuals and commercial vendors will create more applications, which will drive more demand.

Politicians are influenced by contributions. The relevance in this regulated industry is that the rules are largely set by folks with a bias toward the telcos that support them, not the user. In the United States, House Commerce Committee Chairman Billy Tauzin has accepted over $10M from BellSouth and other telcos for his campaigns and those of other Republicans. In turn, he introduced Tauzin-Dingell, a very pro-telco bill, lifting prices and blocking competition. One of the bill's surprising supporters was the nominally liberal New York Democrat Elliott Engel, whose constituents would gain nothing from the bill except higher prices. Engel's campaign reports that Verizon, with $19,000, was his critical campaign donor. In France, telecom competition was blocked by far-left parties, not right-wingers. They were influenced by the labor unions at France Telecom, which became a leading contributor because members were fearful of losing jobs.

Regulators are a lot like politicians, even if they do not accept money directly from the companies being regulated. Most owe allegiance to their political patrons who obtained the job for them, and most come to the job with previous strong ties in the industry. An amazing percentage of regulators go to work in the industry after leaving office; it's hard to act strongly against your possible future employer. Reed Hundt, the FCC chairman who drove the 1996 Telecom Act, made over $10M from his NorthPoint board seat and investments soon after leaving office. Contrary to popular belief, most bureaucrats in this industry are conscientious and work hard to serve the public, but the pressures are strong.

Competition isn't perfect. Information isn't perfect. These terms are crucial for most economic analysis, which assumes that there are many actively competing businesses and that buyers have good information to act rationally. In the real world of telecom, this simply doesn't apply, which means that typical economic analysis is flawed at best.

Two or three companies controlling a market have strong incentive to work together, not compete. Telcos claim that if they have even one competitor, such as a cable company, the market is competitive and doesn't need regulation. That's contradicted by what we learned in Economics 101, that multiple competitors are required to deter abuse of market power. We've seen it again and again, with clear public signaling. SBC raises prices and cable competitor AT&T follows a month later, even though it had no previous plans to raise rates. The week we wrote this, we learned that Verizon was meeting with the cable companies to get support for a bill that would let them raise prices.

Corporations try to maximize profit. You'd think that most folks would accept that assumption, with occasional exceptions. Lots of commentary in this business ignores this principle. If installing DSL in Illinois is profitable, SBC has incentive to do so. That could be affected by rules affecting DSL, but it's not affected by whether the basic phone charge in Illinois goes up or down, contrary to strong SBC comments. The CEO of Qwest is very clear about what determines his company's investment: "I'll invest wherever we earn the highest return, whether it is Boise, Boston, or Berlin," but the consequences of that for Boise and Idaho imply that regulators should be stepping in and ordering performance. Qwest's hurdle rate for return on investment is 35 percent, which implies that the investment must be paid off in full in less than three years. Rational for Qwest, perhaps, but a likely disaster for Idaho businesses that need Internet connections. If low density means that building a DSL network for their state might only earn a return of 15 percent, and take five or six years, that's a reasonable thing to demand from a telco monopoly.

Change is hard, and things go wrong. Everyone in DSL learned this old lesson the hard way, as every deployment in the United States had far more problems than expected. Bell Atlantic, for example, expected to reach 100,000 customers in 1999, and missed by 70 percent. The next year, they were off by 30 percent. Many of the problems occurred because it is hard to retrain tens of thousands of employees in new systems, and that's what it takes to deliver millions of lines. This reinforces the typical telcos' resistance to change. The risk, if something goes wrong, can be enormous, making it extraordinarily hard for them to adopt new ways of working—even ones that would appear a better way to make money. *Bellheads* (the folks with a telco bias) are typically seen as dinosaurs by *netheads* (the Internet/IP people), but some of their reluctance to move fast is smart caution.

Projects are usually late. We know this well in the computer world, but in competitive telephony many companies were burned because others didn't deliver on time. Plans to offer competitive consumer DSL service was dependent on the telcos and competitors making the system work, which took about eight more months than expected. In the meantime, every competitive residential service had crippling problems and costs. Two-hundred million dollars' worth of remote terminals for Project Pronto could not be installed for six months because Telcordia couldn't finish their provisioning software. The more companies involved, and the more complicated the project, the less likely it will come on time.

It's very expensive to lay a new network of fiber or copper. This means that no matter what, it will be very hard to compete with the folks who already have them, whether they abuse their monopoly or follow regulations.

People will use the Internet more. This is clearly true, corresponding to Metcalfe's law and empirical data. The growth rate is not a *doubling every four months* as commonly claimed, but sufficient to require more facilities rapidly. Most DSL networks are underbuilt, and don't have the bandwidth for this growth.

Fiber capacity will increase. Routers and switches will get faster. Result: Tt will be less expensive to provide any of these services.

Adapted from Dave Burstein's speech to the DSL Forum, June of 2000.

The Numbers

Take with appropriate skepticism the projections you read in this book, the *New York Times*, and in $2,500 analyst's reports, especially when they project more than a year or two into the future. Despite that, if you're planning, you need somewhere to start, and not just to fill in missing boxes on a spreadsheet. Table 11.1 is from the equipment team at UBS Warburg in New York, who maintain a global DSL model. This is a high estimate; our guess is lower. Because cable and DSL are almost interchangeable services, it's difficult to impossible to predict which will win broadband customers, adding another enormous uncertainty to these figures.

The analysts at UBS use this model to forecast equipment manufacturers' sales. UBS projections are informed by the bank's local analysts around the world, who are in close touch with the telcos and the major governments. This gives them some of the best information beyond the United States.

Equipment costs are now so low ($200–400 per subscriber, complete) that it makes economic sense for every telco in the world to upgrade to DSL, and nearly all have announced some plans. Some countries, including China, Iran, and Zimbabwe, have active government programs to restrict Internet

Table 11.1 DSL Projections

SUBSCRIBER BASE (MIL.)	2001E	2003E	2005E
U.S.	5.1	16.7	30.4
Canada	0.9	2.1	3.5
Korea	3.9	5.8	7.1
Japan	1.5	9.0	17.0
China	0.5	8.3	24.8
Hong Kong	0.4	1.0	1.6
Taiwan	0.4	2.0	3.7
India	0.0	0.8	6.7
Germany	1.8	5.5	10.0
France	0.7	3.6	6.1
UK	0.3	3.6	6.9
Other	2.0	12.8	31.6
Total	17.6	71.3	149.5

How a Pro Forecasts

Matt Davis of The Yankee Group has been one of the most accurate in his numbers, and we respect his work, so we asked for his thoughts on the future. Our speech earlier in the chapter, *What We Know and Don't Know about the Future*, pointed out how difficult it is to get things right. There are too many factors, in most cases, to be certain about the future. It wasn't aimed at Matt personally, whom we respect, nor at his intense analysis of the short-run results he describes here. Nor did we go so far as to say that all forecasts were bunk; rather, we pointed out how much uncertainty there was in even the best. These are Matt's comments on the general issues, followed by details of his actual procedures.

"I remember giving a speech at the 2000 *DSL Forum* where I shared the podium with Dave. As the buttoned-up analyst I had my PowerPoint presentation, my statistics and graphs, and pre-written speech. On the other hand, all Dave had was a bunch of hardcopy books, including *Towards the Year 2000*. After my talk on the future of DSL, including a forecast, Dave took the opportunity to deliver a fiery oration describing what pure bunk forecasting was, and how analysts in general really couldn't have any more insight than casual industry observers. In particular, he focused on the regulatory environment and the utter chaos and unpredictability emanating from Capitol Hill.

On many points Dave was right. Trying to predict political maneuvering, ILEC innovation, Wall Street valuations, or FCC decision-making is a losing game. However, once a technology has been trialed, adopted, standardized, and rolled out, a lot of the guesswork is taken out of it. In terms of DSL, after the question of whether DSL would be offered was settled, it really became a matter of how quickly it could be offered. As a result, I and a group of fellow analysts at The Yankee Group base our forecasting on three key criteria:

Footprint: What is the true addressable market for DSL? Not how many people want it, or can afford it, or meet some kind of end-user profile, but in terms of infrastructure deployment, how many U.S. businesses and households could actually receive the service if they were willing to pay for it? We measure this by our own metrics, not what the service providers claim to be able to reach. This includes remote terminal upgrades, estimated number of bridged taps and loaded coils, de facto 12,000- to 15,000-foot DSL ranges rather than lab maximums, etc.

Operations and provisioning: Given that a certain percentage can be reached, what is the capability of the service provider to actually turn up the service? This includes technical and regulatory hurdles, physical impediments, and plain old business model considerations. This is the most complex and difficult stage to measure, and covers a lot of the objections Dave roasted me on.

End-user demand. Only after the first two criteria are satisfied can end-user demand, price sensitivity, desire for bundled applications, etc., drive the DSL penetration process. Of course, end-user demand is also the most powerful of the three forces, because without it, the other two would not be necessary. End-user demand is relatively measurable using survey information and scrutinizing take-rates and back orders.

In addition to these three cornerstones, multitudes of variables go into creating a forecast. The Yankee Group has forecast within 10-percent accuracy for the past three years, and to be honest, we have been a little on the low side. Service providers have exceeded our subscriber expectations largely because we believe that the loop qualification and provisioning process is so immature, that turning up subscribers is a money-losing prospect. We underestimated the amount of money service providers were willing to throw at the problem, and anticipated provisioning being a greater barrier than it has proven itself. However, to truly scale DSL into the millions, we continue to believe that the provisioning challenge remains the biggest barrier to true mass-market deployment. Once the process becomes streamlined, The Yankee Group believes that DSL will become a true mass-market commodity technology, and that broadband will almost completely replace dial-up as the way Americans connect to the Internet before the decade is out. This may not seem to be a bold prediction, but Yankee prides itself on accuracy rather than hyperbole."

Davis is right on about the costs being a crucial obstacle, which corresponds to what users perceive as *DSL Hell*. We hope that problem will soon be behind us in the United States. Korea is rolling more than twice as fast, with fewer problems, so we know it's possible.

access, although the Chinese currently plan to do that indirectly, allowing the Internet as a tool for economic growth.

Within the United States, our guess is that the telcos will be less aggressive than this, because they will suffer less pressure from competitive phone companies rapidly being decimated. The Yankee Group has a prediction closer to 15M in 2005, while Telechoice sees 17M in 2004. Both have been among the most accurate in the past. The failure of NorthPoint in the United States was followed by price increases by SBC and Verizon, which is reducing DSL growth dramatically.

Asia is certain to continue extraordinary growth. Korea passed the U.S. in 2001, Taiwan and Hong Kong are ramping rapidly, and Japanese companies have two million orders about to be installed. All are pricing in the $20–30 range, where demand is likely high. China's rollout is only beginning in 2001, and the structure of the industry is changing rapidly. China Telecom is installing equipment rapidly, anticipating competition from other national providers government policy intends to create. Domestic electronics manufacturers, including Huawei, have begun delivering equipment in volume, and intend to drive prices down. The potential is clear; China has 120M wireless phones, and projects rapid growth in all telecommunications. The government, through *People's Daily*, has targeted a price of 100 yuan, about $12, for the service. At that price, China's emerging middle class may well require 25M DSL lines. India is unknowable, with mega-corporation Tata ready to deploy service but the national telco using enormous political power to resist competition. Australia is under country looking for rapid 90 percent availability, with a telco facing competition.

European subscribers are relatively few as we write, but also poised to grow rapidly if the telcos price for volume. Germany, England, France, Benelux, and Scandinavia are substantially wired, with Germany expecting to be able to serve 94 percent of homes in the near future. The German deployment will set the model for Europe, passing 2 million early in 2002. They've priced at $30–$35, substantially less than the UK or France, so demand is huge. Government pressure will probably create motion in France and England as well. Prime Minister Tony Blair likes to speak about *Broadband Britain*, and will one day wake up and discover the U.K. is actually far behind.

Brazil and Argentina are promised hundreds of thousands of lines by Spain's Telfonica, owner of local telcos, while numerous private companies are working in Chile. Key cities throughout Latin America, especially business districts, will have service choices as soon as the practicalities of unbundling surmount the political process. Telmex and SBC in the U.S. have interlocked ownership, so Mexico can call on the resources of one of the world's largest deployments. Presumably the problem is political; Carlos Slim, controlling shareholder, was on the losing side of the last Mexican election, and looking for bargaining chips to hold power. DSL is apparently a hostage to the political fight. Africa must not be left behind, and innovative companies are starting to deploy in Egypt and South Africa.

If You Really Want to Guess the Future, Ask a Science Fiction Writer

Cleve Cartmill was intensely investigated by the FBI in 1942, because he had done such a good job anticipating the Atomic Bomb. Organ-legging, the illegal sales of body parts, was the subject of a seminal story, *Death By Ectasy* by Larry Niven, in 1969. It is a scandal in the *New York Times* in 2001. *Cyberspace* is a term coined by Bill Gibson in *Neuromancer.* Analysts are trained to take today's trends, and carefully project them into the future. Often, the *surprise-free* model works. However, when there are dramatic changes, like the Asian economic meltdown or the telecom boom, the models break down. For paradigm shifts, like the World Wide Web, you need a different kind of imagination.

Michael A. Burstein won the John W. Campbell Award for best new science fiction writer, and has been nominated for Hugo and Nebula Awards. His book, *Hypospace*, is coming soon. His hopes are more optimistic than ours, perhaps, but dreams should be nurtured.

"In my first published story, *TeleAbsence*, I posit a future Telepresence School, where students from all over the world can jack into a virtual reality environment and interact with each other and the teacher in real time. Today, that's a reality.

DSL will break down the traditional barriers in communication, and render a completely frictionless world of interaction. The ability to teleconference and to look up information from anywhere in the world will be available to the world's 6 billion plus people. Imagine a world where one never has to leave one's house for anything except food, where the barrier between working at home and just being at home is completely eradicated...where you can design your own schedule, and be twice as productive as you are now...where fossil fuel consumption drops precipitously, staving off the dreaded greenhouse effect...where dictators and liars can no longer thrive...but also where it gets harder and harder for your own one voice to be heard among the cacophony."

This is the promise of DSL.

Index